The Psychic Home

CW00349036

The Psychic Home: Psychoanalysis, consciousness and the human soul develops, from a number of different viewpoints, the significance of home in our lives. Roger Kennedy puts forward the central role of what he has termed a *psychic home* as a vital psychic structure which gathers together a number of different human functions. Kennedy questions what we mean by the powerfully evocative notion of the human *soul*, which has important links to the notion of home, and he suggests that what makes us human is that we allow a home for the soul. As an illustration of this concept he explores how it can help us understand a vital element of William Wordsworth's development as a poet.

The word 'soul' is both abstract and yet also powerfully emotive. Kennedy shows that it can be approached from a number of different angles, from psychoanalysis, philosophy, religion, sociology, literature and neuroscience. *The Psychic Home* discusses the mysteries and complexities of the soul and aims to evoke some restoration of its place in our thinking. It illustrates how the word 'soul' and similar key words, such as 'spirit' and 'inwardness', express so much that is essential for humans, even if we cannot be too precise about their meanings.

Insightful, enlightening and broad reaching, *The Psychic Home* brings the concept of the soul centre stage as an entity that is elemental, an essence, irreducible and what makes us human as subjects of experience. It is essential reading for psychoanalysts, psychotherapists, neuroscientists, philosophers and those interested in spirituality and religion.

Roger Kennedy is a psychoanalyst in private practice and past president, British Psychoanalytical Society. He worked for 30 years as an NHS consultant. He is a child psychiatrist at the Child and Family Practice and at Ashwood Associates. He has published twelve previous books, including *Psychoanalysis, History and Subjectivity* (Routledge, 2002) and *The Many Voices of Psychoanalysis* (Routledge, 2007).

The Psychic Home

Psychoanalysis, consciousness
and the human soul

Roger Kennedy

Routledge
Taylor & Francis Group

LONDON AND NEW YORK

First published 2014
by Routledge
27 Church Road, Hove, East Sussex BN3 2FA

and by Routledge
711 Third Avenue, New York, NY 10017

*Routledge is an imprint of the Taylor & Francis Group,
an informa business*

© 2014 Roger Kennedy

British Library Cataloguing in Publication Data

A catalogue record for this book is available from the British
Library

Library of Congress Cataloging-in-Publication Data

Kennedy, Roger.
The psychic home : psychoanalysis, consciousness and the human
  soul / Roger Kennedy. — First edition.
    pages cm
 1. Psychoanalysis. 2. Consciousness. 3. Soul. I. Title.
  BF173.K4146 2014
  150.19'5—dc23
  2013033373

ISBN: 978-0-415-71013-8 (hbk)
ISBN: 978-0-415-71014-5 (pbk)
ISBN: 978-1-315-81553-4 (ebk)

Typeset in Times
by Apex CoVantage, LLC

MIX
Paper from
responsible sources
FSC   FSC® C013056
www.fsc.org

Printed and bound in Great Britain by
TJ International Ltd, Padstow, Cornwall

Contents

Acknowledgements

Thanks to Neil Vickers, who helped with the writing of Chapter Three on Wordsworth and also was very encouraging in the early stages of the book. Stephen Gill generously sent me unpublished Wordsworth poetry to help with Chapter Three. Nicholas Humphrey was very encouraging about the project, as was Michael Parsons.

'Settlements' is taken from *Selected Poems* by John Burnside, published by Jonathan Cape. Reprinted by permission of the Random House Group, Ltd.

Permission is granted from Oxford University Press to quote extracts from Stephen Gill, *William Wordsworth: A Life* (Oxford: Oxford University Press, 1989).

Chapter 1

A home for the soul

Home is one of those simple yet elemental words that can convey powerful feelings of belonging and yearning. I was reminded of this when assessing a little boy with regard to his long-term future. He had spent much of his first year in hospital due to a condition which meant that he was unable to take food by mouth and that his vocalization was delayed. In addition, his parents had significant social and mental health issues, so that they effectively abandoned him in hospital. It took some months of trying various options before at last he ended up with very devoted foster carers; he needed constant care because of his disability. One of the issues was whether or not he should stay with the carers. There was a dispute about this, which necessitated a court process. The local authority had a view that he should be adopted, as they considered this would be in his long-term interests. However, if the foster carers were to adopt him, they would lose all the financial and service support they were entitled to as foster carers, and he needed 24-hour care.

By the time I saw him at the age of 3, he was beginning to become stronger. He could talk but only a word at a time, and he could walk but became easily tired. After half an hour or so of playing with some toys, which he did quite well, he was clearly tired. He had not said very much, and what he said was difficult to understand, although he seemed happy with his carer. But suddenly he uttered one word very clearly to his carer – 'Home'. That one word seemed to convey so much – not only the simple fact of having had enough, but also about where he wanted to be after all the earlier instability. I have to add that when I then talked to his grandmother about possible options for this little boy, she became very distraught at the idea of him being moved from his current placement; she felt that he was alive thanks to his carers' devotion. She described him as a 'dear little soul', who would not last a move from the carers. I felt that she was right, and it was the first and only time that I myself became visibly upset in an assessment. I had a sudden image of what it might be like for him to have to cope with a move, both psychologically and physically; I felt that such a move would be a terrible risk. It was as if his soul hung in the balance. I cannot give details of the ins and outs of the court process, except to say that, rather typically, information from the paediatricians was not obtained for court until the very last minute – I was prevented from contacting them, supposedly as I might bias their response – and they supported him remaining where he was, at the place which had become his home, and the court supported this view. His early life in hospital was a physical space where he could be kept alive but was obviously not a place where he could be emotionally sustained; it was not a home, not a place where he could develop an organizing and sustaining psychic structure.

Much of this book develops, from a number of different viewpoints, the significance of home in our lives. I shall put forward the central role of what I have called a *psychic home* as a vital psychic structure which gathers together a number of different human functions. Along the way, I shall also question what we mean by the powerfully evocative notion of the human *soul*, which has important links to the notion of home; indeed, I shall suggest that what makes us human is that we allow a home for the soul. The word 'soul' seems to be both abstract and yet also powerfully emotive. It can be approached from a number of different angles, from philosophy, religion, sociology, literature and neuroscience. No one discipline has the monopoly on understanding the soul concept. I shall certainly not have the final answer to the mysteries and complexities of the soul but hope to evoke some restoration of its place in our thinking. I shall explore how the word 'soul' and similar key words, such as 'spirit' and 'inwardness', express so much that is essential for humans, even if we cannot be too precise about their meanings.

This desire to explore this field began in earnest while I was visiting the National Gallery. One of my greatest pleasures is to spend time there contemplating a few pictures at a time. An hour or so is generally enough to make contact with a group of paintings, such as the Rembrandts and other Dutch masters, a few Renaissance masters, some of the Impressionists or some other group that may suddenly catch my eye. Rather than skim through loads of paintings in turn, I have learned to focus on a few, finding in them depths of expression and content by means of repeated visits. In some ways, this is like getting to know somebody, gradually appreciating aspects of their character over time. It may even be something like falling in love: opening up to the other and letting the other interpenetrate one's own being.

Intimately linked to the artistic process for any artist or writer is, I think, their ultimate generosity of spirit, so that despite all their personal hesitations and doubts about their capacity to create a new work, there is a willingness to commit themselves, to put it down on canvas or on paper, in a brave and generous act of exposure. With the artist of genius such as Rembrandt, one can see a development of means and technical mastery, in his case, moving from the haughty confidence of youth to the reticent, almost 'shy' knowledge of maturity. In his last paintings, his self-exposure seems to come at a price – that seeing into the depths of one's self, both the darkness and the light, is not possible without having to bear loneliness and suffering. Not everyone can bear such knowledge; few can find the means to express it so movingly and cogently.

As you contemplate a late Rembrandt self-portrait, his eyes seem to take you into the picture, into the depths. Unlike a mirror, which reflects your own image back to you, the Rembrandt urges you to reflect into yourself in the act of being drawn into his image. Repeated visits are like drawing from some primal source of light and intensity, leaving you changed in some way, both uplifted and more melancholy. There is, of course, the presence of Rembrandt's own eyes as well, not only those you see in his self-portrait looking out at the spectator, or rather beyond the spectator to some other region, but also those eyes of his which look inwardly so poignantly at himself, scrutinizing and accepting what he saw with so few illusions.

The effect of such viewing remains, to me at least, something of a mystery. How is it that the portrait of a dead artist can have such life? How can marks of paint, however cleverly applied, still speak to us over and over, continuously drawing us both into the picture and into ourselves? It is as if we are witnessing some source of inner light in the picture itself. What is that elusive something that makes this happen? What is it in ourselves that is drawn out by repeatedly viewing the self-portraits?

I have no clear answer to these questions, but it does seem to me that we are here in the area of the human soul. It is what the psychologist Nicholas Humphrey has recently called the 'soul niche', a 'place where the magical interiority of human minds makes itself felt on every side' (2011, p. 154). Though very much rooted in cognitive science, he quotes with approval the theologian Keith Ward from the latter's book *In Defence of the Soul*. Ward makes the point that the whole point of talking of the soul is to remind us that we transcend the conditions of our material existence; we are not just molecules and genes. Thus,

> to believe in the soul is to believe that man is not just an object to be studied, experimented upon and scientifically defined and analysed, manipulated and controlled. It is to believe that man is essentially a subject, a centre of consciousness and reason, who transcends all objective analysis, who is always more than can be scientifically defined, predicted or controlled. In his essential subjectivity, man is a subject who has the capacity to be free and responsible – to be guided by moral claims, to determine his own nature by his response to these claims.
>
> (1998, p. 119)

Such a view about what makes us human resonates with the psychoanalytic view of the human subject. Sigmund Freud's discoveries were very much about bringing back into the realm of the human subject elements of the mind such as dreams and fantasies which had been devalued as mere objects of, at best, some objective knowledge or, at worst, of no consequence, just debris of the mind. The psychoanalytic encounter is very much about helping the patient *become a subject* through a process of recovery, or discovery, of their unconscious subjective life;

dreams and fantasies, for example, are precious signposts towards capturing the elusive human subject. As described in detail elsewhere (Kennedy, 1998, 2007), I mean by this that the analytic patient brings to their analyst all sorts of different stories, fixed patterns of relating or symptoms, hopes, expectations and resistances. Patients often come with a sense of isolation, of either being alone with suffering or suffering from being alone. And they come to analysis subject *to* various forces in their life, past and present. If the analysis works, then there is the possibility of their becoming subject *of* their experiences and ultimately their lives, with a sense of no longer feeling isolated, while being more in contact with others. Some patients have described this shift as finding themselves, or finding meaning, of feeling real, or of having a centre where before there was chaos or nothingness, and even occasionally that they have found their soul or that the soul has been put back into their lives, which until then had become 'soul-less'.

Everyday language occasionally uses the soul concept in somewhat similar ways in order to express something alive in the human subject. Music can be described as having soul when it hits the emotional core of the listener. And of course there is 'soul music', whose basic rhythms reach deep into the body to create a powerful feeling of aliveness. People talk about occasionally finding their 'soul mate', the person to whom they feel especially close, with whom they can share their most intimate emotions with ease. On the other hand, music or literature can be described as lacking soul, lacking some essential quality of sensitivity or depth of feeling. A person can be described as lacking a soul in the sense of a deep moral sense; some people would 'sell their soul' in order to get what they want, if they have a soul at all.

Saul Bellow went so far as to write in his essay 'A Matter of the Soul' that 'what novelists, composers, singers, have in common is the soul to which their appeal is made, whether it is barren or fertile, empty or full, whether the soul knows something, feels something, loves something' (1994, p. 77). Here he was contrasting the world of the arts with the materialism and disenchantment of the new social, economic and technological order. He wrote that essay in 1975, but it seems even more relevant today, where technology, however useful, has created new dangers for the human soul, ever-new ways of alienating us from ourselves and from ordinary everyday contact with one another. For those who need convincing, I suggest observing passengers in an overground train at the end of day for a few moments. While not denying the amazing usefulness of the mobile phone, to see so many people playing with phones or tablets, needing to keep drawing out the phone from their pocket as if anxious that communication will otherwise cease, and once to even see a young man talking on his phone to his friend nearby rather than face to face, is deeply depressing. Anachronistic thoughts about our souls being sold to the devil even come to mind. We seem to be living in a fragmented new world, what Zygmunt Bauman (2004) calls the era of 'liquid modernity' (p. 12), with our mobile world being cut into fragments and disconnected episodes rather than providing stable experiences. Indeed, it was experiences such as that in the train that have led me wanting to return to the notion of the soul as something that involves an essential aspect of our subjectivity.

It was Bruno Bettelheim who reminded us that Freud himself considered that psychoanalysis was ultimately the treatment of man's soul (German, *Seele*). Freud was not precise about what the soul was. Bettelheim suggested that Freud chose the term 'because of its inexactitude, its emotional resonance. Its ambiguity speaks for the ambiguity of the psyche itself, which reflects many different warring levels of consciousness simultaneously. By "soul" or "psyche" Freud means that which is most valuable in man while he is alive . . . it is intangible, but it nevertheless exercises a powerful influence on our lives. It is what makes us human' (Bettelheim, 1983, pp. 77–8).

Of course, as Bettelheim emphasized, the German use of the term soul is different from that in English and has less obvious religious overtones. Freud was also influenced by contemporary thinkers such as Franz Brentano, for whom psychology was the 'science of the soul', the whole domain of the inner world (1982, p. 163). For Brentano, the soul makes up the unity and particularity of a person but has multiple activities.

German does have another word, *Geist*, or spirit, which is common in German philosophy but which has different and again more religious resonances in English. Spirit seems to merge at times with 'subject', 'mind' or even 'soul'. There can be a world spirit, a spirit of the times or a human spirit. The philosopher Ernst Cassirer wrote how the human spirit has created 'symbolic forms' (1955, p. 78) in the sciences and the arts as expression of its creative intellect.

The point is, I suppose, that there are a number of these powerfully resonant words aimed at capturing some essential human quality; they overlap to some extent in their meaning and history. They may be difficult to define, or their definitions may evolve, but they remain embedded in our culture and seem to speak to us in significant ways.

If we were to take Bettelheim's view of Freud seriously, then it would be more accurate to talk about 'soul analysis' rather than psychoanalysis. The advantage then is that we would be approaching nearer to Freud's human endeavour; the disadvantage in English is that the word soul still has more religious meaning that it has in German. This will not, however, prevent me from endeavouring to explore the use of the word soul in its manifold meanings.

The philosopher William Barrett, in his book pointedly titled *Death of the Soul*, commented that the notion of a soul is more encompassing than the reasoning self and that 'we have a new and more powerful reason to be aware of this with the emergence of psychoanalysis . . . "Psyche" in Greek means soul – a meaning we should not let ourselves forget – and psychoanalysis, accordingly, is a therapy which deals with the individual soul . . . [W]ith the historical appearance of psychoanalysis it is as if the psyche, long submerged by our culture, has become very real and has resurfaced' (1987, p. 19).

Two other areas of experience have recently led me to take up the soul theme: the death of my parents and then renewed thinking after those, and other deaths, about my daily clinical work as a psychoanalyst with patients, which I certainly agree can be seen as very much dealing with the care of the patient's soul.

As a young doctor I often saw people die, particularly on medical wards, which are mainly populated with the elderly. However much one was supposed to remain unmoved and objective as a doctor in training, it was not possible to ignore the intense and complex cluster of emotions surrounding the dying patient. In those days there was relatively less focus on doing everything possible to keep someone alive, less use of technology and more attention to making the patient comfortable during the process of dying. Sometimes the family and patient took part in the death with full knowledge of what was happening; at other times it was clear that the patient had no wish to consciously know what was happening to them. There was usually a discussion with the relatives about what the patient wanted to be told, and a judgement made about what was thought to be bearable. Each person has his or her own death. Some fight to the very end, others give up quickly out of despair; some accept the inevitable with grace, others have no idea what is happening to them, particularly of course when their brain is severely damaged as with a stroke or in dementia.

One cannot escape the reality of the death of the body, but dying, as I have indicated by just a few remarks about the process of dying, is not just a bodily process. The body dies, but what of the person? The relatives have not lost a body but a loved one. Heartbeats and blood pressures can be monitored, but how do you monitor that love? Can you put a figure on the quality of attachment? The ancients distinguished diseases of the body, which can be observed and treated, from those of the soul such as passions, including happiness, misery and madness; the physician was concerned with the former, the philosopher with the latter. However, as Jackie Pigeaud (2006) has pointed out, this division is far from clear; there is considerable overlap and a complex interaction between the fields of the body and of the soul, even in these ancient writings. Thus, from early on in Western thought, the phenomenon of disease and dying brought to light fundamental dilemmas about the encounter between the material body and what it is to be human, and what is lost when dying.

Although I saw many deaths when I was young, it was only being present at my parents' recent deaths that brought back to life some observations that had made no sense at that earlier time. I would summarize these experiences in terms of a 'special light' associated with the person's aliveness going out. It is well known that as the person is nearing death, something goes in the eyes; the eyes no longer reflect back our own gaze. The dying person's eyes may not be focusing well, their physiological functions may be failing and their expression loses its quality, but something else seems to be happening. The person's gaze goes; they are retreating from the other's gaze, becoming ever more distant, leaving us increasingly looking on, until at the moment of death, the light behind the eyes appears to go and there is only darkness; the person has gone, their special light extinguished; the link with us is broken. The end of the dying person's gaze gives us a sense of what in life we call our soul, the place, wherever that is, where *the other's gaze gives back to us who we are*, gives us a sense of our own identity. The focus of where this kind of intersubjective exchange takes place is between the eyes of the participants, but the source of the inner light remains a puzzle, much as it is when looking at a Rembrandt self-portrait. From these sorts of phenomenological observation, I would suggest that the soul is essentially an *intersubjective* entity, emerging from interactions between human subjects, not just an entity involved in a magical 'interiority'. Such a view has resonances with Emile Durkheim's notion of the soul as the 'social principle' (1912, pp. 242–75). On the one hand, one can see the soul as the best and most profound part of our being, and on the other hand, as a temporary guest that has come to us from the outside, that is from society, that lives inside us as distinct from the body, and that must one day regain independence. The soul in the latter sense represents something within us that is other than ourselves; it is the voice of society within.

This experience of the light leaving the person is probably one of the roots of the notion of an immortal soul that inhabits the body and then leaves the body after death. I am certainly not making any claims that this is indeed what happens, and anyway this is not my area of expertise, to say the least, though I think it is clear that what is essentially human, the link with others, dies with the body. I would call *that which links with others* the human soul; that is, I am proposing an essentially *psychological* model of understanding the soul. I would not rule out that what I am describing at death is a reflection of the end of brain function; I certainly think it is clear that the world of human functions is dependent on an intact brain. Certain major injuries to the brain, such as those involving the frontal cortex, are well known to fundamentally change an individual's personality, so that they may be unable to regulate their emotions or safely regulate their behaviour. Furthermore, we are divided within our own brains, between left and right hemispheres, though somehow we try to make a unity of that division, if only as a metaphor of what is possible (McGilchrist, 2009).

It may well be that in talking about the soul, one is essentially describing an important human function to see beyond the physical presence of other people. But because there is overlapping territory at this point between religion and psychology, much of what religious thinkers have to say about the nature of the soul is of great interest and lasting significance, even if one is a thoroughgoing materialist.

And while not going along fully with the claims of religious belief myself, I would also follow William James's suggestion in his *The Principles of Psychology* that

> one cannot afford to despise any of these great traditional objects of belief. Whether we realize it or not, there is always a great drift of reasons, positive and negative, towing us in their direction. If there be such entities as Souls in the universe, they may possibly be affected by the manifold occurrences that go on in the nervous centres. To the state of the entire brain at a given moment they may respond by inward modifications of their own . . . I confess,

therefore, that to posit a soul influenced in some mysterious way by the brain-states and responding to them by conscious affections of its own, seems to me the line of least logical resistance, so far as we yet have attained.

(1890, p. 181)

But do we need the notion of a soul? Can we live without it, and if so is there a price in so doing? Is there too much religious 'baggage' to make its use anything but anachronistic? Do we go along with Gilbert Ryle (1949) and assume that the term soul, like that of 'mind', owes its existence to a form of category mistake, in which we give a name to a collection of functions over and above the functions themselves, like imagining Oxford University is an entity different from the colleges making up the university, forming a kind of ghost university, a shadow of the actual one? Similarly, do we go along with Daniel Dennett who states that 'the trouble with brains is that when you look in them, you discover that there is nobody home' (1991, p. 29)? Alternatively, perhaps we are to accept the detailed arguments of Maxwell Bennett and Peter Hacker, who maintain that while neuroscience can 'discover the neural preconditions for the possibility of the exercise of distinctly human powers of thought and reasoning, of articulate memory and imagination, of emotion and volition . . . What it *cannot* do is *replace* the wide range of ordinary psychological explanations of human activities in terms of reasons, intentions, purposes, goals, values, rules and conventions by neurological explanations' (2003, p. 3).

That is, they argue that only *human beings* think, feel and relate, not brains. That is not to say that one can learn much about brains that may well have some bearing on how we think, feel and relate. Indeed, I shall make reference to such work in Chapter Five. But to explain human activity purely on the basis of neural pathways is a fundamental conceptual confusion. As Bennett and Hacker put it, 'It is human beings, not their brains, that are said to have minds, and to say that is simply to say that human beings have an array of distinctive capacities' (2003, p. 106). Such a view very much echoes the thought of Ludwig Wittgenstein, about whom Hacker has written major works. Thus in his *Philosophical Investigations*, Wittgenstein writes that is only of a 'living human being' that one can say that it has sensations, or is conscious or unconscious (1953, rev. 2009, section 280).

Norman Malcolm, Wittgenstein's student, put this issue very clearly:

Present-day philosophy has justifiably turned away from the Cartesian view, but has proposed instead something equally absurd, namely, that the human brain, or even the computational states of machines, are the bearers of mental predicates. It is as if philosophers *could not believe* that the living corporeal human being is the subject of those predicates.

Human life contains many elements or stages: birth, childhood, family life, schooling, sexual awakening, love friendship, marriage, work, poverty, parenthood, ageing, illness, death. These destinies and vicissitudes are undergone and suffered by *people,* by you and me: *not* by immaterial minds or brains or machines. The human being who encounters those conditions is the *subject.*

(1984, pp. 100–1)

If this view of the limited role of neuroscience in understanding how we think and feel is correct, then a considerable amount of time and energy spent trying to figure out the brain processes involved in creating human consciousness is a waste of time, for such an approach will never understand what makes us human. This is not say that it is a waste of time per se, because neuroscience, such as described by Antonio Damasio (2010), is producing some very interesting findings about the brain and how consciousness may be formed by the interaction of different parts of the brain, and I shall refer to some of these findings in Chapter Five. But that still leaves out what we find significant about our lives, which brings us to the soul territory.

My view is that the soul is a psychological and cultural concept, not a natural science concept. Thus it is of interest what happens in the brain, but it is neither here nor there, although it is important and relevant when, for example, diseases affect the brain and cause disturbances in behaviour and emotional regulation. But it is of only marginal interest to know the composition of the molecules in Rembrandt's portraits, or what pathways in the brain are firing when we enjoy looking at a work of art. We want to know how Rembrandt talks to us humanly and how his pictures impact on us as living human beings, soul communicating with soul. It will be of great interest to know how the brain produces consciousness, and I certainly enjoy reading about neuroscience, but it is irrelevant to understanding the Rembrandt portrait, which speaks to us at another level altogether, that involving the communication between human beings, that is, at the soul level.

I would also maintain that to do without the notion of a soul, even if at the very least it is kept as a metaphorical expression for being alive, would be to lose too much that is precious about being human. Without something like souls, what are we? According to Wittgenstein, we could be automata; but, he wonders, how do we then feel pain? For those of us who deal with the extremes of human mental suffering, it is difficult to understand how people split off areas of their experience, can maintain often very strange states of mind or can behave in what appears to be completely against their best interests, unless one looks for explanations beyond mere physical events.

In addition, living without some notion that oneself and other people are not just physical objects but something different can have disastrous consequences. One can see this with autistic children who may not grasp the notion of another person. This is described as them not having a theory of mind. My experience of seeing many autistic children is that while this is undoubtedly a crucial and diagnostic feature, these children also have the ability to empathize, even if distorted; they are not callous. There is even recent scientific evidence for this observation.

Thus, one might say that they have a mind problem but still have a soul, though a soul in need of coming alive.

Even Dennett, who is deeply sceptical about the existence of a central self, talks about looking in the brain (Dennett, 1991). But who is it that is doing the looking in the brain? Why is the 'third-person' perspective being privileged over the 'first-person' perspective? How do we move from physical-chemical processes to personal experience? How do we bridge the gap between the pattern of firing of neurones in the brain and a person's experience of pain, sorrow and love? Is it by nature unbridgeable, or can we bridge that gap? There continue to be attempts to do just that. For example, Damasio's latest book *Self Comes to Mind* (2010) gives an elaborate theory of how consciousness is created by the brain, a theory that is well worth examining. But when (p. 70) he describes that the mind is the 'consequence' of the brain's incessant and dynamic mapping, we are still no wiser about how this occurs; minds *emerge* from the dynamic interplay of nerve circuits, but we are no wiser as to how they emerge. As the great physiologist Sir Charles Sherrington put it in his book on human nature, physiology has gotten far in examining the electrical activity in the 'mental' part of the brain, but 'has it brought us to the "mind"? It has brought us to the brain as a telephone exchange. All the exchange consists of is switches. What we really wanted was the subscribers using the exchange. The subscribers with their thoughts, their desires, their anticipations, their motives, their anxieties, their rejoicings' (1940, p. 222). Yet we cannot get that latter knowledge from just knowing the electrical circuits, as interesting as these circuits may be. Something more must be found, and that is where the human subject, the first-person perspective, has to come into the picture.

Is there a home for this first-person perspective? Is there a home for the notion of the soul? Or are there, as Donald Davidson (1970) argues, two realms of explanation for human activity – mental and physical events, each with its own set of justifications, each irreducible to one another? Is there, then, an unbridgeable divide between the brain and the mind, the circuits and the subscribers?

There are no easy answers to any of these questions, and even pure materialists can express considerable passion about their passions being only caused by physical events. I will look at some of the arguments for and against a purely physical explanation of human activities in Chapter Five but have decided not to get too bogged down by these sorts of questions, at least at this early point of my narrative. I have decided to take a more 'tangential' approach to this whole field and attempt to approach the soul question in a relatively loose way, assuming, as does Humphrey, that we need such a 'magical' notion as part of our human world. Once I have taken this approach, I will then reexamine the strengths and limitations of using such a concept, by tackling those for and against such a view from philosophical and neuroscientific viewpoints.

***

I would suggest that when we talk about a person's soul, we are touching on something elemental, their essence, something irreducible, what makes them human, their sense of being a subject of experience, what Bishop George

Berkeley (1710, p. 136) called an "active being," their unique *voice*, what goes deep within the person, much of course unconsciously – hence the need for some psychoanalytic understanding in exploring the soul territory.

I would add here that in considering what we mean by the soul, we cannot escape the influence of past thinkers, including those of ancient Greece, because much of what we take for granted in the way we think about such matters bears their traces. Thus, just to take Plato's notions of the soul in the *Phaedo*, an account of Socrates's last moments before being executed with poison – Socrates is described as discoursing on the nature of the soul, its relation to the body and the issue of whether or not it is immortal, and if so, how the soul comes to inhabit the body and then leave it. For Plato, the body is a kind of home for the soul; the soul certainly becomes fastened and welded to the body, but as though in a prison. While the soul has communion with the invisible world of truth, the divine, the immortal, intellectual and indissoluble world of forms, the body is tied down by pleasure and pain, the world of the senses. The soul is weighed down by the body and dragged back into the visible world of the senses; death is a potential release for the soul from this prison house.

One may not agree with Plato's argument for the immortality of the soul, and yet it is difficult not to be moved by his descriptions of the soul and its struggle with the body. These sorts of arguments have certainly become the basis for subsequent thinkers, for example, when considering issues such as whether the soul and body are of the same or different substance; if different, how they relate; if the same, how, if at all, they can be differentiated; whether the body is a prison for the soul or in a more comfortable relationship with the body and so on. Such different views of the soul's nature have certainly influenced my own thinking, as will become clearer.

However, I will start with the assumption that the soul is a description of an important human ability to see beyond the physical aspect of a person, to see more in a human being than physical and chemical processes. I shall be proposing that one way of encapsulating the place of the soul in one's life is to describe a human being as providing a 'welcoming' home for the soul, in contrast to Plato's prison house. This will mean having to look at some length at what we mean by the concept of home, and I will particularly focus on my notion of the importance for life and identity of having what I call a psychic home, an organizing psychic structure central to the notion of personal identity. This is, I would suggest, one answer to Dennett's view that there is 'nobody home' in the brain. As an illustration of this concept, I will explore how it can help to understand a vital element of William Wordsworth's development as a poet. Thoughts about the human soul merge to some extent with those concerning issues of identity and subjectivity; there are overlapping territories or 'fields' of thought, each field adding depth to the others.

The book will look from various angles at some basic aspects of the human condition, including loneliness and solitude, happiness and misery and the complexities of human identity, as ways of trying to explore more fully the soul territory and how such the notion of a soul helps us to feel at home in the world.

Chapter 2

Psychic home

Home and homelessness

Having a home implies both having a physical entity, the physical structure of the dwelling, the house, but also something that goes beyond the building blocks into the area of the interior of the soul. Having an idea of home is just as vital for a person as having a physical shelter; it is one of the most basic human needs. We need to feel at home in the world – it makes us feel secure, it provides the base from which we can explore; the loss of a sense of home is deeply traumatic, as is of course the loss of a house. Yet we need to leave home in order to find ourselves, in order to mature and have a firm sense of identity. If exiled, we may be able to carry the sense of home with us, yet there is often a poignant yearning for the original home. This may be conveyed by that sense of one's physical presence being in one country, but one's soul in another.

The sense of home is so basic that we can take it for granted unless the continuity provided by a stable home is undermined. I often see the way that a lack of a clear home can drastically affect a child's stability while doing assessments for social services and the courts. Children often have to be placed in foster care when their own family has become unsafe. While they may settle well into the foster placement, it is rare not to see how confused and troubled children become, if only beneath the surface, until a final decision is made about their future. Some young children in these circumstances will draw two houses, with little connection. Others may be unable to represent the confusion symbolically and just remain confused and behaviourally challenging. One's original home consisted not only of the bricks and mortar of the building, its physical surroundings and interior structures, but also the memories of relationships. Before describing my own concept of a psychic home in detail, I will look at some of the general issues raised by the meaning of having, or not having, a home, which will provide some of the framework for my ideas.

Renos Papadopoulos (2002), exploring psychoanalytically issues raised by the treatment of refugees, also emphasizes how the notion of home is one of the most fundamental for humans; it is both the place of origin and the destination we try to reach. Thus home and homecoming are basic to many human experiences and much of literature. Already this is clear in Homer, when, for example, Odysseus, near the beginning of *The Odyssey*, yearns to see the smoke from his homeland and then die, setting the theme and the tone for the poem.

One could add that there are a number of famous examples in Homer's *Odyssey* where one can see the resonances of the place of home and homecoming, for example, when Odysseus has finally returned home to Ithaca after nearly twenty years away, disguised as a beggar but also greatly changed physically. As he approaches his home in order to confront the pack of suitors who have intruded disrespectfully into his palace and are vying for the attentions of his wife, Penelope, he is accompanied by a friendly swineherd, who is unaware of Odysseus's royal identity. Nearing the palace, they come across an old dog left abandoned on a pile of mule and cattle dung, hardly able to move. But as Odysseus passes, the dog pricks up his ears and raises his head, recognizing the master who trained him and went hunting with him. Odysseus is unable to reciprocate as he wishes to keep his identity secret but carefully wipes a tear away. As the master passes on, the dog finally gives up his struggle and dies.

Later in the palace and still disguised, Odysseus is offered hospitality by his wife, who still does not recognize him. She asks his old nurse to wash his feet as a token of hospitality. This nurse at first finds him strangely familiar, very much like her old master. But Odysseus manages to fob her off. However, as she prepares to wash him, he has to reveal his thigh on which is engraved an old scar he received from the tusk of a boar while hunting. When the old woman passes her hand over the scar, she at once recognizes who he is and lets the basin fall onto the floor. With tears in her eyes, she wishes to let her mistress know his identity, but Penelope is distracted and the moment passes. Indeed, it is only later, and after he has slaughtered the suitors, that Penelope is convinced of her husband's identity when he reveals the intimate secrets of the marital bed, which he himself had built out of a thick olive tree.

Thus we have here, in Homer's homecoming scenes, so many of the basic issues surrounding that of identity and what I shall later describe as a psychic home: for example, how much a person remains the same over time, how much they change beyond recognition, yet are still capable of being recognized, given the right conditions; what kind of evidence we require to confirm a person's unique identity; what marks out the subject as having that unique identity; how the identity of the subject and recognition by the other are intimately linked; and how one's identity is marked forever by one's home, the psychic home one carries around in exile, during various adventures in foreign climes, as well as when at last one returns to the family hearth. As Papadopoulos describes, 'The fundamental sense of home forms part of the substratum of identity which is structured as a mosaic and consists of a great number of smaller elements which together form a coherent whole' (2002, p. 17). This mosaic substratum provides us with the primary sense of our humanity, continuity and belonging – hence the degree of trauma when a refugee loses their home. I shall return in more detail to the whole issue of what we mean by identity in Chapter Four.

Only a few psychoanalytic thinkers use some explicit notion of home in their work. For example, John Bowlby (1988) emphasizes the importance for the child's future secure attachments of having a secure base from which to explore. The quality of the primary attachment, or home base, affects the quality of the child's subsequent development and sense of security. The little boy I described in Chapter One had finally found that home base after a year of uncertainty. Donald Winnicott (1965, p. 236) laid great emphasis on the importance for development of a good enough, commonplace home. For him this was the basis for a democratic society, where development can take place without undue interference. As he put in the title of one of his books (Winnicott, 1986), quoting from T. S. Eliot's poem 'East Coker', 'Home is where we start from.' Although other analytic thinkers may not specifically refer to the place of home, the need in any theory of development for a starting place for the development of the self or subject is common.

In his evocative book *The Poetics of Space*, Gaston Bachelard examines the meanings of domestic space philosophically and poetically. In his study of human intimacy, he 'poses the problem of the poetics of the house' (1958, p. xxxvi). He uses the image of the house to explore the depths of the soul; for him, 'there is ground for taking the house as a *tool for analysis* of the human soul . . . Not only our memories, but the things we have forgotten are "housed". Our soul is an abode. And by remembering "houses" and "rooms" we learn to "abide" within ourselves' (1958, p. xxxviii).

One could thus say that the physical space of an established home has an important function in helping to shape the interior life, as can also be seen in Diana Fuss's book *The Sense of an Interior* (2004). There, she explores the link between the inner mind and the inner dwelling through exploring the rooms of four writers, including Freud and his consulting room. Interiority is described here as 'a mental structure constructed over time, with inner chambers and inner walls that exceed in strength and resistance the physical supports of any actual building' (Fuss, 2004, p. 7). There is an interaction between the subjectivity of the writer and the interior space where they write. The home is thus both part of the world, an object in the world, and a symbol for the human being and their relationships, a subjective entity.

Simon May has written a comprehensive history of love in its many manifestations. Finally, for him, love is the rapture we feel for people and things that inspire in us the hope of an indestructible grounding for our life. It is a rapture that sets us off on – and sustains – the long search for a secure relationship between our being and theirs.

> If we all have a need to love, it is because we need to feel at home in the world: to root our life in the here and now; to give our existence solidity and validity . . . This is the feeling that I call 'ontological rootedness' . . . [l]ove's overriding concern is to find a home for our life and being.
>
> (2011, p. 6)

This sense of home as the ground of our being, the place we need in order to feel secure, is of course fundamental, and I shall certainly incorporate this sense in my own concept of a psychic home. Yet we often feel to a greater or lesser extent incomplete, divided, and lacking a sense of the whole. There is a yearning for wholeness, for a home where we can feel truly ourselves. Some find this home within, others need something external and still others need a being that transcends daily life, such as a God, in order to feel complete. Whatever the nature of the home we seek, the fear of homelessness is never far from that of the sense of being at home.

Some philosophers have even found a place for the home and homelessness within their structure of thinking. Thus for Martin Heidegger 'being' and coming home are interrelated in complex ways. Although the sense of being homeless, with an accompanying loss of meaning, is a basic given of the human condition, we need to find ways to come back home. 'Home-coming is . . . both the process and goal of authentic being' (G. Steiner, 1978, p. 49). When we become lost in everyday existence, we feel homeless (German, *unheimliche*), unhoused. But in pursuit of authentic being, one begins to truly 'dwell' in the world (Heidegger, 1971, p. 145ff.). Man may inhabit a house, but dwelling there requires something more than mere habitation. 'Dwelling . . . is the *basic character* of Being in keeping with which mortals exist' (Heidegger, 1971, p. 160). In addition, for Heidegger, language is what he calls the 'house of being' (qtd. in Steiner, G., 1978, p. 122), where man dwells.

John Gale (2000) from the charity Community Housing and Therapy (CHT) has developed these aspects of Heidegger's thought in their application to residential community treatment of mentally ill patients. Thus for him, Being is always residential. One exists in relation to a location, even if homeless; this location is a fundamental part of human existence. Schizophrenics, who are given great help in the homes that CHT runs, are dis-located; they experience psychic homelessness wherever they are physically placed. By providing a therapeutic residential setting for such patients, CHT can help them begin to retrieve a sense of location, of dwelling in the world rather than retreating from it.

Madness and being dis-located, or psychically homeless, is vividly illustrated in *King Lear*. Once Lear has handed over his power and authority to his daughters, he seeks to live in each of their homes with his household retinue, his knights. But of course neither Regan nor Goneril will agree to have him, at least on their father's terms, and he eventually goes off into the storm on the heath, mad with grief and homeless. He finds shelter in a hovel, a temporary home, together with Edgar, who is feigning madness to escape death. There, Lear at last, despite of or because of his madness, begins to see the truth behind appearances. As he is finally persuaded by Kent to enter the hovel, he muses,

> Poor naked wretches, whereso'er you are,
> That bide the pelting of this pitiless storm,
> How shall your houseless heads and unfed sides,

Your looped and window'd raggedness, defend you
From seasons such as these? O! I have ta'en
Too little care of this.
          (*King Lear*, Act Three, Scene Four, lines 28–31)

One can see here allusions here both to the loss of a physical home, but also to the loss of reason when the home no longer provides shelter for the mind or soul.

The poet John Burnside constantly questions what it means to dwell in the world. A number of his poems specifically address what it means to have a home. The quest for a dwelling place is not free from difficulties:

1 A Place by the Sea

. . . what we think of as home
is a hazard to others
our shorelines edged with rocks and shallow
sandbanks
    reefs
where navigation fails . . .
          (Burnside, 2000, 'Settlements', lines 1–6)

III Wells

–   there's more to the making of home
–   than I ever expected: . . .
          (Burnside, 2000 'Settlements', lines 7–8)

This poem's very appearance on the page, with indentations and spaces, represents the hazardous nature of the home he is describing, one that both shelters the self and creates dangers for others and ultimately for oneself. His poetry is a 'complex exploration of our place in the world, one which poses a series of questions surrounding what it means to dwell' (Pass, 2011, p. 45).

Burnside, as he described in an interview for the poetry magazine *Agenda*, has certainly read Heidegger. 'We have Heidegger to thank for understanding that the real problem for mankind is our homelessness – and we have centuries of philosophical thought to thank for the recognition that, if something presents itself to us as a problem, our best answer is to embrace it. It may sound perverse of me, but the truth is that I'd rather follow the path of homelessness to wild dwelling than accept the costly shelter of a certain kind of building – building that displaces, violates and domesticates what some have called, in translation and as a kind of shorthand, *the great spirit*' (Burnside, 2011b, p. 23).

Home is a world for Burnside and is both suffused by the commonplace, the world of everyday, yet also determined by the 'spirit', which the participants bring together to make a home. It provides a place in which to dwell and yet is fraught with hazards. Unless one takes account of the hazards, one may lose oneself or be wrecked; home, then, can becomes a catalogue of wrecks. Hence the need to retain a certain flexibility; home may provide a settlement for the spirit, or the soul, but to be too comfortable, too settled, may risk losing what you are searching for. 'In short, the perpetual need for settlement, like the quest for the moment's grace, is necessary because home, like grace, is a temporary, sometimes fleeting thing, and cannot be *occupied* as such . . . [m]y view of home is a bit like some conundrum from quantum physics. Home is there until we try to pin it down . . . It's like happiness, I think. Let it happen, and you're fine, but you can't *make* it come true' (Burnside 2011b, p. 23).

In Shelley Mallett's critical review of the literature on understanding the home concept, home can be seen as a place, a space, a feeling, a practice and a state of mind. It is a multidimensional concept and can function as a repository for complex, interrelated and at times contradictory sociocultural ideas about people's relationships with one another. For example,

> it can be a dwelling-place or a lived space of interaction between people, places or things; or perhaps both. The boundaries of home can be permeable and/or impermeable. Home can be singular and/or plural, alienable and/or inalienable, fixed and stable and/or mobile and changing. It can be associated with feelings of comfort, ease, intimacy, relaxation and security and/or oppression, tyranny and persecution . . . Home can be an expression of one's (possibly fluid) identity and sense of self and/or one's body might be home to the self . . .
>
> (2004, p. 84)

As Susan Neiman points out, the metaphor of being at home in the world is an old one. Kant listed four rather unappealing models of home that different traditions held the world to provide – a cheap inn, a prison, a madhouse and a latrine. Yet home is, 'the normal – whatever place you happen to start from and can return to without having to answer questions. It's a metaphor that may seem to fit reduced expectations. We no longer seek towers that would reach to the heavens; we've abandoned attempts to prove that we live in a chain of being whose every link bears witness to the glory of God. We merely seek assurance that we find ourselves in a place where we know our way about' (Neiman, 2002, p. 304).

But, as she points out, the absence of such assurance is the touchstone of the modern. Ever since the massive destructive earthquake of Lisbon in 1755, our confidence in a world we could trust has been shaken, and since Auschwitz, even more so. Yet, as Hannah Arendt put it in her seminal book *Eichmann in Jerusalem*, we still wish to find a place fit for human habitation (1963, p. 233).

For the theologian Reinhold Niebuhr, the essential homelessness of the human spirit is the ground of all religion, as 'the self which stands outside itself and the world cannot find the meaning of life in itself or the world,' (1941, p. 14). In contrast, William Barrett in *Irrational Man*, his classic study of existential philosophy, charted how in losing religion modern man 'lost the concrete connection with a transcendent realm of being; he was set free to deal with this world in all its brute objectivity. But he was bound to feel homeless in such a world, which no longer answered the needs of his spirit. A home is the accepted framework, which habitually contains our life. To lose one's psychic container is to be cast adrift, to become a wanderer upon the face of the earth' (1959, p. 25).

Deprived of his customary home, man became both a dispossessed and fragmentary being. Existentialism can be seen as an attempt to answer the challenge that this new view of man provides – accepting man's fragility and the threat of nothingness, how then to find meaning? Kierkegaard's answer within religion involves a personal choice, an either/or, where the subject has to make a deep encounter with the self or subject, always hovering around an abyss of despair or dread; the aim is to become a 'subjective thinker'. Nietzsche, harking back to the Greeks, before Christianity had put its blight on human drives, urges a joining together of the Apollonian world of order and individuation with the Dionysian world of intoxication and the feeling of one-ness, loss of self. For Heidegger, the challenges raised by Kierkegaard and Nietzsche are answered through being open to being, facing the reality of man's finitude and his homelessness and then reaching back to being where subject and object meet (Barrett, 1959, p. 237).

Finally, if one is to understand the place of homelessness in the human psyche or soul, then Freud's paper on *The Uncanny – das Unheimliche*, in German, literally, the 'unhomely' – is fundamental. Uncanny experiences include those that are frightening and arouse a sense of horror and dread. Freud traces such experiences back to what is previously known and familiar, and yet which erupt in unexpected ways. The word *heimliche* in German can be traced back to what is homelike, what belongs to the house, but also something that becomes concealed, withdrawn from the eyes of strangers (Freud, 1919, p. 225). Typical uncanny experiences include inanimate objects apparently coming to life, a sudden appearance of a double, the appearance of ghosts and spirits and other hauntings. Something becomes uncanny when the distinction between imagination (Phantasie) and reality is effaced (1919, p. 244). Ultimately, the uncanny is something which is secretly familiar and has undergone repression and then returned from it (1919, p. 245) – hence the double feeling of the strange and the unfamiliar that is indicative of an uncanny experience.

Heidegger, in his early *Being and Time* (1926, p. 223), describes anxiety as a basic state of mind where one feels uncanny, or not at home. We can flee from this primordial sense of anxiety into the state of being 'at home' as an escape, rather than face the reality of not being at home. That is, for him the 'not-at-home' is the more primordial phenomenon. This perhaps contrasts with a different emphasis he makes in his later thought (Heidegger, 1971, pp. 145–61), where dwelling becomes the basic character of being. Dwelling is different from being housed. Man may inhabit a house, but dwelling has a different and more elemental quality, which for him involves some kind of safeguarding of freedom; the house is not just a shelter, but also a place where man dwells at peace and, I think, connected with the world around him in a primordial and open way.

Anthony Vidler in his book *The Architectural Uncanny*, influenced by Freud and Heidegger, explores the uncanny as a metaphor for a 'fundamentally unliveable modern condition' (Vidler, 1992, p. x). With an architectural emphasis, he traces the history of the spatial uncanny through the numerous 'haunted houses' of the romantic period, as well as in the way that it can become a means of understanding a number of contemporary architectural and urban projects. As he points out, the unease felt in the uncanny experience had as a favourite motif the 'contrast between a secure or homely interior and the fearful invasion of an alien presence; on a psychological level, its play was one of doubling, where the other is, strangely enough, experienced as a replica of the self, all the more fearsome because apparently the same' (1992, p. 3).

At the heart of this anxiety about an alien presence, Vidler suggests, is a fundamental insecurity – that of the newly established bourgeois, not quite at home in its own home. Since then, estrangement and unhomeliness have emerged as the intellectual watchwords of the modern, given periodic material and political force by the resurgence of actual homelessness generated by war and/or poverty (1992, p. 9).

There is thus an uneasy tension in the modern soul between feeling at home and feeling estranged. This tension is revealed in uncanny experiences, which one might say remind us of the precariousness of our hard-won sense of psychic organization. The French psychoanalyst Michel de M'Uzan (2009) emphasizes how uncanny experiences commemorate a crucial phase in the development of psychic functioning, a moment which brings to the fore the indeterminate nature of identity, when the self becomes 'strange' to itself.

Home: A history and the emergence of the interior

So far, the notion of a home as something central to us both psychologically and philosophically has been taken here as a given. Yet the notion of an interior space and of a domestic private space within the home has a particular history, which provides the backdrop for the developing notion of the individual's interior or inner world. While the notion of a domestic interior began with the development of Dutch interiors in the seventeenth century, it was only in the early to mid-nineteenth century, following the turmoil of the French Revolution, that developments in England led to the notion of a private place within the household for sleeping and family life, and with this the notion of a domestic home with private spaces. The domestic interior gradually emerged as an entity at a particular moment of history. The emergence of psychoanalysis as a treatment within the confines of a domestic space has to be seen within this historical context. Freud's consulting room became a privileged place where the patient's interior life could be laid bare, questioned and challenged, but that was only possible once the historical conditions were favourable for such an undertaking.

Witold Rybczynski, in his history of the idea of home, describes the way that the notion of home changed over the centuries, linked to social and cultural changes, including the way that the family and children were perceived. The typical medieval bourgeois house combined living and work, while the poor were extremely badly housed. People did not so much live in their houses as camp in them. Even the aristocracy did not have a sense of the comforts of one home; they often had many residences and might travel between them, taking their portable furniture with them. Life in the medieval home was full of people and activity, with large households, and houses were used for entertainment and for transacting business. Life in general was a public affair, and 'just as one did not have a strongly developed self-consciousness, one did not have a room of one's own' (Rybczynski, 1986, p. 35).

After the end of the Middle Ages and until the seventeenth century, the conditions of domestic life slowly changed. Houses became larger and more sturdily built, amenities gradually if slowly improved, and with the development of rented accommodations, people no longer had to work and live in the same building. The house was then gradually becoming a more private place. 'Together with this privatization of the home arose a growing sense of intimacy, of identifying the home exclusively with family life' (Rybczynski, 1986, p. 39). However, within the home personal privacy was as yet relatively unimportant. Rooms were still crowded, and there was no separate space for children.

The transition from the public feudal household to the private family home where privacy was possible gradually got under way. This was a crucial development. 'The growing sense of domestic intimacy was a human invention as much as any technical device. Indeed, it may have been more important, for it affected not only our physical surroundings, but our consciousness as well' (Rybczynski, 1986, p. 49).

It was in seventeenth century Netherlands that the family home emerged uniquely, reflecting the growing importance of the family in Dutch society. Special rooms for sleeping were differentiated, children were given special attention and a 'snug' [a Dutch word] home atmosphere began to be created. In Dutch society, '"home" brought together the meanings of house and of household, of dwelling and of refuge, of ownership and of affection. "Home" meant the house but also everything that was in it and around it, as well as the people, and the sense of satisfaction and contentment that all these conveyed' (Rybczynski, 1986, p. 62).

One can see this transition in seventeenth-century Dutch paintings of domestic scenes, which became popular items to hang on household walls. One can see in them the beginnings of a sense of a separate and special interior space.

Simultaneously, the Dutch home acquired a special feminine atmosphere, thanks to the significant and increasingly dominant role played by women in the home. It must be said that this view of Dutch paintings has been challenged as reflecting later family values projected backwards onto them (de Mare, 1999). Instead, others have emphasized the way that the paintings mark out a new visual space rather than reflecting a new domesticity (Hollander, 2002). My own view is that looking at these paintings, as with my description of an encounter with a Rembrandt self-portrait, provides a new way of seeing the human subject, one in which the subject is beginning to look inwards in a complex way. In this sense, I would agree that comfortable domesticity is not merely being represented in them but something more complex and challenging.

According to Rybczynski, it was in French homes of the eighteenth century that furnishing became increasingly informal and comfortable, with furniture specifically designed for women – such as easy chairs and chaises longues. The idea of comfort took some time to develop and was developed most significantly under the influence of Georgian England (1986, p. 104). The sedentary English bourgeois spent most of their time at home, especially those in their country homes; there, they would visit each other's homes, gossip and play indoor games, and there would be dances and dinner parties. This world is pictured in the newly created form of the novel. In addition, the English garden is created, where pleasant walks could take place. 'Since all these activities took place in and around the house, the result was that the home acquired a position of social importance that it had never known before, or since. No longer a place of work as it had been in the Middle Ages, the home became a place of leisure' (1986, p. 107).

As a result, private rooms for the family began to be differentiated, with children having their own bedrooms. The multiplication of bedrooms indicated not only that there were new sleeping arrangements, but also that there were new distinctions between the family and the individual. 'The desire for a room of one's own was not simply a matter of personal privacy. It demonstrated the growing awareness of individuality – of a growing personal inner life – and the need to express this individuality in physical ways' (Rybczynski, p. 110–1).

As described in the collection of papers, *A History of Private Life, Volume IV* (Perrot, 1990), the nineteenth century was the time of crucial developments in the domestic interior, led by changes to the English home, which were a reaction to the storms of the French Revolution and the radical shifts between the public and private realms. During the French Revolution, boundaries between public and private life became unstable (Hunt, 1990, p. 13ff.). An absence of boundaries between individuals was assumed to be the condition of public life (Perrot, 1990, p. 9). At the same time, the Revolution recognized, in theory at least, individual rights. As a reaction to the turmoil in France, English domestic life turned inwards, establishing the 'sweet delights of home' (C. Hall, 1990, p. 47ff.), where home became a place of tranquillity away from stress and strife. Coincidentally, the Romantic Movement encouraged a withdrawal into the self and the withdrawal of the family into a more clearly defined domestic space

(Hunt, 1990, p 13). This can be seen in the pattern of William and Dorothy Wordsworth's lives, as I shall trace in the next chapter.

Homes that were designed exclusively for domestic living with gardens surrounding them were new. Home became the haven for the harassed and anxious man who had to produce the material wealth on which the home depended (C. Hall, 1990, p. 74). A new category of 'housewife', the guardian of domestic virtue, the homemaker, was created. Religious evangelism with its message of sin, guilt and the possibilities of redemption fed the fear, which had affected the British classes in the wake of the French Revolution. 'Evangelism offered middle-class men and women new identities, new ways of giving meaning to their lives and making sense of some of their experience' (C. Hall, 1990, p. 59).

However, alongside this new emphasis on the safe haven of home, various problems and conflicts began to emerge. Privacy could also lead to secrecy.

> The nineteenth-century family found itself in a contradictory situation. Its power and dignity reinforced by society, which saw it as an essential agent of social control, the family attempted to impose its own ends on individual members . . . Yet egalitarianism was also honoured, and individualism made quiet but steady progress. As a result, the family was subjected to centrifugal forces, which led to conflict and at times to disintegration . . . Defence of the family honour remained the most basic rule. Honour required keeping the family's deepest secrets, secrecy being the mortar that held the family together and created a fortress against the outside world. But that very mortar had been known to create cracks and crevices in its structure. Cries and whispers, creaking doors, locked drawers, purloined letters, glimpsed gestures, confidences and mysteries, sidelong and intercepted glances, words spoken and unspoken . . . The family was an endless source of drama.
>
> (Perrot, 1990, p. 139)

One might add that the home was now ripe for repression and neurosis, once it became the place where private life was walled off into special and sometimes secret places. On the one hand, the home established roots; it was where the family gathered. On the other hand, it was also the place where secret retreats from the world could be maintained. The desire for a private space of one's own reflected a heightened sense of individuality, an awareness of individual personality; it became the fundamental place for the recall of childhood memories, the site of imagination (Perrot, 1990, p. 356–7), and the individual's sense of self gained new depth and complexity (Corbin, 1990, p. 455). But that private space could also become a source of secret fantasies, forbidden pleasures, hidden sexuality, frustration and even abuse and domination.

The sense of identity began to become more distinct, and by the mid-nineteenth century living space had become less crowded. The single bed became a feature of the bourgeois home, as opposed to the communal bed, and this reinforced the sense of individuality and independence, making room for monologue and also solitude. In such homes, people began to have their own bedrooms. A girl's bedroom became 'the temple of her private life' (Corbin, 1990, p. 480). People groomed in private in order to appear in public. Introspection became more common, and diaries flourished. The Romantics had already transformed the imagination, blazing new paths for reverie, enriching the forms of interior monologue and inviting their readers to engage in meditation, contemplation and mystical ecstasy (1990, p. 512). With the developments in the domestic interior, new walls arose 'around private life, stricter hygiene, more strenuous exercise, the new concern with modesty, and closer management of time, [which] must have encouraged some to seek escape through the imagination' (1990, p. 513). Silent reading progressed, as did interest in the solitary pleasures of the study.

At the same time as an increase in individuation, there was an increase in feelings of vulnerability and loneliness, a failure to connect. This 'forced members of the dominant classes to retreat into solitary pleasures; the internalization of ever more strict rules of sexual morality . . . intensified feelings of guilt' (Corbin, 1990, p. 549). Progress towards individuation gave rise to new subjective forms of suffering. The image of the hysteric became increasingly influential, with various debates about its origin, ranging from the influence of the womb, to heredity or, according to Charcot, nervous shock. With sexuality becoming increasingly 'locked' in the private domestic interior, the bourgeoisie began to suffer from its morality. But the nineteenth century became the golden age of the confessional, with doctors increasingly becoming the new confidants. Souls which had been tormented by evil and sin became sick and in need of treatment. It was in this historical context that Freud could find a market for treating hysterical patients.

Charles Rice's book *The Emergence of the Interior* (2007) adds further details to how the domestic interior emerged both as a concept and as a material manifestation of the nineteenth century. Beginning with Baudelaire's prose poem 'The Twofold Room', which charts the twofold experience of his room both as dreamlike and then suddenly as a material reality, merely his hovel and the dilapidated context for his work, Rice uses the poem as emblematic of the interior's 'doubleness' – where it can be both imagined and inhabited. Rice points out that the *Oxford English Dictionary* records that 'interior' comes into use from the late fifteenth century to mean inside as divided from outside and to describe the spiritual and inner nature of the soul. 'From the early eighteenth century, "interiority" was used to designate inner character and a sense of individual subjectivity, and from the middle of the eighteenth century the interior came to designate the domestic affairs of a state, as well as the sense of territory that belongs to a country or region. It was only from the beginning of the nineteenth century, however, that the interior came to mean the inside of a building or room, esp. in reference to the artistic effect; also a picture or representation of the inside of a building or room. Also, in a theatre, a "set" consisting of the inside of a building or room' (Rice, 2007, p. 2).

Thus, the interior emerged in a new way, reflecting as in Baudelaire's poem the world of imagination, reverie and dream, but also a material reality. Baudelaire himself was not only contrasting the dream and reality but also his own artistic hovel with the emerging bourgeois world of comfort and domesticity. One can see how the interior became the sight for self-definition, the space where the complexities and paradoxes of subjectivity would be played out. This development may well have been linked to changes in the way that the bourgeoisie saw childhood, which began to take hold as a history of the self, soon to become theorized by Freud (Steedman, 1995). The interior certainly became the context in which psychoanalysis went to work, as well as providing an analogy for the structuring of the psyche (Rice, 2007, p. 4).

Thus, one could say that the older notion of the interior as the spiritual and inner nature of the soul became, in Freud, wedded to the emerging notion of the double nature of the interior as site of dream and material reality to create a new notion of private life and of the human subject. The psychoanalytical interior, or what I shall put forward as the notion of a psychic home, becomes a revolutionary account of the human subject, one that challenged bourgeois domesticity while providing a comfortable space for exploration of its conflicts.

Authors with an architectural background, such as Fuss and Rice, have paid particular attention to Freud's consulting room as the site of a revolution in the experience of both the domestic and psychological interior. They both point out that, in his *Introductory Lectures on Psychoanalysis*, Freud used the metaphor of a suite of rooms, a bourgeois interior, to explain the structure of the unconscious, with an entrance hall, a drawing room and a threshold in between.

> Let us therefore compare the system of the unconscious to a large entrance hall, in which the mental impulses jostle one another like separate individuals. Adjoining the entrance hall there is a second, narrower room – a kind of drawing room – in which the consciousness, too, resides. But on the threshold between these two rooms a watchman performs his function: he examines the different mental impulses, acts as a censor, and will not admit them into the drawing room if they displease him.
>
> (Freud, 1916–17, pp. 295–6)

Rice points out that this striking spatial analogy doubles the domestic situation experienced by Freud's patients and which often drove them to seek psychoanalysis – 'impulses held on the threshold of rooms, jostling between individuals, acts of guardianship that permit or deny access . . . There is a sense that regulated behaviour in the bourgeois domestic interior offered a powerful explanatory tool in Freud's understanding of the structure and workings of the psyche, and also that this sort of domesticity was the context wherein psychoanalysis went to work' (Rice, 2007, p. 40).

Edmund Engelman (1976) captured the layout of Freud's Bergasse 19 consulting room as it appeared shortly before Freud's fleeing to London. His photographs portraying the detailed layout of the rooms and the many collected objects captured 'what half a century of Freud commentary has overlooked: the location of the analytic scene within the walls of a crypt. When patients arrived at Freud's office, they entered an overdetermined space of loss and absence, grief and memory, elegy and mourning. In short, they entered the exteriorized theatre of Freud's own emotional history, where every object newly found memorialized a love-object lost' (Fuss, 2004, p. 79).

The interior of Freud's consulting room was thus not a passive context for analysis, but actively participated in it. Indeed, it is inevitable that the analyst's consulting room will convey their own subjectivity to the patient; it will convey what I describe below as their own psychic home. Like their patients, psychoanalysts carry their psychic home with them, though it will manifest itself differently. The analyst may not reveal details of their private life to their patients, but they carry their psychic home with them into the session. Their choice of interior design of the consulting room, not to mention the books and any objects, reflects the nature of the analyst's psychic home; there is an interaction between the subjectivity of the analyst and the interior space where they work. An alive psychic home can provide a sustaining space for the analyst, allowing them to cope with the inevitable loneliness of the work.

While the analytic work of analyst and patient carries on in separate localities, the worlds of patient and analyst intertwine in various ways, in a dynamic fashion. Sometimes the analyst may find that their psychic home is invaded by the patient, with little space to think or feel; or else there may be a confusion of spaces, with little sense of a boundaried psychic home.

Psychic home, or the psychoanalytical interior

The main thrust of my own contribution to this field, influenced by many of the authors I cited previously, is to put forward the notion of a psychic home, of having an internal sense of a secure home base, as a key feature of identity. The psychic home provides an organizing psychic structure for the sense of emerging identity. Such a home base must be built up from a number of different elements, as with the physical home, which forms its substrate. There are intrapsychic elements but also intersubjective elements, involving the social world.

1. There is the basic structure of a home as a protected and hopefully welcoming space for shelter, providing the core of the internalized psychic home. The physical space of the home has an important function in helping to shape the interior life, as already described; but at any moment, as in Baudelaire's poem 'The Twofold Room', or in uncanny experiences, the material reality may suddenly bring the human subject face to face with the precariousness of their inner reality. One may say that the psychic home has a dual aspect – as both physical and psychical container.

In this notion of a psychic home, the physical structure of the home has an important part to play in providing an overall, containing structure or psychic container, which becomes internalized as an organizing configuration. Thus, the fireplace creates warmth. Usually the first thing one does coming back to a cold home from being away is to light the fire. The hearth, the seat of fire, the place resistant to heat and combustion, has always been a central part of the home. Interestingly in Latin the word for hearth is *focus*. Thus, referring to focal work with families, Alan Wilson pointed out that 'In a psychological sense, the focus also represents an important functionally organized aspect of resistance, that is resistance to instinctual forces, resistance to processes which the focus makes possible to use' (Wilson, 1986, p. 61). The English word home derives from the Old Norse, *heima*, and perhaps encapsulates something of the Viking longing for home and hearth as a stable physical base to return to after their many voyages of exploration and conquest.

The physical structure of the home has an interior marked out by defining walls. The boundary between the interior and the exterior may be firm and stable or flimsy or permeable; the bricks and mortar of the family home may be loose or secure, with a clear focus or none. One may recall here the story of the three little pigs – only the house built of bricks could withstand the breath of the hungry wolf. Indeed, it was the third pig's fireplace that eventually killed off the wolf as he climbed down the chimney.

The boundaries of the house also have to be seen in context, within a community of other homes, and within a society. The home must be permeable to external influences, or else it will become the source of unreal relationships.

At the same time, one could say the division between the interior's inside and outside mark the boundaries of the soul or human subject, a theme which will be developed in more detail in Chapter Five.

2. There is already a preestablished intersubjective symbolic space predating the building or setting up of the home. The home-to-be already has a place in the family history and narrative, already situated as an element in a complicated network of relationships. There is a lineage, reaching back generations. The individual in a family is already situated before birth in a complicated, mostly unconscious network of symbols, or kinship structure. Influenced by the work of Claude Levi-Strauss on how unconscious social laws regulated marriage ties and kinship, structuring them like language, Jacques Lacan called this network the 'Symbolic Order' (Benvenuto and Kennedy, 1986, p. 89). It is the Order into which the emerging subject has to structure themselves, language, for him, being the key element through which this structuring takes place. I would want to add the vital contributions to the emergence of the human subject of the rich pre-verbal world, the world in which language is beginning to take shape.

3. The contents of the psychic home, its mental furniture, consist essentially of identifications with family members making up the home's interior. In the secure home, the parents provide continuity over time in their homemaking, providing a supportive base for the children to eventually leave, and ultimately to build up, their own home. A stable psychic home involves individuals being recognized as being autonomous yet dependent, and receiving respect for their own individuality with secure attachments. One can perhaps see most clearly here how the psychic home is integral to the notion of identity with the adolescent, for whom

identity formation is a crucial task. They need the home base from which to explore but also they need it to be there for their return. This is perhaps why it can be so traumatic for the adolescent when their parents split up at this crucial point in their development, supposedly as they are now old enough to be able to cope.

One can also see how a sense of individual identity depends upon the mutual relationships in the family being respectful of personal autonomy; that is, boundaries *within* the home need to be respectful, with individuality being respected and recognized.

For any individual, alternative psychic homes will develop in time, particularly if the family of origin is unstable or rejecting. Work for many people can become one such place; the workaholic can be locked into a sense of only being at home at work, even though it can never really be an adequate substitute for an actual home. At the same time, for those with a core sense of a psychic home, it may be less conflictual to seek alternative psychic homes, to feel at home in a number of different places, cultures, overlapping and interpenetrating. Nonetheless, leaving one's home where one has lived for long periods can still be destabilizing, as vividly described by Salman Akhtar (2007). He shows how the nonhuman elements of the home, such as the child's toys, blanket and elements of the environment, contribute to the sense of security and are formative in our psychic development. He emphasizes how the analyst working with traumatically dislocated individuals must be prepared to 'receive' nonhuman, largely environmental transferences. The way that such a patient brings into the space of the consulting room their sense of dislocation needs to be accepted and understood.

One can see a particularly poignant dilemma concerning the psychic home with adoptions, particularly when the adoptee reaches adolescence, as Betty Lifton (1994) has pointed out. When adoptees reach adolescence, especially with closed adoptions, and when the adoptee cannot find their birth parents, or when the adopted parents deny the reality of the past, particularly difficult issues around identity may arise. 'If your personal narrative doesn't grow and develop with you, with concrete facts and information, you run the danger of becoming emotionally frozen. You cannot make the necessary connections between the past and the future that everyone needs to grow into a cohesive self. You become stuck in the life cycle, beached like a whale on the shores of your own deficient narrative' (1994, p. 65). If the adopted parents do not *respect* the reality of the child's past, adoptees can grow up with a divided self, walling off essential aspects of themselves, and emotionally frozen, not feeling sufficiently *recognized* for who and what they are. They may remain hungry for a psychic home, bereft of the links to such a home.

There may be some overlap in conceptualization here with John Steiner's notion of 'psychic retreats' (1993). These are pathological organizations in more disturbed patients, referring to when patients can withdraw or retreat into states of mind experienced as if they were places in which the patient could hide. Such states of mind may appear as literal spaces, such as a house or a cave. One could add here, that if the patient makes a retreat, then presumably they are retreating from something, from live contact with the other, or from some living psychic home.

4. The ordinary home consists of activities; it is not a static or frozen entity. What could be called the 'work of the day' (Kennedy, 2007, pp. 246–60) takes place within the home. This refers to significant events, which require thought and/or action. The ordinary work of the day, structured around everyday activities, involves attention to all the significant, and at times deceptively indifferent, thoughts, feelings and experiences that occupy us during the day and provide the raw material for thinking and for dreaming. Much of this psychic work carries on automatically without us being particularly aware of its regular occurrence or of its everydayness. It is usually taken for granted, unless the family has major problems, of the kind where the family home has broken down, and where ordinary family life cannot be held together safely.

When home life has broken down, when it is, for example, chaotic or dangerous, one can clearly see how the basic conditions for secure attachments and identifications cannot take place; the internalized psychic home then becomes precarious or dangerous. From such pathology, one can perhaps see how the core of the psychic home is probably linked to early experiences where psyche and soma are beginning to be linked together, when the psyche begins to feel at home in the soma, along the lines described by Winnicott (1949, pp. 244–5). The infant's psyche begins to dwell in the soma, with a sense of being self-centred inside his or her body, and this process depends upon the mother's handling, her ability to join up her emotional and physical involvement.

Thus, one can see how the notion of a psychic home consists of a number of different and interacting elements, including the physical interior of a home but internalized as a psychic interior. The notion of 'personal identity' refers to the development and then maintenance of a person's character, how they put together in some way their various multiple identifications, as well as including wider issues concerning a person's cultural and social influences. I am suggesting that the basic elements of the psychic home can be seen to provide a way of organizing the person's identity, or can be seen as intrinsic to any notion of identity, a theme I shall develop in more detail in Chapter Four on identity.

In *psychoanalytic treatments*, one can see the notion of a psychic home in a variety of ways. Just take a few brief examples from my own practice:

Mrs X, for example, now has a good home, with a stable family, but she never feels secure in herself; she carries around inside some deep anxieties linked to the experiences of her early life. Her parents split up when she was very young, her mother soon remarried and then the patient was sent to boarding school soon after. Until the analysis, she had never questioned what had led to the breakup of the family, or why she was sent away from home. She carries around quite a fragile sense of a psychic home, afraid of expressing dependent feelings, and quite emotionally inhibited as a person.

She struggled for a long time with the analytic setting. She wanted to come to sessions, but as soon as she arrived, feelings of dread and despair would quickly arise, making, as she said, the couch uncomfortable. She managed her discomfort by a sort of freezing, with her body stiff and immobile on the couch. The analytic setting for a long time thus became a necessary but dreaded place. She would often wonder why she wanted to come, when on entering the consulting room she would feel so awful.

One of the main themes was an almost complete absence of early memories, particularly after the breakup of her parent's marriage. She could recall losing a precious soft toy, and that her mother took her to an expensive store to replace it, but no substitute was found to be suitable, though she made do with some hard toys. However, bit-by-bit over the years, some early scenes came to her mind, after we had gone over some of the difficult feelings she had experienced at boarding school. There, she often felt lonely, cut off and not one of the group. She began to make connections with some of her current fears about intimacy and those boarding school experiences. One session seemed to convey something of a turning point. It was the first time that she had made a stand about coming to her analysis.

She began in a fairly animated way. She was annoyed because at work there was a new computer system, and she had been told that she will have to set aside some full days to learn it. That would mean missing both personal commitments and her analytic sessions. She was angered by her (female) manager who expected this of her. However, she was not going to go along with this and would leave early to come to her sessions. My patient was also annoyed that she herself was made to feel neglectful by not going along with her work's expectations.

I was immediately struck by her making sure she would come to her analysis despite the pressure to miss out.

She was also worrying about a vulnerable client who was angry about having their invalidity benefit being removed. She was not sure what he would do to himself. There were also worries about a close family member who was ill and still in hospital.

I said that she was telling me about a number of outside pressures that had to be overcome. She did overcome them when she had decided she would come to her analysis.

She said that in fact her manager was normally reasonable, but what annoyed my patient was that the manager herself was being put under pressure from above but that she could not stand up to it. My patient did not want to be the one who made a fuss. She feared both standing out and any retaliation – the latter was a *real* fear, as someone in the team had in fact been effectively excluded for making a fuss previously.

I said, 'You mean, do people make a fuss, or do they have to put up with whatever comes their way.'

This comment made her think of her relative's treatment and how they had put up with whatever was done to them, even if the staff were incompetent.

(I was thinking, 'Do I put up with her or make a fuss? What kind of manager/analyst am I for her?')

She continued – her relative would not find out what is happening to them. Typically for her family, they just give themselves to the doctors.

I said, 'Well, there is a doctor here, and maybe you fear giving yourself up to me.'

She agreed. She talked about it being difficult here, with issues of control and power. She has to fit in with the holiday dates I had recently given her. Though she also sees they are reasonable, given the reality of the summer holidays and her own children's school dates, but there is an imbalance of power. She cannot make me say things. She does not know when I will say things. She wants me to say more. She has 'zero control' over me. She added that she often had a sense of deprivation here; she felt deprived much of the time.

After a pause, she said that she was having thoughts about mothers and babies, and all that babies get from their mothers in terms of physical contact and visual stimulation, as much as talking.

I linked what she told me about her own possible early deprivation experiences as a baby or young child, with a mother who came and went, and how she could not make a fuss; she had to put up with what she was given, the hard toys for the soft ones.

She said that when I do speak, she can feel in contact, and that does give her enough to keep going, but the feeling of deprivation is still often there. So she felt better about being here, even though it was also difficult.

I acknowledged what she had told me and then finished the session.

While of course there were many different elements to the session and to what was going on in the analysis at that time, I would point to the fact that it was a new experience for her to take a stand about her sessions. This did seem to be linked to a developing, if fragile, sense of being more at home in the analysis, even though that meant having to experience difficult feelings. Given the fact that home for her was so full of conflict – with a mixture of loss, displacement and rejection, I did feel this was a significant development.

For Mrs Y, home is not a place she can easily identify with. Her own mother was exceedingly narcissistic, never having recognized the patient's own individuality. The family was not one where emotions were easily expressed; they had to be buttoned up. There was great emphasis on good behaviour and not complaining: the typical stiff upper lip. She was also sent to boarding school, where she felt happier on the surface in some ways, at least able to find a way of relating which did not demand having to accept mother was always right. Though she married and had children, she has always felt it difficult consciously to identify with a sense of home; home has always reminded her of being unacknowledged. She has always felt more at ease out of the house, socializing or working. Home was not somewhere where she could find peace and calm.

In fact, she quickly became committed to her analysis and moved into attending sessions five times a week as soon as possible. Her analysis became the place where she could express herself and feel understood. Yet the analysis was not without many difficulties. From the beginning of the analysis, there was a profound fear of being dependent on me, while at the same time a frantic search for live contact with me. In the initial years of analysis, a certain amount of analytic work took place during the week, but by Friday desperation would arise about the coming weekend. By Monday, it felt as if we had to start from scratch. This became a constant and worrying feature of the analysis, making it difficult to build up a sense of continuity.

Building up the picture of life at boarding school, the 'institutional home', became therapeutic in that it clarified how she had turned to an 'institutional mother' as a way of coping with feelings of abandonment and rejection. Being compliant and well behaved disguised her deep-seated feelings of anger and betrayal towards her parents for agreeing to send her away and for not having the capacity to understand her desperation. The work of building up a detailed picture of what might have happened at the time when she lost her sense of a home life went hand in hand with looking at how this scenario was repeated in the transference to me from week to week. It was important that I recognize the quality of her desperation about being left. Gradually a sense of the past week developed; the weekends remained difficult but not unbearable. She no longer had to create her world from scratch each Monday but could feel that she had something to hold onto from the past weeks.

In a later session, the theme of her unhappiness at home, despite a number of significant positives there, came to the fore. It was then that I put to her the suggestion that it was not her real home that was troubling her but something internal, linked to what we had discussed about her feelings of having to turn to an institutional mother when she found her own mother was unresponsive. The notion of a psychic home made a lot of sense to her; indeed, she felt that in some ways she has spent her life moving away from a psychic home, and yet yearning for it. It seems to encapsulate her own problematic particularly cogently. She also felt that her analysis had become her psychic home, or at least the place where she could begin to feel a sense of aliveness for the first time. That seemed to have helped her find more contentment with her own home life.

Ms Z has had quite severe mental health problems, probably of the borderline kind. Though educated and intelligent, she has found it difficult to work and finds close relationships challenging. Her family is important for her, indeed a continuing and major influence. They want her to live near them, outside London, and continue to offer incentives for her to do so. However, the atmosphere at home is quite deadly. Independence is discouraged, the parents are very intrusive about personal matters, and there is little sense of a differentiation between generations. One sibling is probably schizophrenic and lives at home; another has only managed independence by living far away and by not having much contact with the family. A psychic home for the patient is fraught with the danger of breakdown.

In the analysis, these issues have come to the fore very intensely. Early on, sessions would involve quite large swings of emotion, between despair and a manic buildup of excitement. I found myself having to be calm and composed, as if I were trying to manage being in a very unsteady sea. She did find this helpful, though also frustrating; she had a constant critical internal voice, which undermined her, and also found it difficult to believe that I was not mocking her.

Among the many elements of the analysis, one which contributed to her feeling steadier and more able to function socially was using the direct experience of what she was feeling in the analysis as a way of understanding the volatility of home life and the impact it had on her. Due to my calm stance, she was able to begin to explore her inner world without massive feelings of panic and fear about intrusion and abandonment. However, she also found it difficult to trust the analysis, often being drawn back to the disturbed family environment, even though when she actually stayed at her parents' home, she felt increasingly anxious and out of touch with reality. Part of the difficulty is that she is very sensitive to shifts of mood; she can feel as if spinning out of control when her parents argue or show direct anger towards her.

There has often been an oscillation between the stable psychic home represented by the analysis and her unstable family home, where emotions could not be regulated effectively. There seemed to be some progress when she managed to sustain employment where her sensitivity with people could be used. However, I still have the sense that her psychic home is precarious.

For Mr W, work as a professional is the only place where he has relationships. From his description, his own flat is a complete tip. It is hardly ever cleaned and is grossly neglected. He has never asked anyone back there, and outside of work events he has no social life. He has never had a close relationship, only friendships. Such an existence would probably surprise his colleagues, who respect him and his work. He keeps his home life secret from them all; I only began to know the details over a period of time as he felt able to trust me.

He has an intense and highly conflictual relationship with his mother, who is demanding of his attention. His father, to whom he felt very close and whom he resembles physically, died many years ago. Indeed, he describes feeling as if he stopped developing psychically at that point. It is as if he lives in a dead world, in perpetual mourning, like Miss Haversham in Dickens's *Great Expectations*. The psychic home for him has never moved on; it remains full of dead introjects. Everyone carries the psychic home with them; for Mr W the only escape from this dead weight is at work. There is a real terror that the psychic home might come alive, and that he, like his father, might have an early death.

I have chosen samples from various analyses to illustrate the way that one may think about the notion of a psychic home in the analytic session. Clearly, I have only selected small samples from the work and have excluded much else. A major reason for this is the great problem about maintaining patient confidentiality.

I would say that over the years the way that I listen to patients has been significantly influenced by the fact that I worked for nearly thirty years as consultant to the Cassel Family Unit (until its unfortunate closure in 2011). Working with highly troubled families meant having to focus quite minutely on the 'work of the day', the family's everyday life and activities. I became acutely aware that a therapist could only attend to a fraction of the patient's life, even when seeing them five times a week. However, one can listen to the way that the patient uses the everyday, how they manage the work of the day in the 23 hours or so of not seeing their analyst in the week, or over the weekend. It is difficult to describe how this listening differs from other kinds of analytic listening. I should say it does not replace other forms of listening but is additional. It pays attention to the quality of the psychic home, the psychological bricks and mortar, as it were.

In the next chapter, I shall focus on how important it was for William Wordsworth and his sister, Dorothy, to find a psychic home, important both for their personal lives and for his poetry. This will also be another opportunity to illustrate what I am trying to convey about the notion of a psychic home.

Chapter 3

The importance of a psychic home in the life and work of William Wordsworth

One of the most persistent themes in William Wordsworth's poetry, particularly in his early work and during the years he wrote his greatest poetry – between about 1795 and 1805 – is that of home. He writes of yearnings for home, loss of home, intense homecomings, homes that are ruined and may become a shelter for the homeless and characters who have lost homes or who are homeless. Coincidentally, his life began to change significantly when, in 1794 he and his sister, Dorothy, set up home together for a few weeks, sealing their coming together after years apart, with her having led a life of drudgery in other peoples' home, and he having led an itinerant life in England and France. It was not long before they were living in a permanent home, eventually settling back in the Lake District, their childhood home, where Wordsworth wrote his most intense poetry, including *Tintern Abbey* and the early versions of *The Prelude*. After years of wandering, he found the stability he needed to fulfil his potential as a great writer, and she found what she considered her first real home in her life with her brother. I have described the emergence of the bourgeois domestic interior after the turbulence of the French Revolution in the previous chapter. One could see Wordsworth's personal journey as reflecting a general trend of that time. In the end, he found a physical setting for his writing, which became a major theme of his poetry.

Of course, home was not the only space that Wordsworth found to be a source of creativity. The other space to which he returned again and again was that of the vast exterior space of nature as a source of imagination and intense feeling. These two spaces, home and nature, the bounded and unbounded, were to be major sources of inspiration.

The theme of home is so persistent that one must look for an explanation of its importance in Wordsworth's life and poetry beyond merely a wish for domesticity (Page, 2003), as important as that was for Dorothy and him, given the fact that they had lost both parents when they were children. There seems to have been at work something psychically deeper than the mere idea of home, something which one can recognize as a psychic space that provided a structure for his emotional life and thereby his poetry – that is, a psychic home. Using evidence from Wordsworth's life and poetry, one can see how the notion of a psychic home can illuminate his development as a poet, as well as illustrate its existence as a persistent psychic structure.

As I have described, a psychic home is a concept arising out of clinical work with patients in psychoanalysis but also from wider sources. The psychic home can be seen as an organizing structure in the mind central to the overall sense of personal identity, involving elements from within the mind, from interaction with others in the social field and from nonhuman elements, physical objects.

In order to see how the concept of a psychic home can be applied to Wordsworth's life and work, one can start with some basic biographical facts about Wordsworth and his sister, which set the context for their creative life together. On the first page of Gill's life of the poet (1989, p. 1), Gill notes that he faces the task of trying to write a biography, given that the poet himself spent a lifetime sifting, selecting and reordering much of the material available himself, even though much of the most significant material remained unpublished during his lifetime; these unpublished works included pieces such as *Home at Grasmere* (1800), which was a celebration of his life with his sister, and the various versions of his great autobiographical poem *The Prelude*, the poem which represents the growth of his mind.

Because of the death of both parents in Wordsworth's youth, the shape of his life has been described as having a 'pattern of severances and ruptures counterpointed with periods of continuity and calm, which began in a childhood that seemed to give a solid start to life and to promise a secure future but denied both in his most formative years' (Gill, 1989, p. 13). He described his earliest years as involving a positive memory of his house, when as a 4-year-old, he played in the garden and the fields and admired the distant hills (J. Wordsworth, 1995, 1799 *Prelude*, lines 17–26). But in the opening of the 1805 *Prelude*, he moves straight from that early period to his time at his boarding school at Hawkshead, when he was 9 years old, thus significantly eliding what was an unsettled period.

The basic facts of his life include the death of his mother in 1778, when William was 7 years old, and when he and Dorothy had been farmed out to their rather overly strict grandparents, a frequent occurrence, partly as a result of their father often being away on business, and their mother evidently finding it difficult coping with the children. It does seem that these early years were troubled as a result, though he and Dorothy turned to one another for comfort. However, after their mother's death, Dorothy was separated from William and her other brothers and did not see him again for nine years, at the end of his school days, a major blow.

Wordsworth's school, Hawkshead, near the Lake District in the vale of Esthwaite, provided him with a real home for eight years. He lived in the cottage of an affectionate woman, Ann Tyson, to whom he pays tribute in *The Prelude* (1805, IV, lines 19–28). He regarded the whole region there as a paradise, and it was from there that he would get a glimpse of 'what he was to make his own first real 'abiding place', Grasmere (Gill, 1989, p. 23). It was when he was there, too, that his father died in 1783 when William was 13. Memories of this event surface in the long poem he wrote at the end of these intense school days, *The Vale of Esthwaite*, as well as in the 1799 *Prelude*. But what is striking is that 'in both poems what Wordsworth recalls is not the actual death of his father but the intensity of his own longing to be home' (Gill, 1989, p. 34). For example, there is a passage in the *Vale of Esthwaite* which refers to his father's death. In the passage, Wordsworth is waiting with his brothers for a horse to take him home for the holidays.

> Long Long upon yon steepy rock
> Alone I bore the bitter shock
> Long Long my swimming eyes did roam
> For little Horse to bear me home
> To bear me what avails my tear
> To sorrow o'er a Father's bier.
>   (Wordsworth, 1977, lines 431–7)

Then, a little farther, there is a reflection in the present on that past trauma.

> Nor did my little heart foresee
> –She lost a home in losing thee
> –Nor did it know – of thee bereft
> –That little more than Heav'n was left.
>   (Wordsworth, 1977, lines 445–8)

This section of the *Vale* 'strives to define what "home" means and to seek reparation for its dissolution' (Wu, 2002, p. 7). It was also significant that, following his father's death, the large family home was sold, so that he and Dorothy in reality had no actual home to go back to, something she was to bitterly complain about in a letter written in 1787 (Wu, p. 8). Even in 1793, Dorothy complained to a friend that their parents' loss meant that 'we in the same moment lost a father, a mother, a home' (Wu, p. 10).

The various versions of *The Prelude* also describe this incident and his reaction to his father's death. Thus,

> Ere I to school returned
> That dreary time, 'ere I had been ten days
> A dweller in my father's house, he died,
>   (J. Wordsworth, 1995, 1799 *Prelude*, lines 349–51)

The latter phrase seems 'notable for its biblical ring and for its impersonality. Wordsworth had been born in the house, and spent his childhood there, but the reference hardly makes it sound like home' (J. Wordsworth, 1995, p. 547, n. 351). There is certainly some evidence here of a profoundly ambivalent relationship with his father, not merely anger at his death and guilt about having angry thoughts towards him. Indeed, there is no evidence in *The Prelude* of the father–son relationship being warm or close (Ellis, 1985, p. 19). Wordsworth says that after his father's death, he remembered it as an 'anxiety of hope' (J. Wordsworth, 1995, 1805 *Prelude,* line 371), but this was probably no more than an eagerness to go home (Ellis, 1985, p. 19). Yet subsequently in his poetry Wordsworth repeatedly reveals a profound sympathy for, and identification with, displaced people – those who are without a home, widows, beggars or those cut off, as he was, from the parental home.

Dorothy and William were finally reunited at this time, though not yet permanently, causing her considerable frustration: she had to remain in her unhappy and unwanted situation in her grandparents' house while William went off to Cambridge, a place which was 'to provide a lodging but not a home' (Gill, 1989, p. 36). At Cambridge he was unable to fix on anything. Instead,

> I was detached
> Internally from academic cares,
> From every hope of prowess and reward,
> And wished to be a lodger in that house
> Of letters, and no more . . .
>> (J. Wordsworth, 1995, 1805 *Prelude*, Book 6, lines 29–33)

Yet at the end of his time there, he completed a poem, *An Evening Walk*, which reveals elements of his greatness as a poet. In it, he yearns for the sights and sounds of the Lake District, but it begins with an address to his sister, who from now on becomes increasingly central to his life, despite subsequent wanderings.

> Far from my dearest friend, 'tis mine to rove
> Thro' bare, grey dell, high wood, and pastoral cove . . .
>> (Wordsworth, 1977, lines 1–2)

After leaving Cambridge, Wordsworth began a period of apparent aimlessness, walking around Europe and then remaining in revolutionary France, where, in 1792, he met Annette Vallon, who bore him a daughter, though they will be soon be separated for some nine years due to the revolutionary wars, and he became politically radical. Clearly, the experience of revolution in France was both intense and life changing, producing a revolution in his own thinking about the world, questioning his beliefs and assumptions, which would become integrated into his finest poetry; indeed, three books in *The Prelude* are devoted to his French experiences. On returning to England in 1793, he spent part of the summer walking alone across Salisbury Plain and composed a poem which captures some intense period of brooding, influenced by a number of writers, including Rousseau and

Spencer, and probably reflecting his turmoil about being separated from Annette and his daughter. His poem, *Salisbury Plain*, begins, echoing Rousseau, with the proposition that, for the naked savage,

> Hard is the life when naked and unhoused
> And wasted by the long day's fruitless pains.
> (Gill, 2004, lines 1–2)

The poem describes a story of a woman, driven out of her home, robbed by war of her husband and children, wandering aimlessly with 'no house in prospect but the tomb' (line 393).

While Wordsworth's life was in chaos, Dorothy's continued to be stifling, stuck in a life of domestic bondage, while both desired to live together and to find a resting place. What radically changed their lives and in the end provided this peace, a physical and psychic home, was an offer they received in April to May 1794 to live together at Windy Brow, a farmhouse near Keswick. For her, it marked the end of her drudgery, and after a year, she remained with William in various stable homes for the rest of her life. For him, it seems that 'it was a time of equal importance. Drinking in pleasure from the landscape and resting in the stability of his relationship with Dorothy, he seems to have begun the attempt to establish what really mattered to him and to take more command of his life,' (Gill, 1989, p. 80). His poetical activity was certainly intense at this time with his undertaking of substantial revision to *An Evening Walk* and *Salisbury Plain*.

However, it was only a year or so later, after Wordsworth had spent months in contact with London radical thinkers, that he and Dorothy were able, in part thanks to a legacy, to move together to Racedown, a substantial house in the West Country, in September 1795; soon after, he met Samuel Taylor Coleridge, an event which would also, of course, have lasting significance for his life and poetry. William and Dorothy stayed there for two years before moving back permanently to the Lake District, and it is of some interest that they also took with them the child Basil Montagu, age 2-and-a-half, whom they would continue to bring up as one of their own family, not wishing him to experience the early disruption in his care that they had experienced.

From accounts of that period in *The Prelude*, it seems that Wordsworth retreated into himself after the stimulation of London, but that Dorothy's care for him and his contact with nature produced a healing effect. Perhaps this was a time of breakdown, certainly crisis, which the intense coming together of brother and sister did much to resolve. With a stable home, for the first time in their lives, William was able to channel his feelings of guilt towards Annette and his daughter, as well the conflicting feelings concerning radical politics – on the one hand, he was sympathetic to the poor and downtrodden, but on the other hand he had personally experienced what radical politics could lead to: the terrors of the

French Revolution, which of course had a personal significance as the war with England made it impossible for him to see his daughter.

Wordsworth wrote a play, *The Borderers*, at this time, which Gill (1989, p. 101) describes as ushering in a new period beginning the exploration of themes which would absorb Wordsworth until his death. Gill asks how such a breakthrough had occurred and answers that the reason for it is not clear. In Book Ten of *The Prelude*, Wordsworth describes this time as one when he was torn by conflicting emotions as the French Revolution took its chaotic course, betraying its original ideas, and also by the increasing repression in England. He describes how he was rescued from his crisis by the presence of his sister and also by turning to nature, which revived in him feelings from his earlier life. There is no doubt that there was some sort of deep transformation at Racedown, as he shared every part of his life with Dorothy. He became more self-assured, and by 1797, Dorothy describes him as 'cheerful as any body can be . . . the life of the whole house' (qtd. in Gill, 1989, p. 103). She in turn describes Racedown as the first home she had ever had (1989, p. 104).

The Borderers itself begins 'an exploration of human suffering and of the nature of Nature in its widest sense which is to motivate his finest work in the near future' (Gill, 1989, p. 115). Interestingly, the play ends without a resolution in what one could describe as the loss of a psychic home. The play's main character, Rivers, states that

> I will go forth a wanderer on the earth,
> A shadowy thing, and as I wander on
> No human ear shall hear my voice,
> No human dwelling ever gives me food
> Or sleep or rest . . .
>   (Wordsworth, 1977, lines 2312–16)

While it still may not be clear what led to Wordsworth's breakthrough at this time, it would seem pretty clear that his circumstances were crucial. Finally, he and Dorothy were reunited. At last, he had stability, a place where he could recover from the turmoil of the previous years, his wanderings, and the turbulent period in France – and the key themes of his poetry emerged with more clarity and substance. It would seem clear that it was not just domestic peace that led to this transformation, as important as that was, but something deeper. As he conveys in his poem *The Prelude*, Wordsworth, in retrospect, points to the importance to him then of the rediscovery of feelings and memories from his earlier life that helped him recover his balance. While his feeling for nature had a part to play in this process, it would seem that the recovery of a deep sense of home and its significance, something that reached back to his early life, was equally important. He found his role as a poet within the 'life of the whole house'. This psychic home provided him with a structure to manage his tortured feelings, so that they could be represented in poetical form; he had found a home for his feelings, a home for his soul, and of course his soul mate, Dorothy.

Subsequently one can see how home and the loss of home became central themes, coincidentally with the emerging of his most creative period, one in which he at last found his poetic voice. He later described this period as one when he was liberated from some kind of bondage. Thus the opening of the 1805 *Prelude* begins

> Oh welcome messenger! Oh welcome friend!
> A captive greets thee, coming from a house
> Of bondage, from yon city's walls set free,
> A prison where he has been long immured.
> Now I am free, enfranchised and at large,
> May fix my habitation where I will.
> What dwelling shall receive me? In what vale
> Shall be my harbour? Underneath what grove
> Shall I take up my home, and what sweet stream
> Shall with its murmurs lull me to my rest?
> (J. Wordsworth, 1995, lines 5–14)

These were lines he composed in 1799 just as he found Dove Cottage, which marked his permanent return to the Lake District, his childhood home.

While of course the themes of loss and guilt are important in Wordsworth's life and poetry, for example, the death of his parents, the guilt about his daughter, and the loss of the parental home (Wu, 2002), the counter to these losses is at least equally important. First of all there is the creation of a new home with Dorothy, which was to be finally consummated in Dove Cottage. Then there is the intensity of his friendship with Coleridge, with whom he would form a personal and poetical partnership, however strained it would become later. The final return home to Grasmere enabled Wordsworth to look back and face his losses. Of course much remained unresolved, but his conflicts seemed to become at this point the source of creative tension, providing the motivation for his poetry and giving it its intensity and power.

The return home to the Lake District and the creation of the new, permanent home with Dorothy enabled William to look back at his life and development and see a shape from his earliest days. 'Deliberately distancing himself from the political centre, from publishers, and the whole professional world of literature, he had chosen his home, not as a negative retreat from the "real world" but as a positive commitment to an austere and dedicated life amidst the elemental forms of nature' (Gill, 1989, p. 174).

By early 1800, Wordsworth was at work on his poem *Home at Grasmere*. This was originally conceived as the opening of his great philosophical poem *The Recluse*, which he and Coleridge had planned for the future. *Home at Grasmere*, though a significant poem, remained unpublished, and *The Recluse* was never composed, except as fragments of different poems. Yet *Home at Grasmere* reveals much about Wordsworth's joy at finding a centre to his life.

> 'tis the sense
> Of majesty, and beauty, and repose,
> A blended holiness of earth and sky,
> Something that makes this individual Spot,
> This small abiding-place of many men,
> A termination, and a last retreat,
> A Centre. Come from wheresoe'er you will,
> A Whole without dependence or defect,
> Made for itself, and happy in itself,
> Perfect Contentment, Unity entire.
>   (Gill, 2004, lines 161–70)

In contrast to this discovery of a state of contentment, Wordsworth also describes a situation in several of his poems, when a man has no resting place, no stable psychic home. There are ruined cottages, various crumbling homes and places laid waste, scattered all over his works. But for Wordsworth, Grasmere became the centre, a true psychic home where his identity as a poet became consolidated.

In this poem, however imperfectly executed at times, Wordsworth 'draws on what are to be the richest sources of all of his poetry: first, the strength of his attachment to a particular place and his yearning for some *localized home* [my italics] for his imaginative activity; second his conviction that his own feelings, his experiences of friendship, loss, or desire, demanded exploration in poetry' (Gill, 1989, p. 32).

The poem is also a joyous celebration of, and tribute to, Dorothy, who, sharing the home, underpinned his sense of purpose and power as a poet.

> Shall gratitude find rest? Mine eyes did ne'er
> Rest on a lovely object, nor my mind
> Take pleasure in the midst of happy thoughts,
> But either She whom now I have, who now
> Divides with me this loved abode, was there,
> Or not far off. Where'er my footsteps turned,
> Her Voice was like a hidden Bird that sang;
> The thought of her was like a flash of light
> Or an unseen companionship, a breath
> Of fragrance independent of the wind . . .
>   (Gill, 2004, lines 104–13)

While *Home at Grasmere* celebrates the retrieval of home with Dorothy as inspiration, the unpublished poem 'Composed When a Probability Existed of

Our Being Obliged to Quit Mount Rydal as a Residence' speaks about the fear of collapse of home (Gill, 2012, personal communication) when Wordsworth panicked as for a while it seemed a possibility that the lease would not be renewed. The Wordsworths had moved to Rydal Mount in 1812 after the traumatic loss of his daughter's presence and then son and the breach with Coleridge. The move marked the beginning of a new phase of domestic life when, in addition, money worries were lessening. 'Over the years both the place and the idea of Rydal Mount attracted a powerful cluster of feelings in all of the family, who cherished the house, the garden, and its atmosphere as a habitable domain . . . To lose Rydal Mount would have been to lose not just a house but a spot entwined with the reconstruction of their lives' (Gill, 1989, p. 298).

The poem is an elegy to a spring near Rydal Mount, called Nab Well. The intensity of his attachment to the well conveys his deep attachment to the place, which had become a new psychic home.

> Pellucid Spring! Unknown beyond the verge
> Of a small Hamlet, there, from ancient time,
> Not undistinguished; (for of Wells that ooze
> Or founts that gurgle from the moss-grown side
> And craggy forehead of this cloud-clapped hill.
> Their common Sire, thou only bears't his Name)
> One of my last fond looks is fix'd on Thee . . .
>   (Wordsworth, unpublished, lines 1–7)

And later in the poem, he recalls his observations of the well.

> And O how much of all that Love creates
> Or beautifies like changes undergoes,
> Suffers like loss when drawn out of the Soul,
> Its silent laboratory. Words should say,
> Could they but paint the wonders of thy cell,
> How often I have mark'd a plumy fern,
> Bending an apex towards its paler self,
> Reflected all in perfect lineaments,
> Shadow and substance kissing, point to point.
>   (lines 45–53)

Then, at the end of the poem, having extolled the well as a natural phenomenon, which yet has provided him with inspiration and many associations, he takes his leave.

> The cloud of rooks descending from mid air
> Softens its evening uproar towards a close
> Near and more near, for this protracted strain
> A warning not unwelcome – Fare thee well,

Emblem of equanimity and truth,
Farewell – if thy composure be not ours,
Yet if thou still, when we are gone, will keep
Thy living chaplet of moist fern and flowers
Cherished in shade tho' peeped at by the Sun,
So shall our bosoms feed a covert growth
Of grateful recollections, tribute due,
(Not less than to wide lake and foaming rill)
To thy obscure and modest attributes,
To thee, clear Spring! And all-sustaining Heaven.
                                   (lines 88–101)

As powerful as is this elegy to a natural phenomenon, the poetry is tinged with anxiety and fear of loss. As much as Wordsworth is the poet of homecomings, he is also the poet of lives ruined and homes lost. But while there may be loss, he also repeatedly creates a powerful vision of retrieval and renewal, embodied in the mystery of words.

Visionary Power
Attends upon the motions of the winds
Embodied in the mystery of words.
There darkness makes abode, and all the host
Of shadowy things do work their changes there,
As in a mansion like their proper home . . .
    (J. Wordsworth, 1995, 1805 *Prelude*, lines 619–24)

He faces the dark but dwells in the light, the light and dark together making 'a sense sublime . . . whose dwelling is the light of setting suns' (*Tintern Abbey*, Wordsworth, 1977, p. 360, line 98). And he has another sublime gift,

that serene and blessed mood,
In which the affections gently lead us on,
Until, the breath of this corporeal frame,
And even the motion of our human blood
Almost suspended, we are laid asleep
In body, and become a living soul:
While with an eye made quiet by the power
Of harmony, and the deep power of joy,
We see into the life of things.
                                   (lines 42–9)

The poem thus describes becoming a 'living soul' – through the power of love, love of nature and of his sister, who underpinned his security. Particular places become not only sources of wonder and inspiration, but often remind him of attachments to loved people. The particularity of place is important, but not just as a physical space; places become emblematic of a psychic space, interweaving past and present, with a yearning for something that will last. Thus in the *Poems on the Naming of Places*, a brook leads him to imagine nearby a cottage where he and his sister (called Emma in the poem) might dwell and will become a lasting memorial of their love.

> –Soon did the spot become my other home,
> My dwelling and my out-of-doors abide.
> And, of the shepherds who have seen me there,
> To whom I sometimes in my idle talk
> Have told this fancy, two or three, perhaps,
> Years after we are gone and in our graves,
> When they have cause to speak of this wild place
> May call it by the name of EMMA'S DELL.
> (Wordsworth and Coleridge, 1805, lines 40–6)

And in another poem of this sequence, he describes an eminence:

> 'Tis in truth
> The loneliest place we have among the clouds.
> And she who dwells with me, whom I have loved
> With such communion that no place on earth
> Can ever be solitude to me,
> Hath said, this lonesome peak shall bear my name.
> (Wordsworth and Coleridge, 1805, lines 12–16).

A brief poem from 1842 points to almost everything that had been central to Wordsworth's imaginative engagement with words and things and seems to summarize the central role of a psychic home in his creative life.

> Glad sight wherever new with old
> Is joined through some dear homeborn tie;
> The life of all that we behold
> Depends upon that mystery.
> Vain is the glory of the sky,
> The beauty vain of field and grove
> Unless, while with admiring eye
> We gaze, we also learn to love.
> (qtd. in Gill, 2004, p. xvii)

Thus, the living soul, what Wordsworth also called 'the spirit of life' (qtd. in Gill, 1989, p. 196) in the 1802 preface to *Lyrical Ballads*, depends upon the mysterious joining of old and new through a loving attachment to home.

Chapter 4

Towards the soul

The identity issue

Identity is a term used in many different ways and by a variety of disciplines. It has become a central issue of concern in contemporary debates about politics, ethics and culture, as can be seen for example in Kwame Appiah (2005), Amartya Sen (2006), Kathryn Woodward (1997), Edward Said (1993), Stuart Hall (1990) and Stuart Hall and Paul du Gay (1996). Issues of identity also touch upon the soul territory, that of each person's unique sense of who they are. Appiah even goes as far as to call 'soul making' the 'project of intervening in the process of interpretation through which each citizen develops an identity' (2005, p. 164). However, before specifically addressing the literature on the soul, I shall focus on the issue of identity, which will form a backdrop to subsequent chapters, as well as bring together issues already raised by the discussions of the centrality in our lives of a psychic home.

Identity is a term that is of great relevance to issues of race, ethnicity, nationality, gender and sexuality. Identity matters in very immediate ways, when it becomes a question of belonging, of inclusion but also of exclusion. The issue of identity has become a focus for various kinds of radical feminist literature, much of it challenging traditional psychoanalytic thinking, though also deeply influenced by it, even if in opposition, as with the work of Judith Butler (1990). The phenomena of terrorism and fundamentalism mean also that we need to look at how identities are formed, sustained and can be distorted. The existence of the Internet and the place of globalization in addition mean that larger forces are more and more eroding individual identities. It has become increasingly difficult for people to assert their own local identities; there is a constant risk of people becoming subservient to powerful interests.

Though identity has become a central issue of concern in the humanities, it seems to have become of less interest to psychoanalysts, even though it was a major topic of interest from the 1950s to the 1970s. Indeed, some of the ideas generated then, particularly by Erik Erikson, have become central to current pre-occupations in other disciplines.

I will argue that identity is a vitally important but complex and at times elusive or indeterminate concept. There are various fixed or constant elements in the development of identity, which can become the source of integration and of a sense of permanence, of achievement and coherence, whether that be as a person and/or as a psychoanalyst; and there are still issues about the nature of identity that challenge our thinking, such as its link with the processes of identification, the question of whether or not unity is an illusion or a real possibility. De M'Uzan has suggested that one can talk of a 'spectrum of identity' (2005, p. 18), that the sense of I-ness is neither in the ego nor the other, but distributed along both, a theme I shall return to later, and which matches my own picture of the human subject as being organized between the individual and the network of others.

I would suggest that one of the constant elements is that of the psychic home and that this provides a basis for a sense of identity, for crucial questions such as 'Who am I?' 'Who do I look and act like?' 'Which religion and nationality am I?' They indicate a search for a place in life, an identity which provides a relatively stable sense of home and one that supplies the core of the elusive and precarious notion of identity, whatever its complex vicissitudes, however much the human subject is distributed between other subjects.

Psychic home and identity: Some general issues

While in psychoanalytic thinking identity has come to have specific uses, particularly in understanding adolescent and earlier development, it has also come to be used as a general term for weighing up a psychoanalyst's stage in their career development. The phrase 'identity crisis', first described in detail by Erikson (1959, p. 56), is now very much in the public domain when referring to adolescent turmoil and their search for themselves, but it is also now applied to other stages of the life cycle, including middle and old age. That is, identity is a lifelong process, a matter of becoming as well as of being.

For psychoanalysts, there is the specific issue of what it means to have a psychoanalytic identity: how one becomes an analyst and maintains one's analytic stance, and how past generations of analysts have contributed to contemporary analytic identity, a topic I shall come to later in more detail.

Identity matters in immediate and indeed practical ways. For example, if you wish to renew your UK passport, you now have to apply to the Identity and Passport Office, which will authenticate your personal details and confirm your identity as a UK citizen, or not. Having a home is vital to this. Without an address, you cannot really be a citizen. This dilemma was especially poignant after World War II. Tony Judt (2005) has charted in his groundbreaking book *Post War* how there took place a massive movement of millions of people due to the aftermath of the concentration camps and also the civil wars that soon took place in what became communist Europe. Not only had there been, as a result of Stalin and Hitler, the uprooting, transplanting and deportation of some 30 million people between 1939 and 1944, but after the war Europe had to deal with an unprecedented exercise in ethnic cleansing and population transfer. Untold millions were displaced or were refugees. The distinction between displaced persons, assumed to have somewhere, a home to go to, and refugees, who were classified as homeless, was one of the many nuances that were introduced by the authorities trying to deal with this trauma. Its legacy remains to this day, marking the European identity.

The impact of these post- and indeed prewar migrations, of course, greatly affected the history of British psychoanalysis. The fact that the controversial discussions took place both at a time of war and with a number of those who had been displaced from their homes must have had a considerable influence on both the form and content of the discussions, focused around half-conscious notions of whose home was the most suitable to house psychoanalytic truths. Feelings about lost homes, about lost German or Austrian identities, idealized hopes for the new home or inevitable disappointments about establishing a home in exile may have crept into the apparently scientific arguments, and indeed, I suspect, remain still in current concerns about the functioning of the British Psychoanalytical Society.

Identity has always mattered, at least in Western society, certainly since the ancient Greeks, even before passports and the Internet. There are a number of famous examples in Homer's *Odyssey*, which brings this to light, where one can also see the resonances of the place of home and homecoming in the appearance of identity issues, as I have already described in Chapter Two.

In contrast to Homer's epic grandeur, if one were to capture the modern concern with identity artistically, one could do no better than consider the troubling pictures of Francis Bacon. He highlights in a disturbing way how our modern, or indeed postmodern, notion of identity is precarious. There is a permanent sense of unease in his pictures, marking the fragile sense of human identity. Faces and whole bodies intermingle and merge, sometimes are transformed into animal forms; mouths scream, bending figures cry out or are threatened, sexual encounters are anxiety ridden, identities are uncertain. Home is no comforting place here, rather the site of terror, cruelty, perversion and crude sexuality. In his book *Looking Back at Francis Bacon* (2000), David Sylvester describes Bacon's *Study for a Self-Portrait* (1985–6), a brilliant triptych, depicting the artist from three viewpoints. Bacon here seems to alternate between masculine and feminine identities, in one panel with his legs tucked primly under the chair like a modest lady, and in another panel more macho, emphasizing his massive arms and broad shoulders. Sylvester quotes the critic Richard Dormant when he states that in our 'struggle to achieve a separate and secure identity' we have to learn 'to distinguish between our own bodies and those of others, to work out that our bodies not only have weight and mass, but also boundaries, limits, perimeters'. If the figures in this triptych 'are seen as embryonic shapes desperately trying – and failing – to form a single, secure identity, then they speak of a universal human condition, the aboriginal calamity with which we struggle all our lives – and this is the stuff of the greatest art' (qtd. in Sylvester, p. 223–4).

While Bacon's triptych may reveal the struggle to form a single secure personal identity, contemporary politics reveals a real danger when people claim a single and overarching social and cultural identity rather than a looser sense of crossing a number of different identities. The fundamentalist dangerously owns a singular identity, excluding the rest of humanity, with potentially hateful and explosive results. They are no respecters of other peoples' homes. Identity can be homicidal when it becomes singular and disrespectful of differences. Much safer is to recognize that we belong to a variety of groupings, with a plurality of affiliations, including language, gender, profession, religion, class, interest groups, political associations and belief systems (Sen, 2006). Identity can then be humanizing when it respects otherness. Thus, a 'positive' notion of identity, respect and recognition of difference go together, as do a 'negative' notion of identity, disrespect and misrecognition of otherness.

Perhaps a psychoanalytic overview of this complex field can add something useful to current debates about identity, even though it is now often stated that psychoanalysis itself is in its own identity crisis, faced with the challenge of alternative therapies and the constant pressure to provide convincing evidence of its effectiveness. If it is any consolation, one could say that psychoanalysis is not alone in being in a crisis – it seems to have become a way of life at the moment; we are all in some kind of identity crisis, financial or otherwise. Perhaps identity is the kind of concept to which one only pays particular attention at moments of crisis, when fixed patterns of identity formation begin to break down, such as during war situations, institutional change or personal trauma.

What is identity?

The dilemmas of personal identity were first put forward philosophically by John Locke (1690, p. 331ff.), who remains the seminal influence in the field. He placed his account of personal identity in the context of the general nature of identity. The identity of a physical object depends on the identity if its constituent parts; if one part is removed, the object is changed. But with a living thing, the parts may change as in growth, but the living thing remains the same, so that identity in a living thing consists in the *organization* of its parts, the capacity to remain the same in the midst of change. The identity of a human being consists in the organization of their body. Personal identity consists in the unified consciousness of the self's present and past thoughts, and it is consciousness and memory that ground personal identity. However, Locke also highlighted certain dilemmas about such identity, including the periods when consciousness is disrupted and we lose a sense of continuity. He even raised the possibility that one body could house more than one consciousness.

Recent studies of 'split brains' involving severely epileptic patients, as well as experimental monkeys and cats, who have had the connections cut across the corpus callosum uniting right and left cerebral hemispheres, provide further evidence of the complexity of how we view personal identity. In fact, each hemisphere has the capacity to process information separately from the other hemisphere, and conflict may arise between the sides of the brain. According to

Thomas Nagel (1979, pp. 163–4), these studies challenge the notion of a single subject of consciousness.

Indeed, most recent studies on brain functioning highlight how much integration occurs both at the cellular level and in parallel pathways, challenging any notion of an overall single integrating mind. For example, individual neurones in the visual cortex respond to particular inputs, such as vertical or horizontal movement. The cells do not care if the stimulus has, say, different colours; it just responds to verticality or whatever orientation it is set to respond to. So already at the cellular level there is abstraction (see Zeki, 2009). Evidence from work with the visual cortex reveals that each different area of cortex is capable of considerable integration, such as areas involved with colour or movement (Zeki, 2004). Different aspects of visual perception are integrated separately and indeed at different time intervals. This has major implications for our understanding of consciousness and hence of personal identity. There is no single, integrated visual consciousness, but rather several different consciousnesses coexisting at the same time (Zeki, 2004, p. 197).

How then do we have any unity of experience if there is no single place where things come together, and when integration occurs in parallel at many local levels? There are, of course, multiple and reciprocal connections between areas of the brain; areas are not isolated from one another. But accounting for the functioning of the whole is a major puzzle. Perhaps identity and some sense of unity of the whole person consist in having the various areas available, not coming together as such. When the brain is damaged severely, then particular areas are no longer available, and integration is diminished. Severe damage to the frontal lobes definitely alters identity; the individual, incapable of deep emotional responses, appears to be another person, not themselves. Does this kind of damage indicate that identity and the capacity for emotional responsiveness are intimately linked? With a severe prefrontal brain lesion, the person cannot place themselves in time and place; they have no sense of home. Perhaps one can say, then, that the prefrontal cortex is the main site of the psychic home function. Of course, this remains a speculative thought.

Paul Ricoeur (1990) distinguishes two basic forms of identity – identity as *sameness* (Latin, *idem*) and identity as *selfhood* (Latin, *ipse*). Selfhood is not sameness. This is illustrated in Shakespeare's *Comedy of Errors*. The plot of the play, with the confusion between two sets of twins, master and servant, both sets coming together after a period of exile for one of the sets, illustrates how human identity is an elusive and precarious entity; nothing about it can be taken for granted, and perhaps we rely too much on things being or looking the same for reassurance about who we are. The plot of the play emphasizes how having an identity and being identical is not the same thing. One twin looks like the other but has a different role and personality. We may rely on things being the same but identities can be easily transformed. It does not take much for despair to set in, and with a sense that one has lost the ground for being certain about one's own identity. One subject can easily turn into another subject, while appearing to remain the same. The 'plot' of life, one might say, involves a constant play of subjects.

Appiah (2005) links identity with J. S. Mill's notion of an individual 'plan of life'. The life plan is an expression of individuality, who I am. As Frank Sinatra put it – 'I did it my way'. However, this needs to be complemented by the realization that the idea of identity is linked to that of recognition by others, that individuality and sociability are interlinked. Identity provides us with a source of value, one that helps us make our way among options. To adopt an identity is to make it mine, give it a home, and to see it as structuring my way through life, as well as allowing myself to feel solidarity with other like-minded people.

For Charles Taylor (1989), identity designates the ensemble of understandings of what it is like to be a human agent, including the sense of inwardness, freedom, individuality and being embedded in nature. The term is also defined 'by the commitments and identifications which provide the framework or horizon within which I can try to determine from case to case what is good, or variable, or what ought to be done, or what I endorse or oppose. In other words, it is the horizon within which I am capable of taking a stand' (Taylor, 1989, p. 27). Thus, for him, identity is linked with making choices. His use of horizon here would seem to have similarities with that of a foundational psychic home.

Woodward (1997) discusses the tension between essentialist and nonessentialist perspectives on identity. The essentialist account suggests that there is one clear, authentic set of characteristics which account for identity, such as where one belongs culturally or ethnically. A nonessentialist definition, however, would focus on differences as well as common and shared characteristics. She emphasizes how identities are not unified, and yet we need to examine how people take up various fixed or flexible positions and identify with them in order to see our way through tensions between people. This means having to explore the nature of difference, as well as psychoanalytic understanding of how our subjectivity is invested in various kinds of identity positions. Woodward's overall view is that we need to have a broad and inclusive, fluid and flexible, generous and respectful notion of identity if we are to escape the dangers of sectarianism.

Flexible and fluid pictures of the self are common in much modernist literature, famously in James Joyce's and Virginia Woolf's 'stream of consciousness' narratives. There is a striking description of the diversity and unity of the self in Virginia Woolf's *Mrs Dalloway*. Near the beginning of the novel, Clarissa Dalloway has returned from her walk around central London and is preparing for a party that night. She looks in the mirror.

> How many million times she had seen her face, and always with the same imperceptible contraction! She pursed her lips when she looked in the glass. It was to give her face point. That was her self – pointed; dartlike; definite. That was her self when some effort, some call on her to be her self, drew the

parts together, she alone knew how different, how incompatible and composed so for the world only into one centre, one diamond, one woman who sat in her drawing-room and made a meeting-point, a radiancy no doubt in some dull lives, a refuge for the lonely to come to, perhaps; she had helped young people, who were grateful to her; had tried to be the same always, never showing the a sign of all the other sides of her – faults, jealousies, vanities, suspicions . . . Now, where was her dress?

(Woolf, 1925, p. 35)

The writing, both in its content and in its form, expresses simultaneously the flowing of the self and its coming together, into what Woolf describes as a diamond, a multifaceted and precious object.

Bauman describes how finding identity comes along with 'a bunch of problems rather than a single-issue campaign' (2004, p. 12), a feature he shares with most people these days, living in what he calls the 'liquid modern era'. By the latter, he means that 'in our liquid modern times the world around is sliced into poorly coordinated fragments while our individual lives are cut into a succession of ill-connected episodes' (2004, p. 12–13). The modern dilemma is to be wholly, or in part, out of place, or one might say, not quite at home. 'Identities float in the air, some of one's own choice, but others inflated and launched by those around' (2004, p. 13). One can 'even begin to feel everywhere *chez soi*, "at home" – but the price to be paid is to accept that nowhere will one be fully and truly at home' (2004, p. 14).

We in the liquid modern world, 'seek and construct and keep together the communal references of our identities while *on the move* – struggling to match the similarly mobile, fast moving groups we seek and construct and try to keep alive for a moment, but not much longer' (Bauman, 2004, p. 26). One is reminded here of the suitably named mobile phone, to which we have become powerfully addicted, and without which communication can only be slow and uncertain. What did we do without it? Well, we obviously had slower communication, longer waiting times before knowing what others thought or wanted. We had to wait hours or even days for messages to be answered. But there is a price to pay for being in a liquid world; our identity is also liquid, and, like liquid, difficult to tie down and shape, unless kept in a solid container.

On the one hand, we long for a secure identity, yet becoming 'fixed' and identified gets an increasingly bad press (Bauman, 2004, p. 29). Yet having too much flexibility is not conducive to 'nest building'. But we live in a world where it is increasingly difficult to feel one belongs to a workplace or neighbourhood, or even family. There is instead an emphasis on being on the move, having a 'network' of connections, swapping identities. 'We talk these days of nothing with greater solemnity or more relish of "networks" of "connection" or "relationships". Not only because the "real stuff" – the closely knit networks, firm and secure connections, fully-fledged relationships – have all but fallen apart' (Bauman, 2004, p. 93).

While flexibility may be a useful capacity, 'floating without support in a poorly defined space, in a stubbornly, vexingly "betwixt and between" location, becomes in the long run an unnerving and anxiety-prone condition. On the other hand, a fixed position amidst the infinity of possibilities is not an attractive prospect either' (Bauman, 2004, p. 29).

While Bauman here does not offer solutions to the dilemmas he so clearly defines, there is an underlying sense that these dilemmas are directly related to the loss of 'fully-fledged' relationships, where there is a living attachment to home and to the workplace.

Psychoanalysis and identity

Psychoanalytic thinking around the issues of identity first flourished in the 1950s and 1960s, beginning with the work of Erikson, who was well aware of ambiguities and dilemmas in the very notion of identity. Perhaps the fact that he had been adopted made him particularly sensitive to the identity issue – his mother did not reveal that, having been abandoned by Erikson's father when she was pregnant, her husband adopted him. Erikson (1956) pointed out that Freud used the term only once when trying to formulate his link to Judaism; he spoke of an 'inner identity' which links the individual with the unique values and history of his people (Freud, 1941[1926], p. 274). It also refers to something in the individual's core which links up with the group's inner coherence. 'The term identity expresses . . . a mutual relation in that it connotes both a persistent sameness within oneself (self-sameness) and a persistent sharing of some kind of essential character with others' (Erikson, 1956, p. 56). In order to clarify the subject matter of identity, Erikson approached it from a variety of angles, predominantly with a developmental theoretical perspective, but also using literature, sociology and clinical work. Identity, then, appears to refer to a conscious sense of individual identity, an unconscious striving for continuity of personal character or as maintenance of an inner solidarity with a group's ideals and values.

The adolescent is consciously striving for an identity, as one can see in their various fads and enthusiasms, ways of dressing, kinds of music and so on. This compares with the emerging and more unconscious identity of the mature adult. Processes of identification and identity formation are intimately linked. But identity formation involves the selective repudiation and mutual assimilation of childhood identifications, and their absorption into a new configuration (Erikson, 1956, p. 68), which also involves the processes by which a society recognizes the young individual as somebody who had to become the way he or she is, and who is accepted for being that person. Identity refers to knowing where one is going, feeling *at home* with oneself and in one's body, gaining assuredness, respect and recognition from others who count.

While at the end of adolescence there is an overt identity 'crisis', identity formation neither begins nor ends with adolescence, for it is a lifelong development, largely unconscious to the individual and to his society. Its 'roots go back to the first self-recognition: in the baby's earliest exchange of smiles there is something of a *self-realization coupled with a mutual recognition*' (Erikson, 1956, p. 69).

The process of identity formation 'emerges as an *evolving configuration* – a configuration which is gradually established by successive ego syntheses and resyntheses throughout childhood; it is a configuration gradually integrating *constitutional givens, idiosyncratic libidinal needs, favoured capacities, significant identifications, effective defences, successful sublimations, and consistent roles*' (Erikson, 1956, p. 71). Identity formation involves a gradual integration of self-images. Phyllis Greenacre (1958) considered that the developing body image was the core of self-image and hence of the sense of identity. Identity implies both a being equal to and a being different from. The sense of identity comes into some kind of preliminary working form in the phallic-oedipal period, when the child is aware of himself existing in world of others, owns his or her own thoughts and memories, has knowledge of sexual differences, knows the names of body parts and is aware of himself or herself as a unit in a group. Although having a stable core, identity is subject to change roughly approximating the stages of body maturational achievement, with their accompanying emotional problems. Hence, identity formation cannot be completed fully until adolescence is assimilated, and indeed continues throughout life.

Edith Jacobson understood identity formation as a 'process that builds up the ability to preserve the whole psychic organization . . . as a highly individualized but coherent entity which has direction and continuity at any stage of human development. Normal identity formation . . . depends on the effectiveness of the synthesizing, organizing functions of the ego; but . . . the processes of organization are operative in all structure formations of the psychic apparatus, including the superego' (1964, p. 27). The notion of identity, with its focus on the individual's self realization, potentialities and role in society calls special attention to the relations of identity to the ego and superego identifications and their final vicissitudes during and after adolescence. While she agrees with others that the early mother–child relationship is crucial to the struggle for identity, she also highlights the importance of considering the role of aggression in developmental processes, where the assertion of the individual arises in the service of differentiation.

For Jacobson, the child's discovery of their identity occurs around the age of 2 to 2-and-a-half, when with the 'child's ego maturation, his ability to walk and to talk, the ever-widening scope of his perceptive and locomotor functions, his increasing manual accomplishments, his weaning and cleanliness training, etc., have advanced enough to bring about the startling discovery of his own identity, the experience of "I am I"' (1964, p. 59). But, of course, this discovery undergoes many changes; there is an increasing sense of direction and continuity as the psychic organization grows, becomes differentiated, structured, organized and reorganized, via adolescence, until maturity is reached. The finding of one's sexual identity begins early on but is the task of adolescence and postadolescence. For normal identity formation, the integration of the superego components for her is vital, providing safety and protecting the self from dangerous instinctual stimuli. Identity problems arise when the different elements of the psyche fail to integrate. Adolescence is a time when the self is particularly vulnerable due to the fluidity of the psychic organization, which is both an opportunity for growth and a danger to the self. How these processes are negotiated in adolescence will in turn affect postadolescent identity formation, leading to a stable or pathological psychic formation.

For Heinz Lichtenstein (1977), identity refers to the capacity to remain the same in the midst of change, and emerges from the symbiotic relation to the mother. The mother–child unit is the nucleus out of which identity emerges. The mother releases the child's identity. The specific reflection received from the mother conveys to the child a primary identity. The thematic identity will be developed in the course of a life as an infinite variety of identity transformations, as a simple musical theme is developed into a symphony. Thus, the mother imprints upon the infant an identity theme, which is irreversible but capable of variation. Clinically, one can tease out various identity themes in the patient. What makes for success or failure of integration is the patient's ability to confront the identity theme, not as merely an imposed and passive part of the self, but as something that can be open enough to lead to new developments and moments of integration. That is, one could say that there can be rigid or more flexible identity themes.

Winnicott was obviously concerned with what constitutes the sense of self and how this comes into being. Identity seems to be linked to the capacity to be alone, a stage of development where the individual is established as a unit, the 'I am', so they can say 'I am alone' (Winnicott, 1965, p. 33). This capacity to be alone is a sophisticated one, with many contributory factors, and is closely related to emotional maturity. The basis for this capacity is the experience of being alone in someone's presence; that is, there has been good enough reliable ego support from the early parent. For the establishment of unit status, the whole person has to have a sense of an inside and an outside, living in the body, more or less bounded by the skin; for this to happen there needs to have been a successful negotiation of the stages of dependence. A crucial aspect of the establishing of unit status, and hence identity, is the process of *personalization*. This describes the process when the person of the baby starts to be linked with the body and the body functions (Winnicott, 1965, p. 59), with the skin as the limiting membrane. The infant's psyche begins to dwell in the soma, or, one might say, feels *at home in the soma*, with a sense of being self-centred inside the body, and this process depends upon the mother's handling, her ability to join up her emotional and physical involvement. Here, then, one may see possible early roots of the sense of a psychic home.

The core of the self emerges out of the early mother–child relationship and implies body–mind integration. One could say that the merging of the mother's and infant's identities is basic for subsequent differentiation. In addition, around the various identifications, one could envisage a kind of containing membrane, holding them together in some way, akin to the notion of the safeguarding structure of a psychic home.

Subsequently, adult life for Winnicott begins when the individual, climbing out of dependency, has found a niche in society through work and is settled in some pattern; here there is a compromise between copying the parents and defiantly establishing a personal identity (Winnicott, 1965, p. 92).

The work of Lacan (1966), influential for feminist thinkers on identity, *deconstructs* identity. The human subject for Lacan is not an entity with an identity as such; instead, the subject is radically split, a fragmented subject with no sense of unity, almost no sense of a psychic home. Any sense of unity in the subject is an illusion. The unconscious for Lacan undermines any sense of certainty and stability, making the subject precarious. The subject can be grasped in language, but one cannot find from language any sense of a total unifying self; that is, the ego's role is that of giving an illusory sense of permanence and stability. Such a view can be seen to arise from Lacan's notion of the mirror stage, where the young child sees a total reflection of themselves. This reflection, bringing with it the appearance of wholeness, produces a feeling of jubilation and fascination, but is the source of alienation, the illusion of wholeness and an imaginary relationship with the body. The subject moves from fragmentation and insufficiency to illusory unity; psychoanalysis challenges our identity as unified subjects. This view contrasts with Winnicott's view of the mirror experience with the mother, or the mother's face, which can provide a sense for the child of being recognized. The mother gives back to the baby the baby's own self, allowing the baby to begin to feel real (Winnicott, 1971, p. 117). This is in complete contrast to Lacan, for whom there is no possibility of anything except an imaginary sense of wholeness, of a complete identity.

Thus, what is for Winnicott *recognition* is for Lacan *misrecognition.* For one the mirror is restorative; for the other it is alienating.

Lacan's theory was taken up by radical feminists challenging the hegemony of the phallus in the account of sexual identity. However, it must be said that Lacan himself was faithful to Freud's account of the development of sexual identity, where the presence or absence of the phallus has a pivotal role in the subject's insertion into the Symbolic Order and hence the assumption of sexual identity. Butler, in her book *Gender Trouble* (1990) – with the telling subtitle, *Feminism and the Subversion of Identity* – challenges the notion of a unifying feminine identity, which she sees as too often based upon the establishment of a 'heterosexual matrix'. She challenges any fixed notion of identity, seeing feminine identity as distorted by the dominance of masculine ways of seeing women. The aim of her text was '. . . to open up the field of possibility for gender without dictating which kinds of possibility ought to be realized' (1990, p. viii).

For Butler, psychoanalytic theory offers a story about gender acquisition, which effects a narrative closure on gender experience and a false stabilization of the category of women. Instead, gender identities emerge and sexual desires shift and vary so that different identifications come into play, depending upon the availability of legitimizing cultural norms and opportunities. It is not always possible to relate these shifts to a primary identification.

Much of this debate seems to hinge around the meaning of 'difference'. Is difference primary, as Juliet Mitchell maintains (1982), or something that comes with culture?

I would suggest that, rather than be drawn into polarized positions around the whole issue of sexual identity, these various debates highlight that identity has two faces: the restorative one of Winnicott but also the alienating one of Lacan. Identity is precarious; integration can occur but is also elusive. Thus, as Dana Breen (1993, p. 28) points out, the boy is particularly vulnerable in terms of his masculine identity, as he has an intense early involvement with the mother, whom he has to turn away from during development. This situation contrasts with the girl, whose identification with the mother helps her establish her feminine identity. There is in both a need for a positive identification with the pre-oedipal father to help dis-identify with the mother. All these processes of identification and dis-identification are potentially fragile and capable of going wrong. There is the possibility of integration and the establishment of a satisfactory sexual identity, but at the same time there are many different paths towards such an identity, with potential disturbances along the way.

Of recent analytic thinkers, Rosine Perelberg (1999) tackles the distinction between identity and identification. Identification is a process that takes place in the unconscious and is the source of fantasies. As with Freud, identificatory processes are fluid and shifting. Identity, in contrast, is, rather as in Lacan's work, an attempt that each individual makes to organize these conflicting identifications in order to achieve an *illusion* of unity, which allows an individual to say they are 'this' and not 'that'. Perelberg's paper then addresses how some violent male patients, overwhelmed by the extreme fluidity between masculine and feminine identifications, try to repudiate their feminine identification in order to establish an identity.

Overall, one can see with various thinkers that the issue of unity as an illusion or as something genuine becomes a crucial one. My own view is that is plainly absurd to rule out any notion of unity or integration. The issue is where and how the integration occurs and under what circumstances. I have mentioned the evidence from brain research for integration at the micro level; even neuronal cells are capable of generalization and abstraction. But how all the systems come together in an overall unity, and whether or not they do, is another and more complex issue. Here one comes up close to the area of the human soul as described in religious and philosophical literature.

My own picture of the human subject is also relevant here (Kennedy, 1998, 2007). This is of a subject where multiple paths are possible, holding together in some ways and not in others. Being able to tolerate the shifting and multiple elements of the psyche, bearing degrees of fragmentation, is crucial to the individual's subjectivity. I coined the notion of a *subjective organization* (Kennedy, 2007, pp. 83–108) as the psychic organization that structures the subject, involving individual and social elements, distributed along both, rather as in de M'Uzan's 'spectrum of identity' (2005, p. 18). Such an organization can become pathological in the sense of being defensive and held together by perverse forces, as with the pathological organization. But under normal conditions, the subjective organization remains the organizing structure involved in one's sense of I-ness, as well as that involved in the way that the subject is organized in the social field (Kennedy, 1998, p. 193–4). One of the essential aspects of the subjective organization is that it involves subjects in interaction with other subjects. The subjective organization is a dual structure made up of individual and collective elements in a complex interrelationship. I think that becoming a subject must intimately involve having the stable sense of a psychic home as the basis for psychic shifts. This situation could be understood by borrowing a musical metaphor, that of the modulation between tonic and dominant, say in sonata form, or with the resolution of dissonance when music returns to a home key from various musical excursions in related keys.

Bob Hinshelwood emphasizes that the basic experience of having a mind and sustaining its constituents is difficult, and the person remains vulnerable throughout life to primitive mental mechanisms, such as splitting and projection. The traditional unitary notion of personal identity is too static, not taking into account the discontinuities as well as continuities within and between people. Identity for Hinshelwood is what he calls a 'locus of belonging', that place within which mental entities can be gathered as sets of possessions, as well as eliminated through splitting and projection (1997, p. 195). This does not prevent us searching for illusory completeness, coherence and permanence, or in perhaps a more realistic way for the 'thread of life' as Richard Wollheim (1984, p. 10ff.) put it. The individual creating narratives of their life can achieve such a thread. In this sense, identity is a description of a particular kind of unified narrative that the subject can create about themselves. The locus of belonging and the psychic home seem to have a similar pattern.

Identification and identity

I mentioned in citing Perelberg that identity is concerned with uniting in some way different identifications. In *The Ego and the Id* (1923, p. 34), Freud tackles the issue of this unification of identifications in relation to the Oedipus complex. He describes identifications as ambivalent from the beginning. This is an interesting and complex idea, which can be interpreted in various ways. In *The Ego and the Id*, the ambivalence is shown when the boy identifies with his father, wants to become like him, and yet then displace him; thus love turns into hate. In Freud's book *Group Psychology and the Analysis of the Ego* (1921, pp. 105–10) identification is partly seen as the earliest or primal form of the emotional tie with the object or other. Thus, identification is in one sense of the term a primal way of relating to the other, involving both some kind of imitation yet also elimination of the other. Identification in this sense behaves like a derivative of the oral cannibalistic phase of development.

The essential ambivalence of identification can also be seen in Freud's earliest published account of the nature of identification, *The Interpretation of Dreams* (1900, pp. 146–51), when he describes the dream of a patient who affirmed that she had dreamt a dream that went against his theory of dreams as wish fulfilments, that is she wanted to put herself in place of Freud, or displace him.

In the dream, the patient wanted to give a dinner party but only had a little smoked salmon. She was unable to find any since it was Sunday and the shops were shut, and so she had to abandon the wish to have a party. Several themes arose as a result of the dream analysis. The patient's associations first of all centred on her husband, 'an honest and capable wholesale butcher' (Freud, 1900, p. 147), who said he had wanted to lose some weight – so not having the dinner would tie up with that. But then there were associations concerning the patient's friend, whom her husband had praised. Fortunately, that friend was skinny, and the patient's husband preferred more plump women, like the patient herself. That friend had expressed a wish to put on more weight. So the dream was also saying that there was no way that the patient would invite the friend around to a dinner party so the friend could get fat and be sexually attractive to the patient's husband. Smoked salmon was in fact her friend's favourite dish.

But Freud describes how there was also another and 'more subtle' interpretation. Her friend had wished to put on weight, and so it would not have been surprising if the patient had dreamed that the friend's wish was unfulfilled. However, in fact, the patient dreamed that her *own* wish was unfulfilled. That is, she had put herself in her friend's place; that is, she had 'identified' with her. By doing this, the patient appropriated the friend's wish, and in a sense eliminated the wish, nullified it and also the rival friend. Identification, then, is not merely imitation but also what Freud calls 'assimilation'. Through this means, she wins back her husband, or makes sure that the husband still desires her – 'my patient put herself in her friend's place in the dream because her friend was taking my patient's place with her husband and because she (my patient) wanted to take her friend's place in her husband's high opinion' (Freud, 1900, pp. 150–1). Freud does not make too much of the fact that there was also a subtle relationship between the dreamer and himself and why was she so triumphant about bringing a dream that was supposed to counter Freud's own theory of dreams. Nor did he make any comment about a butcher's wife dreaming about fish, which the butcher was not selling; nor that the honest butcher wanted to be thin like the friend, thus expressing a feminine identification. But, of course, we only have a small portion of the actual session material.

In his later work, *The Ego and the Id*, Freud describes the various kinds of identification grouped around the child's mother and father at the time of the Oedipus complex, involving complex feelings of love, hate and rivalry. The outcome of the struggle with these two different identifications is that they form a 'precipitate,' or formation, in the child's developing ego, *'consisting of these two identifications in some way united with each other'* (1923, p. 34).

It is not specified how this unification occurs, except that it happens 'in some way'. There is a similar description in Freud's *Three Essays on the Theory of Sexuality*, when he tackles how the subject can gradually, through development, organize the bodily drives. For Freud, this is a gradual process, which is only complete after puberty. Freud describes how the drives in childhood are not unified in any way, but consist of a number of different components or 'partial drives', each with a special connection to an erotogenic zone, a part of the body giving rise to a form of sexual excitation. Using evidence from, for example, the perversions where the partial drives fall apart, Freud describes how the sexual drive is normally put together from the various partial drives into what he calls a firm 'organization'. This only happens at puberty, where the primacy of the genitals is finally beginning to be established. This new organization is a result of the combination of the partial drives into a unity, though there is the constant possibility that the sexual drive may be fragmented into its components. Once again, it is not clear how this unification occurs and what it consists of, except in terms of a somewhat precarious final sexual organization.

Hans Loewald (1971) did suggest one way that the drives can become unified. He saw the drives as psychic motivational forces which become organized developmentally through interactions within a field consisting originally of the mother–child psychic unit. That is, the drives are organized through a relationship.

I think that the point is that these considerations imply that there are different ways that identifications may come together, or fail to come together, and that will make for different character structures and different issues for the human subject's own sense of identity, including sexual identity. That is, there are all kinds of ways that identifications can sit around in the psyche, lodge there, feel alien, or feel more settled and at home, various ways that the identifications can be bound together in some kind of containing membrane, various ways that the identifications, within and between subjects, interact. For this reason, identity can be fluid, stable or unstable, open to change or resistant to change, depending upon the way that the identifications are organized.

The identity of the psychoanalyst

John Klauber tackled the complex issue of the analyst's identity in an International Psychoanalytical Association (IPA) symposium dedicated to the topic in 1976. He comments on two other papers first, by Edward Joseph and Daniel Widlocher. For Joseph, the identity of the analyst is marked internally by the capacity to think, feel and react as an analyst. Years of training and practice allow the precarious analytic identity to become autonomous, through continuous efforts of self-analysis and education throughout life in order to maintain its autonomy. The latter is buttressed by entry into a psychoanalytical society, where attacks and invasions from within the society and from the external world have to be withstood.

For Widlocher, what lays the foundation for the analyst's identity is the nature of the psychic work, which is demanded from him or her with the unique and difficult practice of handling transference and countertransference. This identity is linked to a narcissistic doubt as our practice is constantly being threatened, taking us away from the essence of the Freudian experience. Widlocher discusses how analytical societies not only have the purpose of training and scientific communication, but also a function of reassuring the group about their analytic identity in the face of doubts.

Klauber points to two strains, which these papers underline. The first strain is the quest for a new experience of truth and the location of the analyst's position in this search. Klauber, like Widlocher, stresses the centrality of the human encounter in this search. 'This is where the mystery takes place, in which one human being understands another, and the sense of wonder is engendered at the persistence of unconscious patterns without which no psychoanalyst can feel at home in his profession' (Klauber, 1981, p. 170). Thus identity is linked here to feeling at home in one's professional role, as well as finding a professional home in a psychoanalytical society.

The second strain is that which responds to the pressure for therapy and even cure, with all the pressure from the external world for results.

These two strains play a part in the 'crisis' of identity that psychoanalysts often experience. For Klauber, the central problem of psychoanalytical identity formation seems to lie 'in finding a balance between the years of training necessary for a student often approaching mid-life or past it to master a highly exacting conceptual system and technique and the stultification of originality by the weight of authority' (1981, p. 176).

For him, the sense of identity of the analyst depends upon an intense experience of the analytical process, which involves the analyst having 'fire in his belly'; it is a very personal process, involving the analyst as a person, their being able to link up the personal with the technical aspects of psychoanalysis – something which may take years to accomplish. In this sense, it may take years to feel at 'home' with practicing psychoanalysis.

For Michael Parsons, the identity of the analyst has a double meaning – 'what it means to be an analyst cannot be isolated from how an individual analyst's personal identity is achieved, through a process of becoming that is unique to that analyst' (2000, pp. 69–70). What most distinguishes the identity of the analyst is the relationship that they develop with their own unconscious. A trust in the unconscious is central to the analyst's identity, even if the route we have come to get where we are can be complex and follow many different paths. The sense of authenticity, of being highly trained and yet able to use analytic concepts and technique with appropriate freedom and flexibility, is central to Parson's approach.

Parsons highlights various polarities,

> ... between, on the one hand, spontaneity, the sense of mystery, openness to the unexpected and trust in the unconscious processes, and on the other, rationality, adherence to fundamental principles, conceptual rigour and consistent, disciplined technique. These two aspects of psychoanalysis pull in opposite directions and psychoanalysts become the analysts they are by the ways they find of sustaining a creative tension between them.
>
> (Parsons, 2000, p. 4)

Thus one could say that a psychoanalytic identity involves both feeling at home in one's role, and, hopefully at one's institution, but that there is a also a necessary pull away from feeling too settled in one's position; it does not pay creatively to be too comfortable with one's position. Indeed, it is not that uncommon for the most creative analysts to feel, at times at least, rather on the margins of their parent institution; they seem to have a need to pull away from a psychic home, though of course there is also the need for the home, however frustrating, to be there to pull away from.

Culture and identity

One cannot ignore the now massive literature on how culture affects one's sense of identity. Said's work is pivotal to this field. In his classic *Culture and Imperialism*, he defines culture as meaning two things. First, it means 'all those practices, like the arts of description, communication, and representation, that have relative autonomy from the economic, social, and political realms, and that often exist in aesthetic forms, one of whose principal aims is pleasure' (1993, p. xii).

Second, culture is a concept that includes a refining and elevating element, the best that is known and thought in each society. However, and this is one of the main threads of his study, culture can be used aggressively by a nation state in order to impose itself on others, differentiating 'us' from 'them'. Culture in this sense is a combative source of identity (Said, 1993, p. xiii).

His own approach in the book, through a detailed examination of the work of various writers, such as Jane Austen, Charles Dickens, Joseph Conrad, Rudyard Kipling, Albert Camus and William Butler Yeats, is to challenge a static view of identity which has been the core of cultural thought during the era of imperialism (Said, 1993, p. xxviii). Rather than see culture and identity as unitary, he proposes throughout his book that all cultures are involved in one another: 'none is single and pure, all are hybrid, heterogeneous, extraordinarily differentiated, and unmonolithic' (1993, p. xxix). That is, he argues for a flexible, open-minded notion of identity, which can embrace different cultures and not impose on them from the outside. Such a view contrasts with that of imperialism, which was essentially about acquiring territory and imposing a particular way of life on other cultures, that is about acquiring *other homes*. Imperialism is the attitude of a dominating metropolitan centre ruling a distant territory. The attitude of those who ruled the colonies, creating an imperial culture in these other homes, reflected the various tensions and injustices in the home culture. There arose a complex relationship between the home culture, which needed to be stable and prosperous, and the overseas territories, which were greatly exploited. Thus Thomas Bertram's slave plantation in Jane Austen's *Mansfield Park* is shown to be mysteriously necessary to the poise and beauty of Mansfield Park.

Imperial possessions are usefully *there*, in some other space, with an unnamed population, whose identity is scratched out, erased; such places become the site for adventurers, disgraced younger sons and travellers who sow wild oats or collect exotica. Said describes how in the great Victorian novels, 'home' and 'abroad' became crucial dimensions for analysing the nature of English society. Abroad 'was felt vaguely and ineptly to be out there, or exotic and strange, or in some way or other "ours" to control, trade in "freely", or suppress when the natives were energized into overt military or political resistance. The novel contributed significantly to these feelings, attitudes, and references and became a main element in the consolidated vision, or departmental cultural view, of the globe' (1993, pp. 87–8).

Said shows how there was, in fact, considerably more resistance to the imperialist impositions than was openly admitted. He also describes how in the course of time, decolonization was very much about *reclaiming homes* which had been usurped. In these acts of reclamation, all nationalist cultures become dependent on the concept of a national identity. As necessary as this process is in the act of liberation, there is of course a danger of mirroring the dominating culture from which they wish to be liberated.

At the end of his book, Said argues for a new concept of identity, one which respects different cultures, different homes, where connections are made between cultures, other languages and geographies, where it is accepted that none today is *one* thing (1993, pp. 407–8). Identity in this sense is about inclusion not exclusion.

Stuart Hall (1990) faces similar issues to those of Said in his exploration of visual representations of Afro-Caribbean and Asian 'blacks' of the diasporas of the West – the new postcolonial subjects. Such subjects have to face complex identity issues. Historically displaced from their homes, they are not in a position to reclaim their homes, as those living in the colonies could do; they are, to use a term often associated with the history of the Jews, subjects of a diaspora, a dispersal. They have found other homes and yet still have fundamental connections, through culture, history, myth, narrative, fantasy and transmitted memories, to their origins. Dispersal and fragmentation is the history of all enforced diasporas, and these clearly involve trauma and loss of identity. Such loss can only begin to be healed when forgotten connections between past and present are brought to light and once more set in place. That is not to say that there can be a return to what was; people's identities have moved on and have a life of their own. There are similarities but also differences between then and now, which have to be recognized. Hall rethinks the positionings and repositionings of Caribbean cultural identities in relation to at least three 'presences' – the African presence, the site of the repressed; the European presence, which is the site of exclusion and expropriation; and the American presence, the beginning of diaspora, diversity, hybridity and difference. There is no simple way that these presences can be harmonized or unified in a comfortable identity. Rather, these presences, which represent different discourses, meet at various junction points; they can become the site of different subjective positions or sites of temporary attachment to different subject positions.

Yet, at some point, these attachments may become permanent. The Lebanese author Amin Maalouf, who was born in Lebanon and lives in France, in his book *On Identity* asks,

> So am I half French and half Lebanese? Of course not. Identity can't be compartmentalized. You can't divide it up into halves or thirds or any other separate segments. I haven't got several identities; I've got just one, made up of many components combined together in a mixture that is unique.
>
> (1996, p. 3)

He points out that identity is certainly made up of a number of allegiances, but that it is necessary to emphasize that identity is also singular, something that we experience as a complete whole. 'A person's identity is not an assemblage of separate affiliations, nor a kind of loose patchwork; it is like a pattern drawn on a tightly stretched parchment' (Maalouf, 1996, p. 22).

Maalouf is also realistic about how identities are not always positive; they can be lethal, especially when 'tribal', based upon narrow and sectarian allegiances which deny difference and diversity. Such a view matches the theme of Amartya Sen's recent book, *Identity and Violence*. Identities may become 'reactive' when, for example, a country which has freed itself from foreign domination creates its own identity as a reaction to what has been left behind, rather than seek or create a different and more open form of identity. Reactive self-identities can lead to dangerous fundamentalism. Instead, Sen talks of the need to pay attention to 'our common humanity' (2006, p. 119), or what one might consider to be the soul territory. Such an approach counters the tendency to neglect an economic and social analysis of the influence of any sense of identity with others, and of what we value and how we behave – what he calls 'identity disregard'. And such an approach also counters what he calls 'singular affiliation' (2006, pp. 1–17) – the tendency to assume that the any person preeminently belongs to only one collectively, thereby obliterating people's natural multiple loyalties and affiliations. It was one of Sen's great achievements to show how an economic theory which obliterated such differences, such as by merely focusing on a free market without any notion of people's capacities and welfare, cannot address modern economic realities in the developing countries.

In conclusion, I think that what has come out of considering the various psychoanalytic and other contributions to identity is how identity as an issue is complex and potentially precarious, involving steering a path between different polarities, different sources of identification, but that in addition, charting a course along this difficult path requires holding a creative tension between possible positions, not holding fast to just one single way. However, feeling at home with a flexible notion of identity does not appeal to everyone. People vary as to how much the psychic home remains for them the only true home, how much they need to pull away from it.

What contemporary accounts of identity in other disciplines repeatedly focus on is the notion of identity as plural, multiple, merging one with another rather than as if it were facing each other from separate corners. In addition, though identity involves individuals, their identity is formed under multiple influences. Identities involve having a position within our society and in relation to a history, a lineage. Certain markers of identity may be visible or can appear through inquiry – whether that is from a country of origin, racial, religious or ideological standpoint.

One can see an identity as involving the taking up of a particular position, depending upon different social roles or different histories. But taking up a position requires a starting point, or a frame of reference or at least some scaffolding. This is where I would suggest the notion of a psychic home comes in, as the starting point for the complex and indeed lifelong task of forming an identity, whether as a psychoanalyst or outside one's professional life.

These considerations naturally lead on to more detailed discussion of how the notion of a soul can enrich what we mean by our common humanity.

Chapter 5

The soul and its home

The Props assist the House
Until the House is built
And then the Props withdraw
And adequate, erect.
The House support itself
And cease to recollect
The Augur and the Carpenter –
Just such a retrospect
Hath the perfected Life –
A Past of Plank and Nail
And slowness – then the scaffolds drop
Affirming it a Soul –
   (Emily Dickinson, 'Poem 729' in Vendler, 1995, p. 307)

I have so far touched upon the nature of the soul from time to time in a preliminary way, suggesting that whatever we mean by talking about our souls, the word
has powerful resonances. Although it is an abstract word, the word speaks to us;
it gives voice to something essentially human. In the words of Helen Vendler, the
literary critic, in her book *Soul Says*, the lyric poem is the home of the soul,
'where the human being becomes a set of warring passions independent of
time and space' (1995, p. 5). The title of her book is taken from a poem of the
same name by Jorie Graham that closes her collection, *Region of Unlike* (1991).
The soul seems an 'abstracted voice of the whole person, body and mind, riven
by the feelings always coursing from the senses to the passions, struggling to say
what words, when formally arranged, can say as the experience of the inner life
makes itself articulate and available to others' (Vendler, 1995, p. 8).

Vendler interprets the Emily Dickinson poem that prefaces this chapter in her
fascinating book of commentaries on Dickinson's poems (2010, pp. 307–10). It
is a poem about spiritual growth, the way that the soul is formed, likening that
growth to the building of a house. The house needs props as it is being built, but
then when it can support itself, the house passes from instability to strength. Along
the way, it has to take account of the hammer and nails of suffering. By the

'ability to do without "Props," the House affirms itself a Soul. The scaffolds seem to know when the work is finished, and "drop" of their own accord as soon as they perceive the presence of the perfected Soul, its suffering completed' (Vendler, 2010, p. 310).

This chapter will look in more detail at the soul concept from different perspectives, looking at some of the 'props' that make up the human soul.

Etymologies and histories

The word soul seems to be both abstract and yet also powerfully emotive. It can be approached from a number of different angles, from philosophy, religion, sociology, literature and neuroscience. No one discipline has the monopoly on understanding the soul concept. It is also a word which even hardened materialists can be attracted to. Thus Francis Crick (1994) subtitled his book on the materialist exploration of human consciousness, *The Scientific Search for the Soul*.

The *Oxford English Dictionary* defines 'soul' in a variety of ways, just to give a selection – as the principle of life in humans and animals, or the principle of thought and action in a person, regarded as distinct from the body, a person's spiritual as opposed to corporeal nature, the spiritual part of a person, the seat of the emotions, deep feeling and sensitivity. These definitions merge with those of 'spirit', which is also the life-giving principle of humans and animals, the immaterial part of a corporeal being, a disembodied and separate entity surviving after death, a soul, the active power of an emotion, the seat of action or feeling. Then we also have 'psyche', which is breath, life, soul, mind and the spirit. And 'mind', which is defined in many ways, including as the faculty of reasoning, thinking, intending, remembering, a way of feeling, the seat of awareness and even the spiritual as opposed to the corporeal part of a person.

All these words, then, cover similar territory, reflecting both subtleties and confusions. Soul and mind are derived from Old English with Germanic origins, spirit ultimately from Latin and psyche from Greek, reflecting the complex history of the English language. We are now faced with the 'debris of centuries of reflection accumulated between the ancient Greeks and ourselves' (Padel, 1992, p. 32).

Ours is not the only language to have such overlapping words for such elemental concepts. Ancient Greek itself, which still provides us with so many of the basic tools for thinking, also spreads meanings over several words – *thumos*, *phren*, *psyche* and *nous*, for example (Padel, 1992). *Thumos* and *nous* can be translated as 'spirit' and 'mind'. *Thumos* derives from *thuo*, 'I seethe'. It is a site of feeling, of spirited emotion, of righteous anger, of desire, of heart. *Psyche* can mean life, the sensual, emotional self, the essential 'you' or the soul (Heraclitus), which is potentially immortal, as well as spirit or ghost as in Homer. *Psyche* is derived from the word *psychein*, 'to breathe'. It came to stand not just for breath but for that which generates life. *Nous*, usually translated as 'mind', is an essentially perceiving element, intellect and intelligence. *Phren* is the heart or mind; the *phrenes* are around the heart and contain emotion, practical ideas and knowledge. This is just to scratch the surface of the many different and shifting meanings of these words used to account for human action and emotion in ancient Greece.

Furthermore, when one examines many ancient accounts involving descriptions of the soul, we find them embedded in an examination of human life in its complexity, not isolated from the human context. Such explorations are tied to human values, the nature of a good life, virtue and justice, not split off from human endeavours. That is, considerations of the soul in ancient thought tend to be embedded in looking at the citizen's life as a whole, not at the soul in isolation, as is the tendency of modern thought.

It is not my intention to provide a detailed history of the soul concept; that is provided elsewhere, such as in the book *A Brief History of the Soul* (Goetz and Taliaferro, 2011) and the collection of papers *The Soul Hypothesis* (Baker and Goetz, 2011). These are books that start with the view that there is no agreement about how we can explain human beings without taking account of the soul.

I will, however, emphasize three crucial 'moments' in the history of the soul: (1) Plato's foundational picture of the soul in his metaphor of the cave, in addition to his tripartite division of the soul linking up the soul with both the pursuit of knowledge and an ethical pursuit of the good; (2) the place of the soul in Hellenistic and then Christian thought and its linking with spiritual transformation, or *transformation of the soul*; and (3) the gradual disconnection of the soul from spiritual transformation with the scientific revolution, the development of a mercantile culture and the thought of Descartes. The latter, what Michel Foucault called for convenience the '*Cartesian moment*' (2001, p. 68), has had profound effects on how we picture the soul. Until that point, philosophy and spiritual transformation, knowledge and human value, tended to be linked. From then on, there develops a radical *split* between knowledge and spiritual transformation, between the world of the spirit and the material world, a split which I would suggest needs some sort of attention.

1. There is no way one can avoid the overwhelming influence of Plato, whose explorations are basic to any consideration of the nature and place of the soul in our lives. Plato, through the mouth of Socrates, explores the nature of the soul in a number of dialogues. Foucault (1994, pp. 93–6) highlights one particular theme of particular relevance to my narrative, that of *epimeleia sautou*, or the *care of the self or soul.* He traces this notion through much of ancient Greek and Roman thought. He chooses Plato's early dialogue *Alcibiades* (Plato, 1927) as a natural starting point for his exploration. The phrase *epimelesthai sautou*, taking care of one's self, or taking pains over one's self, first appears in line 127d of the dialogue, when Socrates is trying to guide the young Alcibiades in a favourable direction while he is still young and before age makes it more difficult.

Socrates makes various, almost 'clinical' observations of Alcibiades at the beginning of the dialogue. The young man cannot keep a lover; they keep running away from him, due to his excessive spirit, or *phrenes*. The good-looking Alcibiades justifies himself by his self-regard, but this is not an attitude that can lead to a successful public life, where one has to pay attention to the care of others. Before attending to others, one must take care of one's own soul. Knowledge of the soul (*psyche*) is the way to achieve this sort of care. That knowledge is found by looking at that part of the soul in which virtue (*arete*) occurs – wisdom (*sophia*) (133b). Wise attention to one's own soul is a lifetime's activity. It consists of a turning towards the divine, which in later Plato will become the eternal forms; this movement of the soul will also become the basis for Christian spirituality.

In Plato's *Apology* (1914), he has Socrates criticize the Athenians in his speech for his defence. Socrates says (29D) that Athens is the greatest city, the most famous for wisdom and power, not ashamed to care for the acquisition of wealth, for reputation and honour, but not for mindfulness, truth and the *best care of the soul.*

Foucault points out that subsequent thinkers, such as Seneca, Plutarch and Epictetus, urge a similar process of the soul turning to itself, while also being drawn aloft towards the divine. The ultimate purpose is for the person to settle into themselves, 'to take up residence in oneself' and to remain there (Foucault, 1994, p. 96). This is a therapeutic or healing process, a kind of *therapy of the soul.* Yet this can only happen with the aid of a teacher, or another soul who can give direction, as shown in the Platonic dialogue. Philosophy is, then, involved with the healing of souls. This becomes very much the theme of later Hellenistic philosophy (Nussbaum, 1994) and profoundly influenced Christian thinkers.

Plato himself, of course, had a complex picture of the human soul, most fully developed in his later dialogues such as *The Republic*, the *Phaedo* and *Phaedrus*. His picture of the soul remains pivotal for all subsequent philosophical and religious thinkers; it provides much of what will become the essential language of the soul.

The metaphor of the cave in *The Republic* remains central to his thought. Plato uses the cave to describe the soul's ascent to the intelligible realm, where it ultimately sees the idea of the good. The men in the cave can only see the shadows of things as they are and not the true light of reality, though they at least can huddle together and keep each other from being too lonely. They have had their legs and necks fettered since *childhood*, remaining in the same spot, unable to turn their heads, so that they can only look in front. They have been thus bound and unfree since childhood. Plato then imagines one of them obtaining a release (*lusis*) from the bonds, enabling them to leave the cave and come into the light, where gradually he accustoms himself to things as they really are.

Plato uses these images to conceive of how such men may be produced by the city-state (*polis*) and how they may be led upwards to the light by a sort of *transformation* of the soul from darkness to light, from the shadow world of becoming to the bright world of being, of that which is to the idea of the good. Essential to this process of transformation is the freeing of the prisoner's bonds so that he can move from the prison into the free world of thought and light. Thus Plato intermingles in his imagery a process of the soul's transformation from bondage to some sort of freedom, a process of rational understanding and an ethical pursuit – of the 'good'.

One could say that in psychoanalysis there is a similar sort of transforming process, a freeing of the neurotic bonds, in which the soul is led out of darkness, or rather, paradoxically, it is led into the darkness of the 'unconscious cave' in order to come out again enlightened.

Plato's tripartite division of the soul adds to the richness of his thinking about the soul's transformation. By recognizing that there are *conflicting* elements in the soul, he raises a question that remains relevant concerning the soul's organization. While considering whether or not the soul contains different forms in itself, he writes that this is a hard question:

> Do we do these things with the same part of ourselves, or do we do them with three different parts? Do we learn with one part, get angry with another, and with some third part desire the pleasures of food, drink, sex, and the others that are closely akin to them? Or, when we set out after something, do we act with the whole of our soul, in each case? This is what is hard to determine.
>
> (*Republic*, 1992, 436b)

That is to say, is there a unity in the soul, or are there separate parts, or are there separately functioning parts which can act as a unit? Such questions remain of contemporary relevance, for example with regard to our understanding of brain function. Does it make sense to talk of isolated parts of the brain with specific functions without referring simultaneously to the workings of the brain as a whole? The Russian neuropsychologist Alexander Luria tackles this issue by looking at the brain as a 'complex functioning system', embracing different levels and different components, each making its own contribution to the final structure of the 'working' brain (1973, p. 43ff.). Based on years of working with patients suffering from traumatic local brain lesions from times of war and peace, Luria puts together a complex picture of how what he calls the three components of the working brain – the unit for regulating tone or waking; the unit for obtaining, processing and storing information; and the unit for programming, regulating and verifying mental activity – are in dynamic interaction. However, we still do not know how the organization creates a unified experience.

Plato has the notion of the soul (*psyche*) having different functioning parts, related to some extent but each with its own separate tasks, and each located in different parts of the body. There is the rational part, the *logistikon*, located in the head which contemplates the forms, the realm of higher being, as with the man who escapes the cave; the part which loves, hungers and desires – the illogical, appetitive *alogistikon*, located in the midriff, which makes up the bulk of the soul; and the third part, the *thumos*, located between the midriff and neck, or the principle of high spirit – this is the part with which we feel anger, but it can also help the rational part, unless corrupted by evil.

Aristotle will base his own influential picture of the soul on that of Plato. For him, the soul is the principle of life, the vital principle in living things. The soul is the 'form' of the body; it configures the body into a unifying organization, composed of soul and body in a close relationship. Indeed, soul and body seem to form one substance. This contrasts with the Platonic separation of body and soul. In the Platonic view, as mentioned in the opening chapter, the body is generally the prison house of the soul. There would seem to be one exception to this view in Plato's works, in his dialogue *Cratylus*, which is concerned with the origin of words. In that dialogue, he contrasts the notion of the body as the tomb of the soul with the Orphic or Pythagorean view of the body as an enclosure for the soul, where it is kept safe. In the Aristotelian view, the soul welcomes the body, provides more of a home for the soul. These two views of body and soul – prison and home – become highly influential for all subsequent thought, which alternates between them.

Psychoanalysis cannot escape the influence of Greek thought any more than can other Western disciplines. The tripartite division of the soul resembles the tripartite division of consciousness, preconscious and unconscious as well as ego, superego and id. Psychoanalysis also restored to Western thought the primacy of dialogue, and one could say that there is something of the Platonic spirit in the psychoanalytic enquiry after the human subject's truth.

When all the parts of the Platonic soul are fulfilling their own functions, then they are each in their own way acting with virtue (*arete*). Virtue is then about some kind of harmonious working of the parts of the soul, although how they work together is still hard to figure out. That is, on the one hand, the Platonic soul has parts, but on the other Plato talks about the whole soul acting together, and this ambiguity is never fully resolved, nor has it been since. Plato does, however, talk about there being some kind of *convergence* of perceptions into some kind of unified perceiving centre.

> It would be a very strange thing, I must say if there were a number of senses sitting inside us as if we were Wooden Horses, and there were not some single form, soul, or whatever one ought to call it, to which all these converge – something *with* which, *through* the senses, as if they were instruments, we perceive all that is perceptible.
>
> (*Theaetetus*, 1990, 184c–d)

Taking our cue from Plato, one can say that the soul is the image of convergence; it is what coheres, it is our name for *what makes for the sense of inner unity*, the 'form' of convergence, to borrow from Aristotle, even though we do not understand how this occurs, even though we still do not understand the link between the inner unity and the brain processes occurring simultaneously or in parallel. We are aware of this sense of unity from time to time, particularly when we feel at home in our body and our selves, when the sense of who we are 'takes residence'; for this reason, one might talk of a human being providing a *home for the soul*. But the sense of unity is an elusive experience, difficult to tie down, capable of fleeing from us. It is in part linked to the unified stream of consciousness, but at least since Freud we know that consciousness is only a fraction of the soul's activity and indeed of the brain's activities. Traditionally, one could sense this inner unity when looking into a man's eyes, the eyes being the 'mirror' of the soul. I suggested in the opening chapter that, from the experience of death, what is essentially human, the link with others, as revealed by the nature of the fading gaze, dies with the body. I suggested there that from a psychological point of view, we call *that which links with others* the human soul. The live gaze, that which reflects back to the other, reveals the essence of a person, their character, their depth, their value, the 'weight' of their soul, to use a rather medieval image.

2. The latter metaphor leads onto Christian thought. Saint Augustine, in his book *The Greatness of the Soul*, asks, 'What is the soul's home?' (1949, p. 14). One may disagree with his answer – that the soul's true home is with God – but it is still an important question. One could say that much of Augustine's complex thought turns round the question of the nature of the soul, which continued to trouble him throughout his life. The questions he posed about the soul and its relation to the body, and some of the answers he provided, are still relevant today. As with Plato, questions about the soul are linked to matters of value and meaning, with Augustine the nature of true happiness. For him, the study of philosophy treats two problems – one regarding the soul and the other regarding God. The goal of the first is to know ourselves; the goal of the second is to know our origin. The former is more pleasing to us; the latter, more valuable. The former makes us fit for a happy life; the latter gives us happiness.

Philosophers after Plato were already concerned with how a virtuous life may be acquired through attention to the soul. Thus, the *Meditations of Marcus Aurelius* describes how the soul may be enlarged through a disciplined inward examination of the objects of the world. 'Look within. Do not let the quality or value of anything escape you' (Book 6, 3). The Neo-Platonist Plotinus described how the soul turns inward in order to see the inner world of the Forms and thereby has access to what he describes as the One, the highest unity possible. And we have looked at what Foucault has emphasized as the care of the self in ancient thought. But it is with Augustine that the inward turn takes on its most radical and modern shape. Through turning inward, we find a vast inner world, from where eventually we may look upwards towards God, and in the process the soul becomes *transformed*. The soul's turning inward and then upwards to God in this process of transformation is crucial in the development of subjectivity. For the first time, we have an alive sense of a complex inner world of memory and imagination. This shift is documented in Taylor's book *Sources of the Self* (1989). The principal route to God is not through external objects but in ourselves. We find truth inwardly.

So the light of God is not just 'out there', illuminating the order of being, as it is for Plato; it is also an 'inner' light. It is the light 'which lighteth every man that cometh into the world' (John 1:9). It is the light in the soul.

(p. 129)

Such an inward turn is a radical shift, providing a new language of inwardness. The inner light is the one which shines in our presence to ourselves, illuminating the space where I am present to myself (Taylor, 1989, p. 131). It is my view that this inner light is also detectable in relation to others, as I have described in the introduction.

Augustine describes how the soul has a different reality from the body: mental vision has distinct properties, and the soul occupies a different kind of space from that of the body. Thus, the soul has enormous amplitude, when for example we reproduce within us memories of a city or an expanse of countryside. The memory's amplitude cannot be measured like the bodily dimensions. The soul has a certain greatness, but not that of bodily bulk. It can grow through learning, through the use of *reason*, but again this growth has a different quality from that of bodily growth. Augustine describes seven levels of the soul's greatness. Each level takes the soul nearer to God, with the last level being described as home, where there is true happiness, where we can fully be ourselves while in relation to God. However, Augustine is not clear in the end quite how the soul and body are related, even resorting to the interaction as miraculous and beyond human comprehension (*City of God*, XX1.10). The soul uses the body as a kind of relay of messages, but the precise relationship between the two remains uncertain – a problem that was taken up by Descartes but remains uncertain to this day.

3. In some ways, René Descartes's thought about the soul is close to that of Augustine. Like Augustine, for him, inwardness is the key to discovering truth. However, while Augustine looked inward in order then to look upwards to God, Descartes's inwardness is a self-sufficient kind of inward looking; modern man becomes his own master, as it were. Descartes believed in God and in the importance of the soul; he even thought, mistakenly, that the soul was detectable and was centrally located in the brain, in the pineal gland, rather than, say, within the whole human being. But the grounds for his investigation of the soul are radically different from those of previous thinkers. Instead of looking at the relation between others in an ethical community, Descartes turned to the solitary thinker's search for certainty, his 'I', as the ground for understanding the nature of the soul. The context for his inquiry is also, of course, the new world of science and mercantilism. The world had become one to which the laws of mechanics could be applied with great success. Such laws could be applied to the body, but what about the soul? Descartes, like Augustine, considered soul and body to have different properties. In that sense they were both 'dualists', believing in the separate nature of soul and body. But, for Descartes, what was new was that the essence of soul was its capacity to think. The soul became a thinking rather than a relating substance. Soul soon then becomes redescribed as 'Mind', as opposed to the

'Matter' of the body. Descartes can be seen to invent the mind (Rorty, 1980). Subsequent thought tended to become polarized between Idealism, which took Mind as primary, and Materialism, which saw all mental phenomena as deriving from the body. Descartes, also like Augustine, struggled with understanding the relation between soul–mind and body. Early on Descartes seemed to make a sharp distinction between them, but later, as in some of his letters, he seems to indicate a much closer union between them.

While Descartes himself clearly considered the soul to have an important place in the human being, his thought inevitably led to polarization across the mental–physical continuum, with the result that the notion of an alive human soul gradually seems to die out as a vital force, with materialism increasingly dominating the intellectual scene, with the soul only having an almost ghost-like presence. Glimpses of a human soul occasionally surface, even in what might appear to be materialist literature. Thus with Defoe's *Moll Flanders*, which appears to be a celebration of self-interested materialism, the pursuit of money and marriage of convenience, there are moments when some other world is touched. This can be seen when Moll takes advantage of a fire to invade a gentlewoman's house in order to steal her jewellery, gold and other valuables. As Moll puts it,

> This was the greatest and the worst prize that ever I was concerned in; for indeed, though, as I have said above, I was hardened now beyond the power of all reflection in other cases, yet it really touched me to the very soul when I looked into this treasure, to think of the poor disconsolate gentlewoman who had lost so much in the fire besides . . . I say, I confess the inhumanity of this action moved me very much.
>
> (1722, p. 202)

Of course, her reflection soon wore off, and she soon began to forget the circumstances that led to her robbery.

It was perhaps David Hume who appeared to finally kill off the soul, when he stated that 'what we call a mind is nothing but a heap or collection of different perceptions, united together by certain relations, and suppos'd, tho' falsely, to be endow'd with a perfect simplicity and identity' (*Treatise*, 1740, Book 1, Part 4, Section 2). And, further, that,

> for my part, when I enter most intimately into what I call myself, I always stumble on some particular perception or other . . . I never can catch myself observe anything but the perception . . . I may venture to affirm of . . . mankind, that they are nothing but a bundle of different perceptions.
>
> (Treatise, 1740, Book 1, Part 4, Section 6)

Thus, Hume disposes of any idea of a unity of the self, or of the existence of a self at all. However, Barrett criticizes this view as missing the point about the nature of a person to describe that nature as just involving sensory information.

'Hume is like a man who goes outside his house and looks through the window to see if he is at home. It is (an) error: the philosopher's temptation to take a purely spectator's view of the mind, forgetting that he himself is a participant' (1987, p. 46).

Despite the limitations of Hume's view, it had a profound influence on subsequent thinkers, and the soul as an alive notion received a blow from which it has yet to recover. Even Immanuel Kant, who tried to address Hume's scepticism by emphasizing that we always have to come back to the active and organizing human mind when trying to understand the world, could not rescue the soul. It is true that Kant showed that the self could not just be a heap of impressions, for how else could it organize what it perceived? This is similar to what has been called the 'binding problem', that is, how consciousness has any sense of unity. If consciousness just consisted of a series of perceptions, how can we experience any sense of continuity? There must be something that binds perceptions together enough to provide that continuity.

Kant also placed the moral law within us, so that there must be some internal structure that can take effective decisions about moral issues. But Kant wanted to devise a 'rational science of the soul' (Kant, 1781, p. 318); the soul for Kant is essentially a rational, thinking soul, the thinking I, rather cut off from the body.

As I have indicated, it was not my intention to give an encyclopaedic history of the soul, but merely to sketch some basic trends in Western thought, which still underpin much of contemporary thinking, or nonthinking, about the soul. These trends are also relevant when considering what contribution neuroscience may have to this field.

Neuroscience of the soul

The previous chapter touched on two basic and related problems: how the unity of the person is maintained, and how the physical functions of nerves and brain cells make for a unified thinking, feeling person. There may be some connection between these two problems. Thus the evidence from neurology and neuroscience (Ramachandran, 2011, p. 247) is that the self is not a single monolithic entity that it can believe itself to be; instead, there are many components that go to making up the self, and with no necessary way that they all come together into a unitary organization. But there remains a gap in our understanding of these two problems: the so-called hard problem of the connection between the mental and the physical. As Nagel (1986, pp. 47–8) has put it, mental events have both physical and mental properties, both of which are essential; yet there remains an inability to overcome the apparent contingency between them. Nagel's view in this text is that mental phenomena are the subjective phenomena that can also be described physically; that is, he has a 'dual aspect' approach, similar in fact to that of Spinoza.

In his earlier classic paper, 'What Is It Like to Be a Bat?' (1979), Nagel was deeply sceptical of understanding consciousness by physical means. Being a human being, like being a bat, implies a particular, subjective point of view from which each experiences the world. We have yet to make a sensible physical description of what this means. The whole point about a subjective experience is that it is precisely that: subjective. Once you try to describe the experience objectively in physical terms, the experience gets lost. There is no way to bridge the gap, at least not yet, for Nagel.

John Searle (1997) argues with characteristic clarity that creating rigidly separate categories of the mental and physical has created considerable problems. The materialist tends to deny the obvious fact that we have inner, qualitative subjective states such as pain, joys, memories, feelings and so on. Instead, we need to accept that consciousness with its subjective properties is a natural biological phenomenon. We will understand consciousness when we understand in biological detail how the brain does it. I have already argued in Chapter One that this latter point may well be true, but that it gives limited understanding about the lives of human beings. For example, we do not find it particularly interesting to know what parts of the brain are firing when we appreciate a Rembrandt portrait; we just want to understand the portrait and how it impacts on us. Such knowledge may be useful if we experience neurological symptoms while looking at the Rembrandt picture. If we start to fit, or experience the sudden onset of right-sided weakness and a loss of speech while at the National Gallery, then such knowledge may make all the difference to how we are going to be treated medically once we are rushed to hospital. At that point, the significance of the portrait may seem of less importance.

Thus, I do not think we can completely abandon paying attention to the findings of neuroscience, which will have some bearing on our lives, particularly when we try to understand illness and pathology and when researching into some of the more primitive elements of psychological functioning. For that reason, I would suggest it is important to keep all options open. In addition, certain facts about the brain may shed light on how we think and feel. For example, what is striking about the organization of the cerebral cortex is how uniform is its organization (Zeki, 2009, pp. 9–11). Basic patterns are duplicated throughout the cortex, with only relatively minor variations in cell types. Cells in different cortical areas derive their differences largely from different anatomical connection. Thus, *connectivity* is made a crucial property of the brain thanks to its basic anatomy. Making connections is also a fundamental human activity, essential to creative thought, and also probably to how we relate thinking to feeling, even if we do not know if the anatomy of the brain and the psychology of the person connect up.

Donald Davidson argues for the necessary contingency between the two realms of the mental and physical – that the two realms of explanation for human activity, mental and physical events, each have their own set of justifications, and each is irreducible to the other. Furthermore, he maintains that 'detailed knowledge of the physics or physiology of the brain, indeed of the whole man, would not provide a shortcut to the kind of interpretation required for the application of sophisticated psychological concepts . . . Past discoveries about the nature of the brain, and even more, the discoveries we can expect from workers in this field, throw a flood of light on human perception, learning and behaviour. But with respect to the higher cognitive functions, the illumination must, if I am right, be indirect. There is no important sense in which psychology can be reduced to the physical sciences' (1980, pp. 258–9).

There is no doubt that in the absence of a functioning brain, there are no mental activities. However, as the anatomist J. Z. Young pointed out, this does not imply that events in the brain cause mental events. 'The complexity and adaptability of the brain means that *precise* forecasting of correlations between mental events and physical processes is never possible . . . The fundamental point is that all mental events are associated with events in the brain; and it is a continuing task for neuroscientists of all sorts to follow the cerebral events, especially those that accompany our more interesting and emotional activities' (1987, p. 15).

Thus the neuroscientist can try to 'follow' cerebral events, can look at 'correlations' between cerebral and mental events and can look at 'associations' between cerebral and mental events and what physical events 'accompany' mental events, but cannot actually see how cerebral events cause mental events. Similarly, the nineteenth-century neurologist Hughlings Jackson described the doctrine of 'concomitance' when speaking of the relation between consciousness and nervous states:

> The doctrine I hold is: first, that states of consciousness (or, synonymously, states of mind) are utterly different from nervous states; second, that the two things occur together – that for every mental state there is a correlative nervous state; third, that, although the two things occur in parallelism, there is no interference of one with the other.
>
> (1958, p. 72)

Such a view about the parallel worlds of the mental and the physical in some kind of dependent correlation very much influenced Freud's thinking about the mind and the nervous system, from early on in his thinking, as shown in his early work on aphasia, quoted in the Standard Edition of his works (S.E. 14, pp. 206–8). Ernest Jones (1954, pp. 403–4), in his biography of Freud, writes that though Freud took this view of the relation between mind and brain, he certainly also took the view that there was no evidence of psychical processes occurring apart from physiological ones; that no mind could exist apart from a brain. Freud also considered that physical processes must precede mental events; however, the essential nature of mind and matter were unknown, and so different in kind that it would be a logical error to translate a description of processes in the one into the terms of the other, even though there might be similarities in the way that both worked.

There are various ways of dealing with this 'hard' dilemma. One may come down on one side of the divide – the mental or the physical – and propose either an idealist or a materialist solution; or accept a dualist position, where both the mental and physical are relevant in different ways; or propose a solution where some merger of the mental and physical is posited, some synthesis of both; or propose a solution that we are made of one kind of material, but that we perceive this in two different ways, appearing material from the outside but mental from the inside; or propose a solution common to religious thought where there exists another entity, such as the immortal soul, which is independent of physical properties; or propose yet another way of thinking which does not close off any solution but which *holds the tension* between different proposals without making a final decision. I personally favour the latter approach in a field where there is so much that is still puzzling. If we still cannot even bridge the gap between the nerve impulse and the feeling, how on earth can we be too dogmatic about the nature of mental events? And, in the end, all these considerations only give us a partial view of the human world, which has more to do with the meaning and value of human stories. In the meantime, we need to turn to a variety of disciplines if we are to find some clarity in this complex field.

Ron Britton (2009) deals with this tension by putting physical and mental events at opposite ends of a continuum, which as yet does not meet in the middle. At present the neurosciences are approaching from one end and psychoanalysis from the other end. Freud began by trying to create a psychology for neurologists, in his *Project for a Scientific Psychology* but then abandoned this for a new focus on subjective experience. Britton makes the important point that, though analysts occupy the subjective position, we should be facing towards the other end, not turning our backs on it. Indeed, the temptation at either end of the axis is for each to turn their back on the other. As our patients live in the middle, this would seem to be most unfortunate.

By holding the tension between different ways of viewing events, one is effectively allowing for different stories about how events can be described. The philosopher Peter Strawson asks us to imagine two different ways of describing the history of a human being. On the one hand, it would seem reasonable to assume that 'there is a system of physical law, such that all bodily movements of human beings . . . are the causal outcome of the stimulation of sensory surfaces together with the internal physical constitution of the organism, those movements being causally mediated by electro-chemical events within the organism, and the constitution of the latter being itself constantly modified by events in its own history' (1985, pp. 55–6). Seen from this limited view, one could then tell the whole history of a person. However, that history would 'leave out almost everything that was humanly interesting, either to the subject of it or to anyone else. We have another and more familiar style of talking about ourselves and others, in which we speak of action and behaviour . . . rather than simply limbs moving, and in which we freely use the language of sensations, perceptions, thoughts, memories, assertions, beliefs, desires and intentions; in short, mentalistic or personalistic language . . . the terms employed by such simple folk as Shakespeare, Tolstoy, Proust and Henry James' (1985, p. 56).

There is not any practical possibility of a complete mapping of a personal story onto a corresponding physical story; they are just different stories.

Barrett (1987, p. 20) makes the point that in practice the body we know is rarely sharply distinguished from the soul or the mind, and that in our moods and feelings we are often not sure what part is physical and what not; there is no sharp dividing line between them; that is, as Britton suggests, there is a continuum between the mental and physical. One could also say that the different stories often intermingle. This certainly corresponds with psychoanalytic experience. I have already described (see Chapter Four) the process when the person of the baby starts to be linked with the body, and the body functions (Winnicott, 1965, p. 59) with the skin as the limiting membrane. The infant's psyche begins to dwell in the soma, or, one might say, feels 'at home' in the soma, with a sense of being self-centred inside his body, and this process depends upon the mother's handling, her ability to join up her emotional and physical involvement. Thus, from early on, there is a joining up in some way of psyche and soma, or soul and body. If this developmental process is interfered with, then psychosomatic conditions may result, where communication goes through the body instead of through psychological means.

Freud's early work with hysterical patients revealed a very strange relationship between the body and the soul. His patients complained of various bodily symptoms which bore little relation to anatomical reality. Thus, one can see how the soul is both attached to the body and yet moves across body boundaries – once more we have a sense of psyche and soma, soul and body, having different, if interconnected, realities.

It is difficult to define quite how the body and soul become linked up in development, and it is difficult to find the right words to describe what naturally takes place without any explanation needed. One could describe the joining up in terms of *illusion*. While one meaning of illusion involves deception, holding to a false belief, another meaning is more positive, allowing for the simultaneous holding of different positions, with some 'play' between them. One can see this psychoanalytically in the transference relationship, where a patient may see the analyst as both a fantasy object and as something different, a real person. I have described this (Kennedy, 1984) as the 'dual aspect' of the transference, which some patients struggle to understand. Indeed, some people never grasp the nature of illusion and are tied down to living in a concrete material world. Working with the transference illusion is potentially therapeutic, enabling the patient to work through different aspects of the past and the present. What makes the transference therapeutic is not specifically resolving the illusion but accepting its paradoxical reality; this can be hard for some people.

Similarly, one might say that illusion has a place in allowing soul and body, psyche and soma, to be linked up. One can see the constitutive role of illusion in Lacan's view of the mirror stage in young child's life, as mentioned in the previous chapter. At about 6 months, the infant becomes aware, through seeing their image in the mirror, of their own body as a totality; they see a total reflection of themselves. This reflection, bringing with it the appearance of wholeness, creates a feeling of jubilation and fascination, but, for Lacan, this is the source of alienation, the illusion of wholeness, and an imaginary relationship with the body. The subject moves from fragmentation and insufficiency to illusory unity. As I suggested, this view contrasts with Winnicott's view of the mirror experience with the mother, or the mother's face, which can provide a sense for the child of being recognized. The mother gives back to the baby the baby's own self, allowing the baby to begin to feel real.

Whether or not one sees illusion being the source of alienation or of integration, the point is that illusion has an important place in the way that the body becomes part of the human world, and in the constitution of the human subject. Furthermore, the body is the aspect of ourselves nearest to material reality. We have to have some kind of comfortable relationship with that physical reality, across the divide between it and the soul, across the different probably contingent realms.

Humphrey (2011) argues that illusion has powerful evolutionary value or force. The illusion of having a soul, an area of magical interiority had great evolutionary value; such an illusion improves our lives, allows us to endure hardships and gives us an ability to keep going in the face of difficult circumstances, all of which has immense evolutionary force.

Allan Schore (2003, 2012) has argued persuasively that *attachment* theory provides a way of linking mental phenomena with brain processes. He describes how the emotional interactions of early life directly influence the organization of the brain systems responsible for processing affect and cognition. He proposes that the attachment experiences of early infancy are stored in implicit memory in the early maturing right hemisphere of the brain (2003, p. 257). He has an essentially sociobiological model, emphasizing the intimate relationship between the brain and social experiences. Thus the emotion-processing limbic circuits of the infant's developing right brain hemisphere are *influenced* by implicit intersubjective interactions embedded in the attachment relationship between mother and child (2012, p. 34).

Schore proposes that the right orbito-frontal region of the cortex is essential for self-regulation. The right brain has detailed maps of the body state (Damasio, 1994, 2010), which makes it suitable for regulating subjective emotional experiences. It is the right brain, for Schore, that plays a fundamental role in the maintenance of a coherent, continuous and unified sense of self; it is the primary place where subjective emotional processing takes place. The right brain here almost becomes a soul, the seat of emotions. By looking at the neurobiology of attachment, he aims to find scientific conformation of psychoanalytic thinking, and even for the mechanisms of psychotherapy. However, the basic issues about *how* attachment influences brain circuits remain; Schore has not solved the 'hard' problem, even though he has added to the complexity of the story.

I have mentioned in the introduction that in neuroscience, minds are said to 'emerge' from the dynamic interplay of nerve circuits. In some way, mind emerges from the brain. An emergent property in a system is caused by the elements of the system acting together. It is not a property of any of the individual elements of the system. The classic example often cited is the liquid state of water. Water is made up of many individual molecules that in themselves are not water, but they become water when added together.

Emergence is a property of so-called complex systems. A complex system consists of diverse and often interdependent entities that interact in time and space, such as a city or an ecosystem or a large group of children on a playground. Complex systems are often unpredictable and can produce novel formations. Emergence occurs when the macro organization differs from the micro organization; the emergent phenomena arise from the bottom up, from micro to macro, with no superimposition from above, that is, with no central planner. A common form of emergence is self-organization, such as when fish swim in a pattern. A system self-organizes when the aggregate of individual actions produced a pattern at the macro level. There may be a 'tipping point' when suddenly the individual interactions become organized into a recognizable pattern.

These days considerable attention is being paid in a variety of disciplines to 'networks' and their properties, from social networks to the World Wide Web, to networks of neurones in the brain. Structure emerges out of the interaction between the different elements of the network. Even if neural networks basically run in parallel to the soul organization, they are still of great interest and significance in the life of human beings, as can be seen by the increasing number of popular books published these days on aspects of neuroscience. Stories about the brain remain compelling.

One can see why understanding complexity, emergence and networks may well add to our understanding of brain processes, possibly even psychological self-organization. We do not know how the brain is organized to function as a whole, though we know it appears to do this quite well, in fact remarkably well, mostly at an unconscious level. The many individual elements just do work, both together and in parallel, making sensation, movement and other functions run smoothly. Can it be that consciousness is just the emergent property of networks of neurones firing until a tipping point is reached and a person has a conscious experience? It sounds like an interesting idea, though as yet there is no evidence that consciousness works like this. Indeed, it is still possible that the firing of neurones and having a conscious experience are different and incommensurable phenomena. This is certainly a position held by a number of thinkers, as I have already described.

If consciousness were just an emergent property of large networks of neurones, as many animals have large networks of neurones, this would imply that many animals also have consciousness. This indeed may well be true, though it is hard to prove. But this does leave the problem of *human* consciousness, and what other element is required to distinguish human from animal consciousness. Presumably, language would be a strong candidate for such an element.

One can see that there still remains a problem about how something that is made up of matter, body parts, neurones, and so on can experience human emotions. Some just say well, that's what emotions are, the firing of the neurones. Others say that feelings and so on emerge from the firing of the neurones. At a certain point the resonance, or whatever, of all the parts of the brain firing up produces the experience; the experience emerges as a different and new quality. Others consider that you need something else, an extra something for humans to experience subjective emotions – from God, from spirit, from a nonmaterial world, or, let us just say, from X.

Trying to understand how human emotions and values arise from a physical brain might possibly be similar to understanding how a Rembrandt painting speaks to us so powerfully. After all, the picture is made up of physical brush strokes placed on a material canvas. Yet almost magically a human being is portrayed, and something more than mere physical marks on a canvas emerges, though it must be said that it is a human hand that put the marks there in the first place, not the hand of some unseen God. And when it comes to trying to understand human realities, we are dealing with complex systems that come together to produce meaning (Cassirer, 1955, p. 95).

Encore: psychoanalysis and the soul – becoming a subject

There is considerable overlap between the realm of subjectivity and that of the soul territory. If human beings have a soul, then that implies a subject with a soul, the soul's owner. It is difficult to say I have a subject, but not that I have a soul. In ordinary language, one might talk of someone having soul, meaning that they are capable of deep feeling and responsiveness to others. A lack of soul implies a lack of humanity, callousness or superficiality. The soul thus seems emblematic of deep subjective experience, which goes along with some ownership of that experience, and being marked by experience, allowing experience to impact us in an alive way, so that the experience *takes root*.

In certain kinds of religious thought, the soul is what makes us who we are and also binds us to God. Yet the soul is our own and bears the mark of our experiences. Traditionally, we are to be judged by those marks after death. The weighing of souls at the point of death and having to give an account of ourselves are telling images of how life impacts on the human soul, and this imagery goes back to at least the ancient Egyptians. One may indeed use these images to look at how life itself impacts on the soul, and how giving *an account* of ourselves throughout life plays an important part in our existence as subjects.

The word 'subject' captures a basic dual aspect of the human condition, that we are both *subject of experiences and subject to* various phenomena. That is, the term refers both to our I-ness, who we are, our very soul, the root of our being. It implies that we can be authors of our actions and our history; at the same time, it also indicates that we are subject to various forces outside the orbit of the 'I' who speaks, forces arising both from within the individual and from the environment. Subject is a term that has many resonances, comprising a mixture of conscious and unconscious elements. For example, it refers to the conscious or unconscious subject of discourse, the one who speaks, the subject of a story or narrative; and it can imply a relationship to an object. It seems to include the idea of agency, being the subject of actions, and also, as Jessica Benjamin (1988, 1998) has described, that of authorship, 'the condition of ownership that reflects intentionality and bestows awareness of others' states, feelings and intentions' (1998, p. 39). The term has both philosophical and political resonances. In one line of philosophical thinking, still dominant in much academic philosophy in the United Kingdom and North America, the subject refers to the conscious, thinking subject, the subject of conscious reason. While the political subject is a citizen with certain fundamental rights, such as that of belonging to civil society and having the right to vote, the term implies being subject to a higher authority.

The Freudian subject, a unique construct, incorporates ambiguity, uncertainty and paradox, which follows from the existence of an unconscious. At the heart of our subjectivity, as seen through the psychoanalytic perspective, is an obvious and fundamental paradox: psychoanalysis has shown that many of our most human aspects, which make us passionate, vulnerable and problematic beings, reside in our unconscious and often appear to us as if they came from somewhere else, from an 'It', Freud's *das Es*. We may experience this core of our being – as Freud described the unconscious wishful impulses embedded in the unconscious (1900, p. 603) – as a place outside ourselves in some way, in some objective place, certainly in some other location. Even when we begin to discuss in a formal way the nature of this subjectivity, something always gets lost; we too readily fall into an objective way of thinking, where we may lose the heart of who we are. At the same time, this dilemma highlights what Edmund Husserl called the 'paradox' of human subjectivity (1954, p. 178), the fact that the human being is both a subject for the world and at the same time an object in the world.

A further issue, which underpins much of psychoanalytic thought, is the question of the *location* of human subjectivity. On the one hand, there is the notion, following Descartes, that the essence of human subjectivity is located inside the person, in the 'I think'. On the other hand, there is the counterargument that there is no privileged place where unity is found, as I have already discussed. Indeed, Freud himself, in *The Interpretation of Dreams,* came up with an image of the mental apparatus that highlighted this very issue. In order to capture the way in which the mental apparatus functioned, he disregarded any notion of anatomical locality; instead, he pictured the apparatus as a compound microscope or a photographic instrument.

> On that basis, psychical locality will correspond to a point inside the apparatus at which one of the preliminary stages of an image comes into being. In the microscope and telescope, as we know, these occur in part at idea points, regions in which no tangible component of the apparatus is situated.
>
> (Freud, 1900, p. 536)

Freud's metaphor of the virtual nature of the psychic apparatus suggests that there is something essentially *elusive* about our subjective life that makes it difficult to capture. The quest for the human 'centre', where one can capture the origin of the person, is reminiscent of the search for the locus of the soul, or for the place where consciousness resides, or where memory or language is centrally organized by the brain. Such quests proved fruitless, as we have already seen, until the search for the centre was abandoned in favour of an 'interactional' model, where a function is produced as a result of interaction between many elements or pathways, both within the subject and in relations between subjects, with no one place where everything comes together. Such an approach to the nature of the person is fundamentally different from that which starts out from the individual mind, isolated from other minds, as with Descartes. The latter produced a form of subjectivity that is free floating, in the sense of being cut off from the social world, for only that kind of knowledge formed by the solitary Cartesian ego is certain. Freud's thought at times adheres to this form of thinking, yet there often seems to be a pull towards another kind of thinking, which takes account of the fleeting and ambiguous nature of our subjective life as it exists in relation to a world of other subjects, and which cannot be tied down to the centralized and solitary ego.

There is thus an ambiguity about the nature of psychic locality and hence of subjectivity – whether or not it makes sense to locate the subject in the individual, in the social field, somewhere between, or, as I would now suggest, in some *shifting position* involving both individual and social fields.

Benjamin (1998) has also tackled this kind of issue from a psychoanalytical viewpoint. She points to the need to use a model of the mind that incorporates both intrapsychic and intersubjective positions without privileging either. Furthermore, she suggests that 'the analytic relationship provides some experience with the kind of intersubjective space that allows us to hold multiple positions' (1998, p. 90).

Peter Fonagy and Mary Target have approached these issues from a developmental perspective. They maintain that 'our understanding of the mental world is not a given, is radically different in the young child and crucially depends for its healthy development on interaction with other people who are sufficiently benign and reflective' (1996, p. 217) as providing the philosophical demonstration of this basic position. Thinking for them is inherently intersubjective, requiring relationships between subjects for the individual to develop a capacity for self-reflection.

Lacan offered a more radical view of the human subject, who for him was essentially alienated, 'lacking' and 'fading' (see Benvenuto and Kennedy, 1986). There is no place in his theory for a unified sense of who we are: subject and other are inextricably linked; when the subject appears in one place, he disappears in another. For Lacan, the unconscious appears through a split in the subject, so that the subject is always surprised by what then appears.

I would suggest, then, that subjectivity incorporates both intrapsychic and intersubjective positions, both phenomena within the subject and in the network between subjects in the social field. This notion connects with what I have suggested in Chapter One about the soul being an experience of essential connectedness between people, an intersubjective entity, that which links with others. That is, the soul can be seen to go beyond the individual's inner world, reaching out to the other. This reaching out was striking in the recent exhibition of Lucian Freud portraits at the National Portrait Gallery. Freud would spend many hours with his subjects, trying as it were to distil their essence onto the canvas. Faced by a whole room of portraits, one seemed to feel the unique souls of each of these people, all connected in some way by the artist's vision. Here, one can sense our common humanity, what links us to one another. The material reality of the canvases conveys, or is the carrier of, another reality to that of physical marks of paint. Of course, Freud was deeply influenced by Rembrandt; one might even say that Rembrandt is the only artist to rival Freud's ability use of paint to capture human flesh and the essence of people.

Interestingly, in this context, Lambros Malafouris (2008), an archaeological thinker, points out that the human condition demands that selfhood cannot be characterized and understood according to some internal, fixed and biologically determined bodily properties. Instead, the archaeological record shows how a great deal of cultural parameters operate 'beyond the skin', beyond the boundary of the 'I'. The boundary of this 'I' is changeable and extendable in the outside world, the world of material objects. He uses the example of a gold Mycenaean signet ring, embedded in the social life of the ancient Greeks, to explore how a piece of inanimate matter can be seen as a constitutive part of the human self-system.

I would see the task in psychoanalytic treatment very much concerned with helping the patient *become a* subject, which requires both intrapsychic and intersubjective understanding, understanding of what lies within and beyond the individual. To understand what this means, one may begin with Sigmund Freud's discoveries, which one could describe as being very much about bringing back elements of the mind, such as dreams and fantasies, into the realm of the human subject when these, before his work, had often been devalued as either mere fancies of no consequence, or as inhabiting some kind of objective knowledge. Hence, becoming a subject would entail a process of recovery, or discovery, of unconscious subjective elements. It would also involve a complex mixture of conscious and unconscious elements. Furthermore, the analytic setting itself, with the analyst sitting behind the patient, out of sight and reach, demonstrates literally that the analytic relationship is not an object relationship in the usual sense. With the analyst not being directly available, the analytic setting sets in motion a complex search for the human subject.

What I mean by this is that the patient brings to us all sorts of different stories, fixed patterns of relating or symptoms, hopes, expectation and resistances. Patients often come with a sense of isolation, of either being alone with suffering or suffering from being alone. And they come to analysis subject to various forces in their life, past and present. If the analysis works, then there is the possibility of their becoming the subject of their experiences and ultimately of their lives, with a sense of being no longer isolated and more in contact with others; they may become more part of a network of other subjects.

Becoming a subject, then, involves a shift towards a *subjective position*. This refers to how being a subject involves some capacity to take up different positions without becoming fixed in a kind of frozen state of being. (This is similar to Benjamin's attention to multiple positions referred to earlier.) Being the subject *of* actions and thoughts is different from being subject *to* them, or being in an 'objective position' where actions and thoughts and so on are not felt to be part of the subject's life. In order to be fully in touch with another person, in a truly subjective position, one must begin to grasp the other's point of view; the other is seen as other, a person or a subject, in a context, orientated to others and being affected by others in the social world.

A subjective position involves allowing experiences of the other, at many levels, conscious and unconscious, to interpenetrate oneself so that they make an impact. In the analytic encounter, the analyst may have to bear being in a number of different subjective positions in the session rather than allowing himself or herself to become fixed in one place, although at any moment the analyst may become 'moored' in one place more favoured than another. I would suggest that the analyst's free-floating attention consists of a subjective oscillation between different positions or moorings. This means having to tolerate a considerable amount of ambiguity, uncertainty and paradox. Moments when the patient experiences the impact of the analyst's presence or subjectivity can become key experiences in the process of becoming a subject (Kennedy, 2007, p. 180).

Recently in the psychoanalytic literature, and influenced by the French school, the term *subjectivication* has come to be used (Wainrib, 2012) as a description for the process of becoming a subject. Foucault originally used this term as a key concept in distinguishing how the subject can become objectified, for example a mere object of power, as opposed to coming together with oneself in a 'practice and exercise of oneself on oneself' (2001, p. 333). Such a practice involves the relationship between master and student. Subjectivication involves becoming the subject of truth, being able to speak the truth about oneself. It 'begins with listening to the true discourses proposed' (2001, p. 365) in the relationship between student and master, as in the Socratic dialogue. It involves an open way of speaking, a free way of speaking. While Foucault based these notions on his reading of ancient thought, it is difficult not to imagine that he was also influenced by psychoanalytic thinking, with its emphasis on the relationship between psychoanalyst and patient, the expectation of free association and the search for the subject's psychic truth. Equally, it would seem that psychoanalysis has been deeply influenced at some level by those past ways in which the subject's truth has been under scrutiny.

Subjectivication in the psychoanalytic sense refers to a process of becoming a subject through linking up with others, underpinned by a process of mutual recognition. But this also means facing processes where subjectivication can be undermined, for example, when the subject may fall back into a narcissistic position (Wainrib, 2012) and, one might say, loses something of their human essence.

Spirituality: Religion and the soul

In many people's minds, religion is the true home for the soul. There is, indeed, a religious longing for human beings to worship something beyond themselves, to find a home for that deep longing, which can be described in terms of the needs of the human soul to reach out to God. I have presented the notion of the human subject reaching beyond the individual, not being confined within physical boundaries. Religion makes the leap from this notion of the subject to that of a realm beyond physical reality, an immaterial reality, which becomes the true nature of the human soul. The soul looks beyond the material world for its true fulfilment; it is both a spiritual and an embodied reality. As Ward puts it,

> It is not a ghost behind the scenes, and it is not just the physical brain, in its publicly described properties. It is not an object or event or set of events in the world. It is a point of subjectivity and transcendence, of rational under-standing and responsible action, which comes to be at a particular stage of the emergent interactions of spatial, material substances. Once it is generated, it continues to have a place in those physical interactions, to respond to them and realize itself in them . . . [I]n its understanding the soul relates itself also to that realm of truth and value that transcends the physical, in its interior life of feeling, and perhaps of prayer and contemplation, it expresses a capacity and natural tendency to relate to a purely spiritual realm.
>
> (1998, pp. 148–9)

Thus for Ward, the soul is not some disembodied spirit floating somewhere; it is firmly embodied in the world and yet remains a spiritual subject, which for him means that it is not observable or scientifically definable. The soul can grasp and understand truth and act responsibly, but 'the unique dignity of the soul lies in its freedom to determine itself by such understanding or not' (1998, p. 125).

Of course, materialists would argue that one can still value life without a belief in God. The counterargument is that without some belief in a nonmaterial world, it is increasingly likely that respect for human life and all that we value, our free-dom, dignity and sense of justice, will be lost or diluted.

Rowan Williams, in his book *Grace and Necessity*, reflects on art and love, and makes the point that the realm of art opens up the dimension in which 'things are more than they are' (2005, p. 37). This notion, originally put forward by the Roman Catholic thinker Jacques Maritain, points out that art is vital as it points to an 'excess' of the material environment (2005, p. 37). We are then in touch with a realm beyond the ordinary material environment, with something outside the scope of everyday representation. This is the realm of the sacred; it is what we feel when in a great cathedral or before great works of art. Thus, standing before the Rembrandt self-portrait in the National Gallery, we encounter an excess of meaning, something that reaches beyond the everyday. Williams would link this area of experience to the realm of the sacred and to the role of God. I have described how Rembrandt's eyes seem to take you into the picture, into the depths. Unlike a mirror, which reflects your own image back to you, the Rembrandt urges you to reflect into yourself in the act of being drawn into his image. Repeated visits are like drawing from some primal source of light and intensity, leaving you changed in some way, both uplifted and more melancholy. Repeated visits do not exhaust the depths of the experience; in this sense, the portrait is always 'more' than it appears. Perhaps here one is touching what religious thought would see as the sacred element of the soul.

Judaism and Islam both emphasize the *ascent* of the soul towards God, that is, a process of transformation from lower to upper levels until the soul dwells in a higher state of being. With the Jewish Kabbalah, the soul can move from the lowest and most basic aspect of the soul, the Nefesh, which animates existence and gives the human body its ability to move, towards higher levels involved in creation, ideas and then the spiritual world. The Koran describes five stages for the life of the soul: preworldly existence, earthly life, the grave, the day of judgement and its final home either in paradise or hell. Running through these and most other religions is the notion of a movement, a process in which the soul is transformed when the person becomes renewed, or spiritually alive, or at peace with themselves through struggle. Often, a path towards such transformation has to be taken by means of some guidance, from a spiritual leader or from a religious community, and it may involve commitment, some faith, following some guidelines or laws and a process of enrichment as a result of personal encounter and interchange. Spiritual transformation may occur in isolation, but that is usually only possible with great religious leaders, who may be able to bear the pain of solitary struggle.

Personally, I think one can have spiritual experiences without a belief in God, that, for example, an encounter with the Rembrandt self-portrait is as spiritual an experience as one can get; it is like William's 'excess', a realm beyond the ordinary material environment. It was Augustine, as I have described, who emphasized that by turning inward, we find a vast inner world, from where eventually we may look upwards towards God, and in the process the soul becomes *transformed*. The soul's turning inward and then upwards to God in this process of transformation is crucial in the development of subjectivity. We may still turn inwards and upwards, though God as such may or may not be present as a living reality. Yet, as George Steiner has put it (1989, p. 3), our very understanding of language and how we think, and even the human capacity to communicate feeling and meaning, is underwritten by the possibility of a transcendent presence, Otherness. This notion is near to that of Lacan's distinction between the other and the Other in psychoanalytic and human discourse in general (Benvenuto and

Kennedy, 1986, pp. 86–8). The speech which takes its orders from the ego is addressed to what Lacan calls the 'other', with a little o, the subject's imaginary counterpart. This is 'empty speech'. On the other hand, Lacan described 'full speech', addressed to the Other, with a capital O, which is beyond the language ordered by the ego. The subject of this speech is the subject of the unconscious, which speaks most clearly in dreams and jokes and can be encountered in various symptoms. This is why Lacan called the unconscious the discourse of the Other, to whom true speech is addressed. In order to help the patient discover their psychic truth, the analyst needs to speak from the position of the Other rather than the other. However, there is a constant dialectic between other and Other in the analytic discourse; becoming a subject means, one might say, having to face both full and empty speech and their interrelationship, how just as one approaches full speech and the Other, one is drawn away towards empty speech and the other, and vice versa. Lacan was heavily influenced by Christian thought, however far he strayed from actual religious belief, and this notion of the Other seems to provide a secular description of experiences which merge with the spiritual, or anyway share similar territory. This scheme also provides a psychological model for spiritual struggle, emphasizing the constant pull towards an alienating other when trying to approach the subject of truth, the Other.

Chapter 6

Loneliness and solitude

Introduction: Loneliness–solitude dimension

In Plato's metaphor of the cave, the prisoners remain shackled and cut off from the light, but they are at least huddled together so as to mitigate their loneliness. Once one of them is freed from their shackles and reaches the bright light of true being, they are transformed into a new state, no longer cut off from the light, and in touch with a higher region; their souls have reached a higher stage of development, reminiscent of the religious grades of the soul's upwards ascent. I would suggest that this latter state is less like loneliness and more like solitude; the move from one state to the other is one theme of this chapter.

The transformation described by Plato involves a move of territory, from the restricted world of the cave to the open and dazzling world of light. Yet the cave has been the prisoners' home, where they have felt safe, even if in a state of ignorance. Plato infers that this is a false kind of home, not a true home for the soul, which needs the bright light of true being to be fully alive. I think that one can infer from this that life without an alive sense of one's own soul is deeply lonely. The prisoners in the cave are not happy in their ignorance, even if they are only really aware of this ignorance once they have left the cave. Going along with that sense of aliveness is the sense that there is a depth to one's soul, and that something alive comes up, as it were, from those depths to reach outwards to the world outside the cave. One could also describe this movement from inside to outside in terms of becoming a subject, where one relates to other subjects in the social world and has a full sense of having a psychic home; the opposite pole to this is loneliness, where one is bereft of a psychic home. In this chapter, I aim to define more clearly what we mean by terms such as *loneliness* and *solitude*, which on the surface appear ordinary words, yet which convey considerable complexity; such considerations will also add to the picture of the soul territory.

There is a difference between loneliness and solitude, though with some overlap. Loneliness is about being cut off from others, even in their presence. In solitude, one often requires being alone, yet I am by myself with myself in some kind of *internal dialogue* – very much part of the soul territory. Since loneliness and solitude are so much a part of the psychoanalyst's work, I shall use the psychoanalytic experience to explore the loneliness–solitude dimension.

Much of the psychoanalyst's development has to take place in solitude, which though rarely absolute is certainly relative. We may seek support and supervision, continue our own analysis or go back for a while into analysis, discuss cases with colleagues or turn to writing as a way of dealing with the confusion of the work, but in the end we are on our own with patient after patient in the solitude of the consulting room. This solitude can turn into loneliness. While being lonely and having to tolerate loneliness is part of the human condition, there are aspects of the analyst's loneliness that are particular to the analytic setting and to the analyst's identity formation. There are also clinical situations where the patient's own particular problems with bearing loneliness may well challenge the analyst's capacities.

The chapter will discuss some of the consequences of considering these difficult issues both for the formation of the analyst's identity and for how they perform their clinical work, and how such considerations have wider ramifications beyond psychoanalysis.

Various psychoanalytic and other thinkers have tried to make some distinctions between different states of being alone, sometimes between loneliness and solitude or between different forms of either loneliness or solitude. Though some of these distinctions may be helpful, and I shall emphasize a particular difference between *creative solitude* and a more *passive loneliness*, I think it is in reality difficult to refine these differences because there is quite an overlap. For example, in the *Oxford English Dictionary*, 'loneliness', with its Middle English origins, refers to the condition of being alone, while 'solitude', with its Latin origins, is the state of being alone, being accustomed to aloneness (*soleo*, I am accustomed) – hardly a distinctive difference, except, as so often in English, between a word's roots. What might make for a meaningful distinction is to combine the state of the experiencing subject with the quality of their relationship to the other – with, that is, the degree of isolation of the subject. The degree of their solitude may indicate something about their sense of loneliness. The symbolization of absence makes solitude bearable; merely feeling absence without the capacity to speak about it plunges the subject into loneliness.

Overall, loneliness is more like the feeling state of the subject cut off from others, solitude more the general state of being alone, but with a more secure sense of oneself. As so often in English, the Early English word is closer to basic feeling than the Latin word, which is associated with the more patrician language of invasion – Romans and then Normans. But this may be stretching the difference between the words too much.

Literature on loneliness and solitude

Many writers offer descriptions of loneliness, but there are relatively few who tackle the meaning of the term and its various distinctive properties. I have picked out a few who seem to offer particularly valuable insights into the way that different states of loneliness and/or solitude can be distinguished.

Beginning with the *psychoanalytic* literature, Frieda Fromm-Reichmann (1990), in her posthumously published late essay on loneliness, describes the word as containing a basket of terms – culturally determined loneliness, creative loneliness, self-imposed aloneness, compulsory isolation and real loneliness as seen, for example, in the psychotic patients she treated. She focuses on the severe form of loneliness where there is a deep threat of incommunicable, private emotional experience. This is a disintegrative form of loneliness, which reveals itself in psychotic states, where intimacy is not possible. It renders people who suffer it emotionally paralysed and helpless; it is associated with extreme states of anxiety. She offers vivid descriptions of psychotic patients' experiences of loneliness, with the implication that an important aspect of therapeutic work with such patients is to help them feel less alone and less ashamed of their loneliness. But, of course, such work is massively demanding of the therapist, requiring them to withstand powerful projections and extreme states of anxiety. Indeed, taking on psychotic patients is greatly assisted by being in a regular support group of other analysts. This was certainly my experience of working at the Brent Adolescent Centre in the 1980s when a research programme for the treatment of psychotic adolescents was undertaken (Laufer and Laufer, 1989). In order to make this difficult work feasible, it was necessary to set up weekly small-group clinical discussions where detailed clinical material could be presented and discussed. In that sense, each analyst felt that, though they might be alone with the patient, they carried the support group with them into the session.

Melanie Klein's last paper was 'On the Sense of Loneliness' (1963). She refers to the inner sense of loneliness that can be there even in company. She suggests that this state is the result of a ubiquitous yearning for an unattainable perfect internal state, linked to the infant's early psychotic anxieties. She links loneliness and the incapacity to sufficiently integrate the good internal object. Loneliness can be diminished by various external factors, such as the relation to the parents and appreciation by others, but loneliness can never be eliminated because the processes which lead to integration are never complete and always involve pain.

Winnicott (1958) writes of a sophisticated phenomenon involved in the capacity to be alone, a sign of maturity in emotional development. Instead of focusing on the fear of being alone or the wish to be alone, where the subject withdraws from others, he discussed the positive aspects of the capacity to be alone. The basis for this latter capacity is a secure foundation in early childhood, when the child can enjoy solitary activity such as playing and exploring, knowing that the mother is available as a support, which he describes as being alone in the presence of someone. Once that form of aloneness has been internalized, then there is the possibility of a relaxed form of aloneness. This contrasts with, for example, the hectic and desperate behaviour of the deprived child who is unable to settle to quiet play.

This latter paper can be fruitfully set beside the 'use of an object' (Winnicott, 1969). 'Object-relating' is described there when the subject is an isolate, functioning at an omnipotent level. Winnicott describes a more mature level of functioning when the subject can use the object or other. The change from relating to using involves a particular process in which the subject destroys the object, but the object survives the destruction. Once the object has survived, the subject can move into a new kind of position where he or she can start to live a life in a world of alive objects – that is, they are no longer alone and cut off from others, but in live contact with others.

Jean-Michel Quinodoz (1993, 1996) describes how the analyst needs to acquire a well-developed sense of solitude, which involves being able to work through anxieties about object loss and separation, in order to 'tame' the deep anxieties associated with solitude.

Françoise Dolto (1994) also emphasizes the importance for the young child of periods of secure solitude, where they can explore for themselves, supported by a lively mother who talks to the child. This positive form of solitude is different from isolation, where a child withdraws and may have experienced little positive communication. The former is structuring, peopled by constructive memories; the latter is destructuring, without symbolization.

Sandra Buechler (1998) is one of the few analysts who specifically tackles the analyst's experience of loneliness. For her, the analyst's loneliness with the patient is affected by (1) the patient's loneliness and potential for collaboration; (2) the patient's diagnostic type; (3) the analyst's stance about countertransference; and (4) the other emotions evoked in the analyst by their patient.

She gives vivid clinical descriptions of the analysis of different kinds of patient and how loneliness came into the analysis in various ways, sometimes giving the analyst challenging personal and human dilemmas. She also emphasizes the need for the analyst to bring into the consulting room an 'internal chorus' of identifications to help deal with these challenges. This is similar to what I have described as the need to take into account the 'many voices of psychoanalysis' (Kennedy, 2007, p. 1), the many roles and approaches a psychoanalyst may take, while adhering to the established ideas of psychoanalysis.

There are many *literary* descriptions of the lonely state of mind, though relatively few which look at the meaning of loneliness. The philosopher and theologian Paul Tillich (1963, p. 5) distinguishes between loneliness as an expression of the pain of being alone, and solitude, which expresses the glory of being alone. The pain of loneliness can be overcome by facing solitude, which for him, like Jesus alone in the desert, means facing the daemonic forces.

In Michel de Montaigne's essay 'On Solitude' (1580, pp. 211–22), man is described as both sociable and unsociable. While we should have a wife, children, goods and health, that is, a *home,* we must not bind ourselves to them so much that our happiness depends on them. We must 'reserve a back shop all our own, entirely free, in which to establish our real liberty and our principal retreat and solitude' (1580, p. 214). Thus the home, though important, needs to have a special space to which one can retreat, but in a creative way.

Solitude is thus the source of strength, provided we know how to use it well. There are dangers in retreating to an ivory tower, but without a safe place to retreat to, we are too dependent upon others. One could add that the analyst's consulting room is a place which provides a mixture of the back shop and the 'front shop'. There is the retreat from the social world, for both analyst and patient, and yet it is at the same time an intense setting for working out dependency issues.

A number of writers have expressed the need for what one could call a *creative* solitude, where thoughts can be crystallized, even if the experience can involve much pain and frustration. As Thomas Wolfe describes in his essay on 'God's Lonely Man', 'if a man is to know the triumphant labor of creation, he must for long periods resign himself to loneliness, and suffer loneliness to rob him of the health confidence, the belief and joy which are essential to creative work' (1941, p. 146). Wolfe cites the book of Job as the 'most tragic, sublime, and beautiful expression of human loneliness' (1941, p. 149). And as with Job, the joyfulness of love destroys loneliness, providing Wolfe with some comfort against the 'tragic web of life' (1941, p. 150).

The theme of creative solitude as a necessary feature of the creative process runs implicitly through many writers, from Rousseau's solitary walks and discourses with nature, through the Romantic poets' confrontation with the solitude of landscapes as sources of joy, to modern preoccupations with states of isolation as in Conrad's *Heart of Darkness*, where Kurtz confronts his truth in the 'great solitude' of the jungle.

Paul Auster describes the way, familiar to many authors, that the writer requires essential solitude in order to write, but he links this to the work required of the reader.

> Every book is an image of solitude, the outcome of a great deal of time spent alone in a room. Literature is at once the product of an author's solitude and a means by which a reader reaches through his own and the author's solitude. In reading, an isolated individual becomes absorbed in something beyond his own preoccupations and communes with another mind.
>
> (1982, p. 136)

One might add that the writer needs to have a sense of the reader while he is writing, so that while he is solitary, he needs to reach out to the reader. There is thus a complex intersubjective process at work between the solitary writer and the solitary reader, which provides a point of contact for both of them. As Maurice Blanchot put it, 'The work is solitary: this does not mean that it remains uncommunicable, that it has no reader. But whoever reads it enters into the affirmation of the work's solitude, just as he who writes it belongs to the risk of this solitude' (1955, p. 22).

With the literature in mind, I turn now to the specifics of the analytic relationship. I shall develop the distinction between solitude and loneliness but will also explore more of the essential dilemmas about being an analyst in the loneliness of the consulting room.

Loneliness and solitude for the psychoanalyst

While on the one hand the psychoanalytic encounter can be intensely engaging for both patient and analyst, can tap into deep, often long-suppressed emotions, can become a source of creativity and can even on occasions become both life changing and life saving, the encounter can also be very challenging with regard to what has to be endured by both parties for long periods of time. I will here tend to focus on the more challenging aspects of being an analyst, but I do not wish to give the impression that analytic work is predominantly painful and difficult; there are, of course, many times when it is deeply satisfying, and indeed it is also a privilege to be in contact with another's world in such an intimate and engaging way.

One of the most challenging aspects for the analyst is how to come to terms with the psychoanalytic way of life, which imposes certain restraints. Like the writer, we have to work on our own, but the analyst has particular pressures to bear. Long periods of necessary isolation have to be tolerated so that the patient's inner life can be given special and focused attention, in a space and setting which is protected from external intrusions. While such protection is necessary for the development of the transference, the concentrated restraint required by the analyst does impact on their own well-being. Indeed, one might say that the analyst has only limited protection from all sorts of 'internal' intrusion into their own mental equilibrium. That is, we cannot leave unscathed from our analytic encounters; there is a price we have to pay for doing our work. The increasing focus on using our countertransference, on making creative use of many of these intrusions, adds to the richness of the analytic work, but it also adds to the stresses and strains of maintaining the analytic relationship. Tolerating and understanding projections and disturbance, keeping quiet when tempted to speak out, maintaining an analytic stance under the most difficult clinical situations, not to mention standing up for psychoanalysis and for thinking about the unconscious inner life outside the clinical setting when all around us may be avoiding any such thing, all present challenges to our precious and hard-won sense of equilibrium and analytic identity. We may, for example, have stirred up in ourselves powerful memories as a result of listening to the patient, but we have to keep such memories to ourselves. We have to forego the pleasure of sharing many such intimate experiences evoked by the intensity of analytic listening. In our social life, we often need to refrain from using our analytic techniques to intervene in ordinary relationships, however tempting, otherwise we may undermine defences and create unnecessary antagonism. Yet sometimes the temptation to do a bit of 'wild analysis' is just too much to resist. While occasional use of our skills can be helpful in situations of difficulty or crisis, the temptation to 'show off' our analytic understanding may be driven more by a desperate desire to share our experience rather than maintain our difficult, unusual and lonely stance.

In order to bear this situation, we have to have a capacity to be alone (Winnicott, 1958), but under rather particular circumstances. But that does not take away the reality of the struggle when the analyst has to bear the often acute sense of solitude which accompanies analytic work. A certain amount of detachment is necessary in order to be able to establish and maintain the analytic setting and to make effective decisions about how to intervene, yet that does not eliminate our basic wish for attachment, for relatedness, which we may have to modify considerably.

In order to bear the loneliness of being an analyst, it does seem important for the analyst to be able to have a significant and sustaining life outside the analytic work, even though such work is the core of the analyst's creative life. One can see the dangers of not having a life outside analysis with those analysts who engage in sexual misconduct with one patient. Andrea Celenza and Glen Gabbard (2003), in their account of different kinds of boundary violation, point out that this kind of violation typically occurs when the analyst is in the midst of a life crisis such as divorce, illness or death in the family, when they are cut off from, or cannot use, their usual support networks; they are more lonely than usual. The psychopathology of such analysts varies, but typically they are people who look primarily or even exclusively to professional relationships and activities for sustenance and affirmation of self-worth. Their analytic identity is too much dependent on their professional life. It is as if they cannot bear, at moments of crisis, the pain of being alone with their problems and not having a suitable network to turn to, and unfortunately use their patient as their comforter. Celenza and Gabbard make the point that this situation is much more humanly understandable than the boundary violations involving the psychopathic analyst who has no empathy with the patient and shows no remorse for their actions.

Whatever the precise definitions of the terms, the loneliness–solitude dimension is an inevitable accompaniment of the psychoanalytic setting, with the patient on the couch, turned away from the analyst. It is also a feature of those times when we struggle to formulate interpretations, particularly if under pressure from the patient to make sense of some difficult conflict before we are ready. The periods of contact with the patient can be satisfying for both parties, but there are many in-betweens, of silences, uncertainties, periods of desperation and intense moments of loneliness that have to be tolerated, especially with the more ill patients. Indeed, we may be tempted to interpret too much in order to defend ourselves against feeling lonely. Listening in silence until one is ready to interpret may be just too much to bear. One of my main points is that being able to deal with these kinds of pressures in a good enough way is related to the gradual development of an *analytic identity*. The analyst's own rootedness in their identity mitigates the trauma of the necessary and inevitable periods of loneliness while doing analysis. One may add that the evidence from Celenza and Gabbard is also that having a secure internal analytic identity is aided by having effective external supports, both from within the analytic community but also from elsewhere.

A psychoanalytic identity takes several years to acquire, and involves a gradual process of development, as a result of repeated and extensive listening to patients analytically over several years. In some ways, this development in the analyst requires something like a 'spiritual' growth, something that goes increasingly inwards and in more depth, and involves an inward transformation (cf. Parsons, 2006). One might add that there is something about the special quality of loneliness in the analytic position which matches what Kierkegaard (1846) captures so well – how to express the subject's inwardness, which can be communicated, but indirectly.

Adequate training and analysis is, of course, the basis for the development of an analytic identity. But so is a commitment to undertaking a reasonable amount of analytic work, not that easy these days with all the economic pressures on young analysts. Personally, I am not that convinced by such economic reasons for not developing an analytic practice, as those pressures have always been there, certainly since the 1980s. I suspect that the fear of working alone for hours at a time with disturbed patients – common in the early years of one's practice – may have more to do with the reluctance to do a substantial amount of analytic work. I mentioned my own experience of working analytically with disturbed adolescents. I should add that this took place soon after I qualified. But I had the great privilege of being aided and supported by a wide range of other analysts, several of whom were senior colleagues, who could provide encouragement and support for undertaking analytic work. I am not sure how easy it would have been to develop an analytic practice without their input.

There may also, of course, be institutional reasons that interfere with analytic identity, for example when an institution can demand too much conformity, or on the contrary is too chaotic or split between warring parties. That kind of atmosphere is hardly encouraging to the new analyst.

Whatever the decision about setting up an analytic practice, the path towards a firm analytic identity is never smooth. There are usually a number of fits and starts, with disappointments, knocks to one's narcissism, surprises, traumas and failures. One has to get used to this lonely kind of work, and sometimes the strain involved in taking so much onto oneself can have the effect on many analysts of being overly concerned with their own contributions and importance. The narcissism of the analyst is, I find, a significant feature of the analyst's social presentation. I suspect that this is also a reaction to a number of narcissistic wounds we regularly have to withstand, denigration from the patient being perhaps the easiest to bear. Others less easy to manage include the fallout from unhelpful analytic rivalries within analytic institutions that can at time be very hurtful, as well as the fairly frequent scepticism towards our work shown to us by psychiatric colleagues and the wider public. While Freud often cautioned us to expect resistance to psychoanalysis, reading constant attacks on our work does not exactly help us with our precarious and hard-won sense of analytic identity. But I would suggest that the loneliness of the analyst's work can have an unfortunate side effect, in that there may develop as a reaction formation a tendency to wall oneself off from others in a form of narcissistic character formation, which may manifest itself as an inflated sense of self importance.

Much of the analyst's development has to take place in solitude, which though rarely absolute is certainly relative. As Dolto put it, in her evocative book on solitude, psychoanalysis is a profession where one is alone. 'Everyone is alone, but the psychoanalyst more so, and there is no one else to whom he can refer because no one else can feel what the analysand subjects him to, even if he can be understood' (1994, p. 151).

While, of course, loneliness and its effects are part of the human condition, the analyst has to bear a special kind of loneliness due to their analytic function and the special nature of the analytic relationship. The analytic setting, with the analyst sitting behind the patient, or not providing ordinary social cues in face-to-face meetings, demonstrates literally that the analytic relationship is not an object relationship in the usual sense. That is, on the one hand, the analyst has to hold the patient in mind while being unable to express their feelings towards the patient freely; on the other hand, for the patient, the analyst is enigmatic and frustrating in a way that would be unacceptable in social relationships. With the analyst not being available as a direct object of relationship, then the analytic setting sets in motion a complex search for the human subject, predominantly through contact with the unconscious of both parties. As I have already suggested earlier in the chapter, one could describe the human subject as essentially elusive (Kennedy, 1998), appearing and disappearing as one tries to tie down human subjectivity. One may try to 'capture' the human subject in the analytic encounter, and of course there are moments when this is possible, but then something vital always escapes. This coming and going is what makes for human subjectivity. But it also means that being an analyst, whose function is, as it were, to help the patient 'become a subject' is a difficult, paradoxical and demanding business, certainly at times 'impossible'. One has to tolerate a good deal of uncertainty, paradox and puzzlement, in addition to the more obvious times when one has to withstand aggression and projections. And one has to deal with the patient's intense longings for more than an analytic relationship, which may unfortunately, as I have mentioned, lead the vulnerable analyst to act out a boundary violation.

In addition, it is clear the analyst has a deep need for the patient in order to crystallize their thoughts and to fulfil their own creativity. As I indicated above, there are dangers when this need becomes exclusive. But I also think that we need the patient in other more private ways, even when one has a good support network outside the analytic framework. I think that the use of what I would call our *private area of suffering* is a vital and therapeutic element of the analytic relationship, a helpful aspect of our countertransference. It is what is inevitably missing in accounts of an analysis because it will remain silent. I feel that we need to tap into this suffering, a particular area of our subjective experience, the area of the soul. Sometimes, perhaps often, patients are in touch with this area and use it for their own purposes, to avoid conflict, to get us to collude with them or simply to share their suffering. Thus, our private and lonely sufferings are not only a nuisance, something we hoped our own analysis would have dealt with, but also an inevitable part of the analytic work, which, if used wisely, can be the source of creativity. I think we need to listen to the patient's conscious and unconscious assessment of our private areas of pain and suffering. They may not know what they are reacting to, nor do we have to tell them exactly, but we will hopefully know, provided we do not retain a God-like stance. Our patients reflect back to us our own suffering; they may even wish to protect us from ourselves, which is perhaps particularly seductive and dangerous for the analysis.

It is possible that what I am proposing is related to the function of the area that Winnicott described as the central or 'core self,' which seems to resemble what I have been describing as the human soul. This core self can only come into being, paradoxically, in an authentic way if protected and allowed to remain isolated. As Winnicott wrote,

> The central self could be said to be the inherited potential which is experiencing a continuity of being, and acquiring in its own way and at its own speed a personal psychic reality and a personal body-scheme. It seems necessary to allow for the concept of the isolation of this central self as a characteristic of health. Any threat to this isolation of the true self constitutes a major anxiety at this early stage . . .
>
> (1960, p. 46)

In another paper, 'Communicating and Not Communicating', Winnicott develops this argument further, emphasizing that there is a kind of silence and lack of communication at the core of the individual which needs to be respected and, indeed, preserved in order to facilitate the formation of identity. 'This preservation of personal isolation is part of the search for identity, and for the establishment of a personal technique for communicating which does not lead to violation of the central self' (Winnicott, 1963, p. 190). He does also go on to ask how one may remain isolated in this special sense without having to be insulated. But essentially, this notion of necessary isolation, or essential aloneness, is really quite a radical and paradoxical one, though it does bear some similarities with certain religious and spiritual traditions, where silence has an essential place, at least during moments of deep contemplation. It may also be linked to the positive use of solitude in creative activity. It certainly seems that this state of being in touch with some deep inner self or soul is a special state of being, which requires discipline, quiet, and special focus.

It was Klauber who first asked serious questions about the possible long-term vicissitudes on the analyst of the patient's longings (1976), as well as how analysts deal with the effects of forming relationship after relationship of the deepest and most intimate kind with patient after patient, and the mourning which at some level must be involved for each of them before and after an ending. He asked how the analyst can accommodate themselves to being without the basic cue of human expression, face-to-face contact, for so many hours of the day, and whether or not it imposes a strain on the analyst, and if so, how this strain can be alleviated. Klauber pointed out that the newly qualified analyst is confronted by object loss on several fronts, losing a variety of supports, and how traumatic this may be, particularly as it will take so long for their analytic role to become integrated into a sustaining sense of analytic identity. Here, one may add that such experience points to a fundamental issue that, as Quinodoz pointed out, what makes the analytic work bearable is being able to tolerate object loss, or, one might add, that absence can be symbolized.

I think one could also add that there are different pressures at various stages of the psychoanalyst's life cycle. The relief and excitement of qualification may help mitigate the early strains of building up an analytic practice. The period between qualifying and becoming an 'experienced' analyst may be particularly difficult, when the reality of having to bear hours of analytic listening in the solitude of the consulting room finally hits home. And most difficult of all perhaps is the relinquishing of an analytic practice at the end of one's career, when another form of loneliness hits home with the loss of the setting and the fear of loss of identity.

The issue of what we mean by identity, let alone a psychoanalytic identity, is a complex one, as I have discussed before. Having an analytic identity refers to a sense of solidity in one's core identification with psychoanalysis as a theory and practice, an increasing sense of confidence in knowing what one is doing, even when not knowing what is going on in the session. It is probably about finding one's own *voice* as an analyst, being able to develop a particular quality of listening – both listening to the patient's unconscious communications, but also to oneself, with a complex interaction between the two sides. The analytic voice is not only shaped by the clinical encounter, but also, of course, by other influences – from training, personal analysis, colleagues, reading and life.

Clinical example

There are many times that loneliness may feature in an analysis, but one example may illustrate some of the dilemmas I have touched upon. I shall focus mostly on the transference and countertransference movements.

I am thinking of a man in his thirties who came into analysis with an acute sense of feeling out of things, not part of the group, cut off from others in a deep way, though able to have his own family. One of the main facts about his presenting history was that he had no recollection before the age of 5, when his parents split up. Indeed, much of his early history is still very vague. The mother left his father, taking him and his younger siblings. Before the analysis, my patient had never been told why the mother had left, but on asking his mother recently, he had reluctantly been told this it was because of 'mental cruelty' – though my patient did not find this very convincing. There then began a life of wandering around, and he went to boarding school from an early age, which he found very difficult. He always felt an outsider, on the margins of the group. It was a very lonely time. He would often walk around the school on his own. This period of time, the period of extreme loneliness, is remembered by him, and perhaps can be said to have covered over the earlier and even more painful memories of loss.

In analysis, the patient is not that forthcoming with his associations. There are quite a lot of almost 'Harold Pinter-like' pauses. He will say a few lines, wait, and expect me to say something, which I may or may not, depending on whether I have anything to say. He may wait for a long time for me to speak, and I know now that he then begins to feel more and more detached and in a world of his own. So there is a dilemma about letting the silences go on for too long; it may become counterproductive as he falls into an extreme sense of loneliness. At the same time, I do not wish to intrude or to be controlled into engaging in a way that means I have all the life. So there is an issue of the timing of what I say. In the past, I have tried to understand this interaction in various ways. Some relief came from thinking in terms of my becoming in the transference a withholding mother, which seemed to have some link to his own picture of his mother, who has never been particularly warm. However, that relief was short lived, and the familiar pattern of communication persisted, from time to time leaving both of us in some despair.

At these times, his loneliness can get to me. I feel a mixture of empathy for his plight and irritation at his passivity, which can sometimes leave me feeling cut adrift from my sense of confidence in the analytic process. I then feel really lonely, helpless and disconnected. This is quite different from a more organized sense of solitude, where I can still have an internal dialogue about what is happening. Instead, I don't know what to say, and this can feel quite dismaying. I begin to doubt my analytic identity.

There are times when the atmosphere in the session is particularly detached, flat and even dead. The issue of deadness and aliveness has often been around – how much he can bear having live contact with me, how much he longs for it and yet also avoids it. Some understanding of this feeling in terms of Andre Green's dead mother complex (1983) has been helpful, with the sense of the patient being in the presence in the transference of a depressed or cut off mother, who had once been more alive. This became clearer as I began to understand what was happening as the session was reaching towards its close.

In order to get to that point, I had to reexamine how I had felt intermittently frustrated, controlled and irritated by his withholding. At these times, I was also aware of his deprivation, the emptiness he has had to cope with since early childhood. He has that mixture common to those with such a childhood – of being like an abandoned child craving for love but unable to make the kind of live contact which would satisfy him.

What seems to have begun to make a difference to him is trying to differentiate different states of loneliness, and how he feels I am available for him at the beginning of a session and now for about three-quarters of the session – the length of time he can trust in my being available within the session has gradually increased over time. But then, suddenly, I seem to disappear. He will imagine I am elsewhere, particularly if I do not speak much. This can suddenly produce a terrible sense of despair and futility, which may last until the next session. My own experience of these moments in the session itself can be somewhat disorienting. I can feel I am doing my job reasonably well, and then suddenly I doubt myself; I feel alone in the presence of the other, but not in a healthy way. I just feel lonely and cut off. Using this countertransference emotion in order to name the sudden loss of confidence in my presence as the repetition of an early catastrophic loss seems to have made some impact. We are beginning finally to piece together the unbearable depression of his early years when he lost the security of his home life. In addition, one could understand this sense of my being available and then disappearing to him as the repetition of Green's dead mother, the mother who was once available and then no longer. Whatever the precise nature of the transference constellation, what seemed to bring most relief to the patient was to understand the timing in the session of the sudden states of lonely despair; even to see that these moments had meaning was a relief, that he was not just being abandoned by me but was in the grip of some unconscious process that we could begin to work out together. He was not totally alone in the presence of an abandoning other.

Such early losses with my patient remind one of Freud's *fort/da observation*, which in some ways is about a little child coping with the threat of loneliness while their mother is absent. One could even describe the fort/da as a pivotal organizing framework around which one can understand fundamental developmental processes. It is obviously an observation of a child who has to hold a situation in time until the mother returns. Winnicott (1958, pp. 222–3) describes how the child can deal with the mother's absence when there is active adaptation to the child's needs, so that the child can wait in a state of undisturbed isolation. But when the environment has failed and impinges on the child, the child falls into a state of restless isolation, and I think that captures something about my patient's emotions towards the end of a session, when he has lost confidence in my presence, just as he has to face the prospect of leaving the session and facing my actual absence.

The fort/da observation and the loneliness–solitude relationship

One could see the fort/da game as a kind of description of what takes place regularly in an analysis. With the neurotic patient, there is in the transference a regular kind of coming and going; the analyst is both present and absent for the patient, appears and disappears. Such transference movements do not create massive anxiety or a great deal of loneliness. However, traumatised and borderline patients bring in an intense way the issue of a going away which feels at times total, with no hope of a return, and a traumatic sense of loneliness. And yet they keep coming back to their analysis in the hope that the analytic setting can provide some resolution to their despair.

In order, ultimately, to make sense of these kinds of clinical situations, I shall consider a few analytic thinkers for whom the fort/da either appears particularly crucial or relevant, or whose thought can shed particular light on the observation's significance. Fundamental once more is Winnicott's approach to early development, with his focus on the play area between the child and mother, and how physical objects, whether they be teddy bears, pieces of string or indeed the cotton reel of Freud's observation, can become important to the child as objects transitional between the subjective and what is objectively perceived. Referring to the early development of the reality sense in the child, Winnicott suggests that 'it is assumed that no human being is free from the strain of relating inner and outer reality' (1958, p. 240). For Winnicott, the relief from this 'strain' for the young child comes from an unchallenged intermediate area of experience, which is in direct continuity with the play area of the small child lost in play. Transitional phenomena are allowable to the infant only when the parents intuitively recognize the strain inherent in objective perception, and so 'do not challenge the infant in regard to subjectivity or objectivity just here where there is a transitional object' (1958, p. 241). Excessive strain will thus come into this area of experience when there is not good enough environmental provision, with, for example, a poorly adaptive mother or excessive environmental impingements. But however good the parenting, there is always some degree of strain inherent in the task of linking inner and outer realities; the strain of linking is universal, and needs to be recognized by the parent, and, indeed, by the analyst. Furthermore, as Green has emphasized, the transitional space is not just 'in between'; it is a space 'where the future subject is in transit; a transit in which he takes possession of a created object in the vicinity of a real external one, before he has reached it' (1997, p. 173). Thus, in the transitional area, the human subject is in the process of *becoming* rather than merely being.

Winnicott also highlights the relationship between the transitional object and symbolism. When symbolism is employed, the infant is already making a distinction between fantasy and fact and between inner and outer. One could see the fort/da game as a pivotal step in the process of the child's making sense of time, through finding a symbolic means of coming to terms with the mother's comings and goings. As I suggested before, the symbolization of absence makes solitude bearable; merely feeling absence without the capacity to symbolize it plunges the subject into loneliness.

If, as I have suggested before, subjectivity is essentially elusive, with the subject appearing and disappearing, coming and going, one is then, of course, reminded of the fort/da observation, of the child's making the cotton reel come and go. In this sense, the fort/da reminds us not only of the elusive comings and goings of the mother but also of the precarious way that human subjectivity arises out of the child's shifts between different states.

Green's concept of the 'work of the negative' (1993) and his notion of the dead mother complex (1983) are also pivotal reference points for understanding the nature of the role of the mother's absence in the fort/da observation. The mother does not have to be literally dead, but instead is emotionally dead, unavailable to the child. Then, the dead mother complex is observed in the transference of certain subjects suffering from a particular kind of depression. Green highlights how one characteristic of this depression is that it takes place in the presence of the parental object, which is itself absorbed by a bereavement. Instead of being an animated source of liveliness for the child, the preoccupied mother becomes psychically dead in the child's eyes; her absence is deadly.

Relevant, too is Lacan's focus on the fort/da as an illustration of how the child can enter the symbolic order through coming up with binary phonemes to structure his play of presence and absence (1975, pp. 173–4). The physical object, the cotton reel, becomes transformed into an object with a symbolic function while the child is confronted with the mother's absence and the child's own desire for her to be present. The fort/da is an early manifestation of the child's use of language. In the phonematic opposition, the child transcends the phenomenon of presence and absence by bringing it onto the symbolic plane.

Putting together some of these approaches, I would suggest that there is always a tension, or strain, between the mother as mere physical object and the mother as an elusive human presence, capable of appearing and disappearing when she wants to, or needs to, whether it is to go to the father or elsewhere, the mother who stirs up the child's yearnings and desires. In the fort/da one can see the working out of the difference between mother as material object and the mother as elusive human presence; out of this difference one can see human subjectivity, with all its dilemmas and possibilities, beginning to emerge. The task of the developing child, as well as that of the analytic patient, is, in a sense, to come to the realization that the mother is not a mere physical object, or at least not an object under the child's omnipotent control, but a subject with a mysterious life of her own, relating to other subjects, the father and others. The dawning of this realization is never easy; there is always a certain amount of strain involved in the process of coming to terms with the mother's elusiveness, more so when the mother's absence is prolonged, or her return highly problematic.

Yet before considering the theoretical and clinical relevance of the fort/da in further detail, it is hard to forget the context of the observation, aspects of which haunt it and give it particular and poignant significance. It is placed early in Freud's book *Beyond the Pleasure Principle* (1920, pp. 14–17), following on what Freud describes as the 'dark and dismal subject of the traumatic neurosis' (1920, p. 14). From the terrors of the repetition of war memories, he moves to the apparently lighter topic of children's play, but which reveals a young child coming to terms with the mother's temporary absence. And yet within a short time, as a footnote tells us, as if in passing, we learn that this mother (in fact Freud's beloved daughter Sophie) died some four years after the observation, before Freud wrote his book. One can thus see the observation in a more primeval light: a mother dies and is then resurrected in the text. Furthermore, though we are also told that Freud's grandson had been jealous of a younger brother, we are not told that this brother, Heinz, also died from 'TB' some time after his mother. This child's death, according to Jones, produced 'the only occasion in his life when Freud was known to shed tears' (1961, p. 550). The loss, no doubt coming after his daughter's death and the emergence of his cancer of the jaw, was almost unbearable and produced in him symptoms of depression.

There are also other personal references surrounding Freud's focus on this grandchild of a year and a half, for this was about the age he was when his younger brother, Julius, died (Jones, 1961, p. 36). This death was to haunt Freud; he admitted that the evil wishes he had against this early arrival of his younger brother had aroused self-reproaches which continued to affect his personal relationships. For example, Freud would link his fainting fits around the time of the increasing tensions with Jung to the effect on him of his younger brother's death. One may finally note that around the age of 18 months was the time when the Wolf man was likely to have witnessed the primal scene, the scene of sexual intercourse between the parents, which the child observes or infers on the basis of fantasy and inference (Freud, 1918, p. 37). Thus the significance of the fort/da observation is mutlidetermined, linking the personal and the theoretical, the real traumas in Freud's life to general considerations of the nature of trauma.

In *Beyond the Pleasure Principle*, Freud notes how dreams in traumatic neurosis bring the patient back into the situation of the accident or 'fright', a situation from which the patient wakes up in 'another fright' (1920, p. 13). From the appearance and reappearance of the traumatic situation in the dream, Freud leads onto the appearance and reappearance of the mother in the world of the young child, a situation which, though apparently lighter, is fraught, as we have seen, with dark resonances of traumatic elements in Freud's personal life. From the fort/da, Freud moves onto the analytic patient and then to how the mental apparatus tries to protect itself from traumatic stimuli by means of a protective shield. One might add here that the repetition of the fort/da game is itself a shield against the pain of the mother's loss. Freud then moves onto his new drive theory, with the death drives leading the individual one way, towards certain extinction, and the life drives prolonging the inevitable as long as possible. The life of the individual is described as moving with a 'vacillating rhythm' (Freud, 1920, p. 41), 'ein Zauder-rhythmus', something which lingers or delays.

> One group of drives rushes forwards so as to reach the final aim of life as swiftly as possible; but when a particular stage in the advance has been reached, the other group jerks back to a certain point to make a fresh start and so prolong the journey.
>
> (1920, p. 41)

Could one say, then, that the fort/da prefigures not only the introduction into Freud's text of the tragic fate of the individual desperately trying to prolong the inevitable journey towards death, but also that it represents a pivotal, 'transitional' moment in the development of the human subject, poised between the processes of coming and going, presence and absence, the past and the present, loneliness and solitude, life and death?

There are many ways of viewing the fort/da observation. While the fort/da could be seen as a relatively sophisticated example of the linking of separation and absence by means of early language, it has resonances with earlier experiences of separation, as well as anticipating subsequent developmental moves.

Holding over time

One could describe the fort/da as a pivotal organizing framework, around which one can understand fundamental developmental processes. The *Oxford English Dictionary* defines 'process', in its main meaning, as a thing that goes on or is carried on, a continuous series of actions, events or changes; and especially a continuous and regular action or succession of actions occurring or performed in a definite manner. Time is thus integral to the nature of a process, and time haunts the fort/da.

The fort/da is obviously an observation of a child without its mother, a child who has to hold a situation in time until the mother returns. Presumably, an image of the mother sustains the child through this period of waiting. But after a certain, critical time, this image will begin to fade, and the strain of holding the situation in time will become unbearable. One can see how this image fades in different ways, from a gradual loss of representation due to lack of reinforcement, to its more active and aggressive elimination. Or else, as Green suggests (1997, p. 1081), there may be a destructive negative hallucination of the object; the negative of the object is created and subsequently sought.

Earlier experiences of separation will, of course, be crucial to how the child manages the waiting time. Winnicott (1971, p. 97) describes how the inner representation of the mother is kept alive in the baby by the reinforcement given from the mother and her technique of devoted childcare. The baby may be distressed by the mother's absence, but if she returns within a reasonable time, this distress is soon mended. Trauma implies that the baby has experienced a break in life's continuity, so that primitive defences come into place to defend against the repetition of unbearable, or unthinkable, anxiety, with attendant confusion and disintegration of ego structure.

Winnicott (1958, pp. 418–19) also describes how the young child can deal with environmental disturbances, such as the mother's absence, when there is active adaptation to the child's needs. The child can then be in a state of undisturbed isolation. In this state, the child can make a spontaneous movement, and the environment is discovered without any loss of the sense of self. There is a respect for processes, a sense of continuity, that one experience will follow another; when something occurs in the environment, there is an appropriate reaction.

Thus an absence, a 'fort', produces or is followed by a return. The child can build up memories of a mother who is both actively present and returns when absent.

But when there has been a failure of good enough adaptation, with environmental impingement, the child returns to a state of restless isolation. The absence produces no return, or there is such a long wait for the return that there is a loss of the sense of self, and the child is in a state of solitary and anxious waiting. In extreme cases, with persistent and repeated absences, this situation may lead to various forms of psychosis, where, instead of the persistence of an internal image of the mother, there is merely a gap, an absence of representation. The gap itself takes possession of the mind, erasing the representations of the object that preceded its absence. The adult patient with such psychopathology will often present with a negative therapeutic reaction (Green, 1997, p. 1081).

Such early experiences can help us understand the psychic situation in adult patients. The neurotic can stand absence without loss of the sense of self. The borderline patient goes in and out of states of unthinkable anxiety, but there is still some sense of a return of the mother. But, with the psychotic patient, there is no return, and a sense of utter desolation and emptiness remains. With the treatment of these latter patients, analysis may only repair such fundamental damage by means of the real relationship with the analyst, as the hole in maternal representation will persist.

Winnicott also draws attention to the importance for the young baby of dropping things, a precursor, one might say, of the more organized fort/da experience, to which Winnicott refers in the context of giving a personal account of Klein's depressive position (Winnicott, 1958, pp. 414–17). The stage of the baby playing at dropping things is seen as a crucial stage, around the time of weaning, and when there is the beginning of the capacity to master loss. For constructive play to be possible, the loved person needs to have been near the baby in the first place, in order to survive the baby's various anxieties and projections, as well as offer holding-over time through their adaptive responses and their safe return.

In fact, Winnicott noted (1941, p. 68) that the fort/da stimulated him to make detailed observations of infant's play between about 5 to 13 months of age. In a paper on the observation of infants in a 'set situation', he describes a way to observe infants and diagnose some of their difficulties by presenting them, while their mother is present, with a shiny tongue depressor, or spatula. There are usually three possible stages to be observed. In the first stage, the child begins, tentatively, to show a spontaneous interest in the spatula. In the second stage, after a period of hesitation, the child accepts the reality of the spatula and soon puts it in his mouth. He or she now feels the spatula is in their possession and may bang it on the table or hold it to the observer's mouth, playing at feeding. In the third stage, which Winnicott links with the fort/da game, the baby

... first of all drops the spatula as if by mistake. If it is restored he is pleased, plays with it again, and drops it once more, but this time less by mistake. On its being restored again, he drops it on purpose, and thoroughly enjoys aggressively getting rid of it. The end of this phase comes when the baby either wishes to get down on the floor with the spatula, where he starts mouthing it and playing with it again, or else when he is bored with it and reaches out to any other objects that lie at hand.

(Winnicott, 1941, p. 54)

There are thus *three* main elements of the whole spatula observation; incorporation, retention and riddance.

The third phase, when the infant practices ridding himself of the spatula, can be related, according to Winnicott, to the fort/da game, when the child is mastering his feelings about the mother's departure. He considers that his own observation could be seen as an extension backwards of Freud's observation, and corresponds to the third stage, that of ridding the child of the object.

'I think the cotton reel, standing for the child's mother, is thrown away to indicate a getting rid of the mother because the reel in his possession had represented the mother *in his possession.* When the mother goes away, this is not only a loss for him of the externally real mother, but also a test of the child's relation to his inside mother' (Winnicott, 1941, p. 68).

The game of riddance of the object reassures the child about the fate of the internal mother, that she has not vanished, that her image is still alive, that she is going to return and to play with the child again. There is thus a need for the child to be able to throw the mother away symbolically in order to keep her alive. But, of course, this presupposes that the successful negotiation of the earlier phases of incorporation and retention has taken place so that there is a sense of continuity over time.

Those patients who have had such an experience of continuity are more able to do psychic work; there is an adequate level of symbolic functioning, what goes away can return and they can cope with being on their own. However, in those patients with disruptions in the early holding environment there may be a retreat from the reality of the social world into a private time, or into a state of almost psychotic timelessness; there is little hope that what goes away can ever return, so better to create a state of timelessness where comings and goings are irrelevant. With some traumatised, and often abused, patients, there are also pathological states in which lived time is avoided by a whirlwind of activity, and they may experience rapid changes between extremes in their mental state. The whirlwind of confusion, with so many comings and goings that it is impossible to register any coherent pattern, may be both a defence against experiencing chaos, and a way of re-creating an excited mental state. They may need the whirlwind in order to feel alive, for they have not had the sense of time kept going by the mother.

Different kinds of absence

The absence of the mother haunts the fort/da game. This may be a physical absence, but an emotional absence, both before she goes and when she returns, is just as significant. That is, the quality of the contact between mother and child is crucial to how the child will deal with her absence. There are a number of different kinds of absence. Green's dead mother complex refers to a pervasive and catastrophic absence, with a bereaved and preoccupied mother unable to be alive to the child. There is a void, an emptiness, between mother and child, which leads to a loss of meaning and desperate attempts to patch the hole between them. The shadow of her absence, even when physically present, pervades the child and the analytic patient. This results in a fundamental fantasy: to nourish the dead mother, to maintain her perpetually embalmed. She is never 'thrown away' symbolically as in the fort/da game.

When the dead mother complex is touched in the transference, 'the subject feels himself to be empty, blank, as though he were deprived of a stop-gap object, and a guard against madness' (Green, 1983, p. 162).

There is a difficult task for the patient, who eventually has to mourn the dead mother rather than keep her embalmed, that of letting her go, getting rid of rather than holding onto her. This task means having to face intense feelings of emptiness, for the mother has filled the patient's psychic life as a dead presence. Letting her go, that is, bringing to her life and then mourning her loss, means having to face the paradoxical situation of two losses: presence in death and absence in life.

Other patients may not have the dead mother complex, but the quality of the mother's absence may also be an intense issue. For example, at the more psychotic end of the spectrum, there is the non presence of the object; there is a void, a nothingness, an emptiness and blankness. Even if the object returns, it is not enough to heal the disastrous consequences of its too long absence. The nothingness of this experience is eloquent, communicating a sense of disaster. As one approaches this area in the patient, there may be a futile absence, which may be experienced by the analyst as depression, and brought by the patient through enactments. One might say that with these patients, the 'fort', the 'gone', predominates; with them, there is no 'da', no 'there'. This entails the intense presence of a sense of nothingness, a nonexistent or cancelled subject, with little sense of human agency. The hope is that analytic work can provide a framework for the linking of presence to absence, and with it the possibility of becoming a subject.

Wilfred Bion makes a distinction between nothing and no-thing. Knowledge of loss, of the thought as a no-thing, with a realization of the absent object, can lead to freedom; or else, the patient may be unable to tolerate frustration, and the no-thing may be used as the foundation for hallucination (1970, pp. 16–17): Green calls the latter negative hallucination, and he cites the female patient who said to Winnicott that the negative of him was more real than the positive of him. Parsons also develops this theme when he distinguishes between a constructive and a destructive role for negativity in psychic life. The constructive role of the negative requires a certain psychic mobility, a capacity to shift between negating and affirming, separation and connection (Parsons, 2000, p. 185). One may see this shift between presence and absence in the pattern of the patient's movements of engagement and disengagement in the transference relationship.

I have described (Kennedy, 1984) what I called the 'dual aspect' of the transference, which refers to the analyst as simultaneously the receiver of the patient's projections, or the analyst as fantasy object, and as different from these projections. This dual aspect of the transference refers to the way that the more neurotic patient can oscillate from being identical, in the patient's eyes, to archaic fantasies, and being something else, different. I described how to begin with the patient who revealed a repetitive transference pattern, in which some analytic work was possible but was then thrown away, so that looking back at what had happened one seemed to be left with a series of fragmented weeks and months. But this was not a helpful throwing away, in that nothing came back, and she was left with a feeling of futility. However, after a considerable amount of work, the transference began to have a more dynamic and less rigid feel. I became less merged with her primitive fantasies, and she was able to see me both as a fantasy figure and as different. This coincided with an ability to hold onto analytic work rather than merely throw it away. One is reminded here of Winnicott's observation of a boy's use of string (1971, pp. 15–20) as a means both to communicate and to deny separation. The mother of this 7-year-old was a depressive who had been hospitalised for depression. As a result, there were several extended occasions when the child was separated from the mother. He developed a number of symptoms, including compulsions and retention of faeces. When he was seen for a consultation, he showed a preoccupation with string; at home he would join up the furniture with string, and had also tied string round his younger sister's neck. The function of the string was seen as a way of trying to communicate the child's fear of separation by desperately joining up objects. It was as if he were trying to 'rope her in.' It was not just the mother's going away which was traumatic for the child, but also her lack of contact with him when she returned, due to her preoccupation with herself and other matters, her lack of focus on the child. The string both communicated his wish to join up objects, but also his denial of a painful separation, with an anxious form of attachment. As Green (1997, p. 1074) put it, the string was a positive materialisation of an absent, negative bond.

One can see a variety of disorganized attachments with those children who have been subjected not just to emotional detachment but also to physical and/or sexual abuse. My own experience of working with such children and their families at the Cassel Hospital (Kennedy, 1997) revealed that the children are often haunted by their abuse and unable, without considerable help, to free themselves from its consequences. They often cannot concentrate on a task for long, as if there has been a massive disruption in their capacity to link experiences over time. They appear overstimulated with poor impulse control, and they may have a haunted, driven quality to their relating, and a tendency to be aggressive and test boundaries. Sometimes they may show inappropriate sexual behaviour; they may go in and out of confusional states when they become very anxious, particularly about being abandoned, and they have great difficulty in trusting adults. The parent–child relationships are usually pathological, with varying degrees of disorganized attachment patterns. There is often role reversal, in which the child tries to control the parents' comings and goings, while the parents have problems in maintaining ordinary child–adult boundaries. These parents often have difficulty in being emotionally attached to their children, with inhibition of the capacity to play. In the child, and probably also in the parent, there is a loss of, or failure to develop the capacity to use meaningful symbols, so that, as it were, no fort/da interchange is possible. The parents are often inconsistent, at times cut off and self-absorbed. The children themselves seem to make a particular kind of powerful emotional impact on their parents and other caretakers, as if they are desperately trying to get the parents to acknowledge their needs and accept the trauma that they have experienced.

My own experience of the abused adult is that they can recreate the emotionally absent parent at some point. This is the parent who could not bear the child's pain and vulnerability, and who has left the child with a sense that the environment has fundamentally failed them, and that there is a kind of breach, or unbearable gap, in the parenting experience. An unbridgeable gap may suddenly appear between patient and analyst, which either party may be tempted to deal with by some kind of precipitous action, such as termination. Bearing unbearable emotional pain is an issue in any analysis, but with the abused adult it becomes acutely relevant (see Kennedy, 2007, p. 165ff.).

Different kinds of psychic space

One may ask what happens to the child between the mother's coming and going. Of course, the effect of prolonged separations on the child is well documented in the attachment literature. Anxiety, ultimately leading to despair and depression, has long been known to occur with, for example, hospitalised children left without a caretaker. Such situations, though originally described by James Robertson (1958) in the 1950s, are, unfortunately, still common throughout the world as a result of war and famine, or poor services for abandoned children left unattended in institutions. The space between the child and the mother will become so vast as to be unrepresentable. No cotton reel play can ever bring the mother back, and the play is soon abandoned, leaving the child in a despairing and depressed state of listlessness.

One can see, in less globally damaged children and adults, various kinds of ways of dealing with the psychic space between parent and child. Michael Balint describes two characteristic modes of relating which act as defences against primitive anxieties of psychotic intensity, and which refer to the quality of space between parent and child, as well as a way of trying to understand various kinds of patients who are difficult to reach. In one attitude, the 'oncophilic' attitude, the maternal object is felt to be a vitally important support, but to such a degree that there is no separation from the child. The oncophilic clings to objects, trying to control them. The 'philobat' on the other hand, prefers objectless expanses and the safety in the empty spaces. Objects are considered indifferent or even deceitful and untrustworthy hazards, better to be avoided (Balint, 1968, p. 70). No doubt there are mixtures of the different attitudes, with varying amounts of clinging to the object and avoidance of it. In patients who are too close to their object, treatment may enable them to develop a sense of psychic space; with those who avoid objects, treatment may enable them to begin to relate without excessive anxiety about the object.

Anxiety about the mother's return, and the state when she returns, may become organized in the adult patient through perverse functioning, when, for example, there is an attempt to control the other. For example, a narcissistic man came into analysis as he was having difficulty sustaining relationships. He showed little empathy for others and was exploitative and often emotionally sadistic. He sought my admiration to boost his fragile sense of self-worth, while he was dismissive about my capacities. I was treated like a servant, there to attend to his needs. Women were seen as mere objects to be entered. He would gain pleasure from teasing them, keeping them waiting, stirring them up with desire and then dropping them. However, he also at times, after some analysis, experienced an increasing sense of futility about his lifestyle, with how much he needed to fill himself up with sexual excitement and destructiveness, in order to avoid feeling empty. What soon became clearer was an all-pervading fear of psychical collapse, and a terror of being submerged by me in the transference. The picture of his mother was of a cold, puritanical and panicky figure, brittle and unresponsive. He was left with her because his father was often away from home, and she turned to him for comfort. She became depressed, and he felt he had to bolster her up, a situation which he greatly resented. His sadistic use of women could clearly be related to this early mother–child interaction, in which there was an excessive turning to the child for comfort, intrusion into his psychic space, and a fusion of her needs with his.

Use of the transitional space clearly represents a more satisfactory way of dealing with the mother–child relationship, based on 'good enough' environmental provision rather than excessive anxiety and retreat from active engagement. One has a sense of the playful interaction between mother and child, which can allow her to come and go without excessive anxiety, but also allows the child to play alone in her presence and without her intruding.

However, there are anxious situations, repeated in an analysis of, for example, borderline patients, where there is an issue about the space between coming and going when the subject may feel they can never find their way back to the maternal object. Instead, they may feel lost in the space between coming and going. There is little prospect of becoming a subject as there is little hope of re-finding the object. There is neither 'fort' nor 'da', but a refusal, or absence, of either 'fort' or 'da'.

In Freud's original observation, one can see the fort/da game as a positive use of repetition. The game helped the child cope with the mother's comings and goings, as well as provided a means, according to Lacan, of becoming inserted into the Symbolic Order and into language. In the space between these comings and goings, the child was able to find a place to play; there was a space for representation. The child could let go of the mother once he had found a repetitive but symbolic means of representing her leaving him. This positive use of repetition contrasts with a more compulsive and insistent quality of repetition also described in *Beyond the Pleasure Principle*, which has a more mindless, or 'daemonic', quality, related to the power of the unconscious repressed. One could imagine a delicate balance between these two kinds of repetition, depending on the time for waiting for the mother's return, what state she was in when she left, what state the child was in when she left and what state both are in on her return. Of course, the fort/da game occurs without the mother, and yet there are many occasions when something similar takes place in the presence of the mother. Various kinds of comings and goings occur in the complex interactions between mother and child. The mirroring role between mother and child is of particular significance in this context. For Lacan, the mirror stage plays a pivotal role in his theory as a moment of alienation preceding the fort/da moment of entering the Symbolic Order. The child sees himself as a whole in the mirror, but it is as an imaginary unity that he sees himself. This contrasts with the reality of his helplessness and his lack of bodily mastery. For Lacan, the formation of the ego begins at this point of alienation in the mirror, with the fascination with one's own image (see Benvenuto and Kennedy, 1986, p. 55ff.).

Clearly, this view of the place of the mirror image is quite different from that of Winnicott, and subsequent child and infant researchers, who focus on the role of parental mirroring as structuring the child's affects. For Winnicott (1971, p. 111ff.), how the mother looks at the baby, and what the baby sees when he or she looks at the mother, are crucial to the development of the child's sense of self. The mother has a fundamental role here in giving back to the baby the baby's own self. If, for example, the mother's face is unresponsive, then 'a mirror is a thing to be looked at but not to be looked into' (1971, p. 113). There is, then, no depth to the mother's mirroring role; the child may be left puzzled about what the other's look may bring; they may be left without much experience of ever getting back what they give. With the mirroring and responsive mother, there is a constant process of flexible interchange between her and the baby, so that a kind of primitive fort/da game is already taking place between mother and child, but with her present. If she is unresponsive, then she becomes emotionally absent while present, a traumatic situation for the baby.

Further thoughts on loneliness and solitude

Both Klein and Fromm-Reichmann approached the topic of loneliness at the end of their careers; indeed, in both cases these papers on this topic were their last. For Klein, loneliness was an inevitable state of mind, indicative of the fact that

integration is never fully achievable. While one may mitigate the feeling of loneliness, it is not something that we can avoid. There is certainly a sense in this
paper of an analyst at the end of life looking into the void, of having to face the
pathos and pain of approaching death. There is something of that quality in the
late work of great artists. Said (2006), in his poignantly last and unfinished book,
approaches the issue of 'late style' in such artists. For example, he suggests that
there is something in late Beethoven, as in his late quartets, that remains unrec-
onciled and fragmentary; these quartets acutely express a sense of abandonment,
in contrast to the relentless quality of his second period works, such as the *Fifth
Symphony*. Indeed, one might add that in his last works, he pushes harmony and
form to the limit, moving away from the 'home' key at times so that one may
wonder if home will ever be reached; there are even moments, as in his last piano
sonata, when time itself seems suspended (see Rosen, 2002). The prerogative of
such late style is that it '. . . has the power to render disenchantment and pleasure
without resolving the contradiction between them. What holds them in tension, as
equal forces straining in opposite directions, is the artist's mature subjectivity,
stripped of hubris and pomposity, unashamed either of its fallibility or of the modest assurance it has gained as a result of age and exile' (Said, 2006, p. 148).

Anthony Storr (1988, p. 174), in his book *Solitude*, also discusses late
Beethoven as an exemplar of the late or third period in an artist's development.
The last quartets, for example, are less concerned with communication, are
unconventional in form, display an absence of rhetoric and explore remote areas
of experience. Such work is deeply expressive of deep inward experience, very
much the theme of last works.

One may suppose that as a result of the artist achieving a point in their life
where their identity is firm enough to be able to face their own dissolution, these
last works convey in their form and expression what is unattainable; that human
happiness, while achievable in brief moments, cannot last, though the yearning for it may persist. Faced by approaching death, the artist, or indeed analyst,
becomes ever aware that happiness and integration are transient, loneliness in
some form inevitable.

One may infer from these considerations that solitude as an active state of
mind, as opposed to the more passive experience of experiencing loneliness,
can be creative under certain conditions. The kind of creativity shown in the
last works referred to represent some of the highest human achievements, where
solitude before death becomes the source of illumination. But even long before
death, solitude, as Storr (1988, p. 28) points out, can be facilitated by encouraging deep contact with one's inner world, or what I would describe as the depths
of the soul. This contrasts with much of contemporary Western culture, with its
constant bombardment of the senses, the continuous call of the mobile phone and
the ever-present text message, which at times appear as manic defences against
any possibility of imagining oneself alone. Storr (1988, p. 106ff.) also points out
how solitude can encourage the growth of the imagination, so long as it is not too
extreme. Indeed, it does seem that imaginative capacity tends to become particularly highly developed in gifted individuals who, for one reason or another, have

passed rather solitary childhoods. The point made is that, provided the childhood circumstances are not so severe as to cause lasting and profound damage, a certain amount of solitariness can encourage the imagination to flourish. Though, of course, one may add that with a number of creative artists who have experienced childhood loneliness, their subsequent personal relationships may well have suffered. Storr cites as examples of these kinds of artist Kipling, Saki and P. G. Wodehouse, all of whom had the experience of being 'farmed out' as children, without the experience of a secure childhood home. As a result all three suffered from difficulties in forming close relationships.

In the analytic setting, one may tend to focus more on the relationship difficulties than on the creative imagination. Yet we also touch on at least the roots of imagination, or when it can become blocked. Bearing loneliness seems to me an essential aspect of being an analyst, but also of some analytic work, particularly with patients who have spent periods of their childhood in extreme states of isolation. Helping them to manage their isolation and reach a point of creative solitude may be very important for them. In the main clinical example, the patient reached a point where there was some confidence that he could face the prospect of facing my absence.

Having confidence in a return of a loved one seems essential to the capacity to bear loneliness, even in adversity. I want to finish with a quotation from Dietrich Bonhoeffer's last letter from prison to his friend Eberhard Bethge before Bonhoeffer was taken to a concentration camp, as an example of how even under extreme situations, such love can be sustaining.

> These will be quiet days in our homes. But I have had the experience over and over again that the quieter it is around me, the clearer do I feel a connection to you. It as though in solitude the soul develops senses we hardly know in everyday life. Therefore I have not felt lonely or abandoned for one moment. You, the parents, all of you, the friends and students of mine at the front, all are constantly present to me . . . Therefore you must not think that I am unhappy. What is happiness and unhappiness? It depends so little on the circumstances; it depends really only on that which happens inside a person.
>
> (1970, p. 419)

The next chapter takes up Bonhoeffer's question about the nature of happiness and unhappiness, from both a general and psychoanalytical point of view.

Chapter 7

Happiness and misery

There is considerable interest these days in issues of happiness and well-being. It would seem that happiness has become a fundamental need for the modern soul. I am not sure that this has always been the case. For example, in Simone Weil's account of the needs of the soul, written in 1943, happiness does not appear; instead, there is a focus on needs such as liberty, order, responsibility, equality, security and truth (Weil, 1986). Perhaps this is unsurprising given the context for her essay. At other times, authenticity may have more of a pivotal place in the needs of the soul. Indeed, as Bernard Williams put it, 'Men do, as a matter of fact, find value in such things as submission, trust, uncertainty, risk, even despair and suffering, and these values can scarcely all be related to a central idea of *happiness*' (1972, p. 80).

Bernard Williams also criticizes a simplistic Utilitarian notion of happiness as being essentially about facilitating the happiness of the greatest number. This was based upon Jeremy Bentham's notion that happiness was the basic human condition. Such an account misses out on crucial human values, such as integrity, spontaneity, freedom, self-expression and love, by merging all values into one common currency. Also, Utilitarianism cannot cope with the fact of human tragedy. For example, in ancient Greek and Shakespearean tragedy, we are brought face to face with horrors which challenge our beliefs and our values. The tragic space is one where virtue can still shine through such challenges, but the characters, like the spectators, are not impervious or invulnerable. There is not a happy outcome, but we are still uplifted, and see the world with new eyes.

However, it is accepted that not to be happy for long periods can entail serious consequences for the individual, with the risk of developing depression. In the UK, Lord Layard, using Utilitarian arguments, has shown that unhappiness has considerable and serious consequences for the economy, being a major cause of time off work and inefficiency. His arguments have been so persuasive that the last government put in millions of pounds to provide talking therapies rather than rely on medication for the treatment of mild to moderate depression.

While the latter programme is to be commended and is preferable to having patients unduly rely on antidepressants, as useful as they can be in severe depression, the concept of happiness being put forward here is very simple, and does need considerable modification if it is to have any resemblance to what is a complex human issue. Layard's answer to the age-old problem of human happiness is simple – by happiness he means feeling good, enjoying life and feeling it is wonderful. And by unhappiness he means feeling bad and wishing things were different. He also recommends an extensive programme of cognitive behaviour therapy (CBT) as the solution to many depressive episodes, bar the most severe and those with the most complex problems. As a result of his influence, such programmes have been rolled out extensively. The jury is still out about whether such programmes are in fact as effective in the long term as he and other advocates of CBT maintain. CBT is undoubtedly effective for some conditions, and I personally recommend its use when I see children and families, for example, where it is appropriate, for a variety of anxiety conditions when short-term work is adequate. But my experience is that it is of doubtful value in more complex situations, where a more subtle understanding of ambiguities of the human situation is required. Just as not every problem requires intensive psychoanalysis, not every problem can be cured by CBT.

The notion that there is a simple cure for human unhappiness, while seductive, is hardly convincing. We are, unfortunately, difficult creatures to please, and are easily led into contradictory and self-destructive paths. Even the notion of a person wanting a good experience is fraught with tensions and conflicts; they may want a good experience, but they may equally find ways of not receiving it, or of spoiling it or of turning it into something bad. There is thus a major dilemma if one ties happiness too closely to goodness. Goodness is a fragile concept (see Nussbaum, 1986).

Furthermore, a happy mood, feeling that everything about life is good, may cover up what is really going on with the subject; they may be denying the reality of a situation. One would thus have to look beyond a short-lasting happy mood to really capture happiness; the latter would seem to require something longer lasting, perhaps involving some sort of richness and depth of experience, a life 'well lived,' which does not deny whatever uncomfortable reality may be present. Indeed, happiness may involve the sense of achievement in overcoming difficult and painful situations. One can see already that happiness may involve a number of different and contradictory states of mind and that it will not easily be pinned down. For this reason, any investigation into human happiness needs to take account of our complex psychology, in particular how we constantly trip ourselves up, and that something often gets in the way of our feeling happy. In addition, we need to retain a certain amount of caution when looking at the place of happiness in our lives. Oedipus was no doubt very happy to be married to Jocasta, but his happiness was beside the point; other little problems like incest and parricide were just under the surface.

Freud tackled the complexities of the problem of happiness and unhappiness in his *Civilization and Its Discontents*, where he wrote that 'here are . . . many paths that *may* lead to such happiness as is attainable by men, but there is none which does so for certain' (1930, p. 85). While Freud may veer a bit too far towards the pessimistic pole, nonetheless his examination of the happiness issue is pivotal in trying to grasp the subtleties of the human soul, its twists and turns. This is not to rule out the important place that a reduction in suffering has in facilitating an individual's happiness.

In an earlier paper, 'Civilized Sexual Morality and Modern Nervous Illness' (1908), he had argued that civilization is built up on the suppression of instincts. The renunciation of the fulfilment of sexual instincts has been a progressive one, from the free exercise of sexuality to its more legitimate and ordered form. The price of having to renounce the sexual instincts in the name of civilization can be considerable; suppression of the instincts is seen as a significant cause of mental illness and suffering, hence of personal unhappiness. However, by the time of *Civilization and Its Discontents* (1930), Freud had a much more complex view of the causes of our unhappiness. Our inherent bisexuality, which can usually not be fulfilled, and the innate presence of our aggressiveness, means that our sexual life is inevitably full of conflict and a sense of guilt; any search for human love and lasting human happiness has to take account of these basic facts of our psychic life.

This chapter will start with Freud's detailed breakdown of the notion of happiness, and then consider a variety of other thinkers, in order to explore happiness from different angles, so as ultimately to come up with what I would suggest is an understanding of happiness that more accurately reflects the complexities of the human soul. I think that such a method of exploring the happiness dimension, using a number of different sources, is the most effective way of allowing something significant about a complex and elusive topic to emerge with more clarity than would otherwise be possible.

Freud and happiness

The original title for Freud's book was *Das Ungluck in der Kultur*, or *Unhappiness in Civilization*, and indeed the text contains a subtle and extensive examination of the ways that humankind strives to gain happiness and keep suffering or misery away. Of course, as I have said, he was something of a pessimist. Rather like Arthur Schopenhauer, Freud seemed to see the world as a source of suffering, with life inherently unhappy. Such happiness as was attainable was elusive or even an illusion. This vision is very much the inheritance of the Romantic Movement, with its overturning of the Enlightenment's Layard-like optimistic dominance of the life of reason in determining our state of mind and place in society.

> Happiness is not an ideal, said Holderlin, happiness is 'tepid water on the tongue'; Nietzsche said 'Man does not desire happiness only the Englishman does.'
>
> (Berlin, 1999, pp. 141–2)

So quotes Isaiah Berlin in his book *The Roots of Romanticism*, where he shows how Romanticism transformed the Enlightenment optimism about the power of human reason to achieve answers about life into something more like our own more tentative view of the limits of human reason. Indeed, one could say that the Romantics, poets such as John Keats and Percy Bysshe Shelley, created new forms of despair, linking happiness and misery inextricably. They created pictures of the dark delights of suffering, which certainly has Christian echoes, but invokes a new form of feeling, one to which we are heirs.

Freud and Breuer also famously stated in *Studies in Hysteria* that 'much will be gained if we succeed in transforming your hysterical misery into common unhappiness. With a mental life that has been restored to health you will be better armed against that unhappiness' (1895, p. 305). Of course one may wonder what exactly is hysterical as opposed to ordinary misery, let alone what is mental health, an issue which will be discussed later. But clearly here there is some notion of *unhappiness* being a normal state, as opposed to Bentham's view that happiness was the normal state, and that the task of therapy is to help the patient move from being stuck with abnormal amounts of misery into a position of being able to bear the essentially unhappy human condition.

Not the most uplifting vision, or is it? Could one say that there is something noble in this rather stoical, or even tragic, view of the world? Or is it just realistic, facing squarely the fact that happiness is an ideal more to be aimed at than achieved, and its fulfilment a utopian ideal, rather like that envisaged in the Garden of Eden, where humankind is perpetually happy because ignorant.

The image of a lost paradise, or a sense of unalloyed happiness irretrievably lost in experience, still haunts certain kinds of experience, as Stuart Hampshire points out. 'Attending to some perfect achievement in art, such as Mozart's *Figaro* or Casal's playing of Bach or a painting by Vermeer, very great pleasure may often be combined with an elegiac feeling, of sadness that perfect happiness is lost – that it is nowhere to be found in the unimagined world and that it exists only in the perfect achievements of art' (1989, pp. 152–3). Beauty in art, he adds, has sometimes been interpreted as a promise of happiness, or as a lost happiness.

A similar kind of happiness can also be seen in Marcel Proust's work, where he equates happiness with the recovered reality of a life, found at particular times – *moments bienheureux*, or 'blessed moments'. At the end of Proust's great novel *Time Regained*, he describes intense states of being in which the subject can capture lost time, or capture fragments of existence withdrawn from time (1927, p. 229). Thus, while the narrator returns to the Guermantes' mansion after some twenty years, several times in succession there is reborn in him an intense and veritable moment of the past – the taste of the madeleine cake, the clink of a spoon on a plate, the uneven paving stones under his feet and the stiffness of a starched napkin on his lips. Such moments – these *moments bienheureux* – invoke the illusion of simultaneity, in which past and present merge into one, or past and present sensations flash back and forth. There is something analogous in the psychoanalytic session when analyst and patient are constantly finding moments of being in which past and present scenes and situations interact, merge or shift backwards and forwards, which can then create the possibility of some new connections emerging, or when repressions are lifted. This can be seen in the first clinical example below.

Semir Zeki (2009) goes so far as to propose that brain functioning itself creates misery for us. One of the main functions of the brain is to create meaning, but the brain finds this difficult as it is often confronted with several meanings of equal validity. The brain tries to cope with this by creating unity, seeing wholes where they may or may not be. Love is just such a wish for unity. But such wishes are doomed to fail, and this causes us misery. 'The "unity-in-love" is a brain concept that involves the splendors of heaven. That heaven can never be permanently attained on earth; it is against reality' (Zeki, 2009, p. 133). This does not stop the brain from looking for such illusory wholeness, and the result is human misery as we always fail to achieve this unity. At the same time, the wish for unity and wholeness drives both love relations and the greatest human endeavours in the arts – hence the title of his book, *The Splendors and Miseries of the Human Brain*.

Such general considerations lead one to ask whether or not there is a place in the psychoanalytic encounter for consideration of the 'larger' issues such as the place of happiness in one's life. I would suggest that it is important now and then at least to think about such matters, even if the day-to-day work of analysis is usually concerned with the minutiae of a life and of the analytic encounter itself. However, it is not always easy to find the place of these general issues in the analytic context, and other disciplines often need to be enlisted in support of searching for an analytic approach to broader and at times philosophical issues, which metapsychological concepts may not adequately grasp. Freud himself was exemplary in such undertakings and can provide a model of how to think psycho-analytically about broad human issues.

I would also add that there is currently a great deal of literature, much of it popular, concerned with the topic of happiness, some of it providing some sort of self-help approach to human living which only focuses on 'positive' or 'life coach' thinking, with the avoidance of 'negative' thoughts.

But this linkage between happiness and misery is much too simplistic, eliminating all the complexities of the human psyche, let alone some two thousand years of philosophical thinking about the nature of happiness (see, for example, McMahon, 2006). Furthermore, our experience of those coming for an analysis is that often they are not merely looking for a way out of their suffering, but are also looking for 'deep' meaning and purpose, something that cannot be found in a few sessions.

Freud's arguments in *Civilization and Its Discontents* about the place of human happiness and misery depend upon certain complex assumptions about what makes us happy, which can provide the basis for such a deep psychoanalytic contribution to the understanding of the nature of happiness. Freud's earliest reference to happiness occurs in the Freud–Fliess letters, where he describes happiness as the belated fulfilment of a childhood wish (Freud, 1985, pp. 294, 353). As I mentioned, in his paper 'Civilized Sexual Morality and Modern Nervous Illness' (1908, pp. 179–204), Freud displayed an optimistic notion about the possibilities of achieving human happiness. He maintained that civilization represses sexuality and this makes us unhappy, leading to neurosis or perversion. Potentially healthy and socially viable sexual drives are transformed by civilized morality, such as the demands of a poor marriage or of sexual abstinence, into culturally useless nervous illness. Sex here is seen as essentially beneficial, and freeing it up would make us happier. But in *Civilization and Its Discontents*, sexuality itself, as for example necessarily incorporating aggression, is the cause of unhappiness. Thus, one can already see what a complex field one touches once the topic of happiness is approached.

Indeed, *Civilization and Its Discontents* is, as Darrin McMahon describes (McMahon, 2006, p. 448), a remarkable synthesis of almost the whole history of the philosophy of happiness. One can piece together eleven ways by which individuals strive to gain happiness and keep suffering away (Freud, 1930, pp. 77–85). These in summary are as follows:

The most enticing method of doing this is to conduct one's life by aiming for unrestricted satisfaction of every need, a kind of pure hedonism. But this means putting enjoyment before caution and soon brings its own punishment.

Other methods involve the avoidance of unpleasure and are differentiated according to the source. Some of these methods 'are extreme and some moderate; some are one-sided and some attack the problem simultaneously at several points' (Freud, 1930, p. 77).

Against the suffering which may come from human relationships, one may turn away from the external world into a quiet isolation. But a better way is to become a member of the human community, and try to work for the good of all.

The crudest but most effective method of influence is the chemical one of intoxication, but of course such drugs are also responsible for 'a waste of a large quota of energy which might have been employed for the improvement of the human lot' (Freud, 1930, p. 78).

Another way to avoid suffering is by influencing the drives. The most extreme way of doing this is brought about by 'killing off the drives' (Freud, 1930, p. 79) through practices such as yoga. Alternatively, one may try to control the drive life through the higher psychical agencies, which have subjected themselves to the reality principle, thus gaining a certain amount of protection against suffering (1930, p. 79). However, 'the feeling of happiness derived from the satisfaction of a wild drive impulse untamed by the ego is incomparably more intense than that derived from a drive that has been tamed' (1930, p. 79). Hence, the irresistible attraction of perverse impulses and forbidden things finds an economic explanation here.

Another method Freud outlines is by means of the displacement of libido, where the drives are shifted in such a way that they avoid frustration from the external world. This can be seen in sublimation, gaining most if one can sufficiently heighten the yield of pleasure from the sources of psychical and intellectual work (Freud, 1930, p. 79). Freud emphasizes the special quality of satisfaction that comes from the artist's joy in creating, in giving his phantasies body, and the scientist's joy in solving problems or discovering truths. However, such satisfactions do not 'convulse our physical being' (1930, p. 80), and are only accessible to the few. 'And even to the few who do possess them, this method cannot give complete protection from suffering. It creates no impenetrable armour against the arrows of fortune, and it habitually fails when the source of suffering is the person's own body' (1930, p. 80).

Contemplation of works of art, based on the satisfaction of illusion and the power of the imagination, can give us temporary solace, but for Freud, 'the mild narcosis induced in us by art can do no more than bring about a transient withdrawal from the pressures of vital needs, and it is not strong enough to make us forget real misery' (Freud, 1930, p. 81).

A powerful but dangerous technique for avoiding suffering is to turn away from reality altogether, such as with the hermit. However, reality is so strong that this method can lead to madness. Looking for a certainty of happiness would require a delusional remoulding of reality, which Freud mentions in passing belongs to religions, which he sees as mass delusions.

One of the most powerful ways of gaining happiness and keeping suffering away is through a special kind of 'technique of living' (*Lebenstechnik*), involving love relations. The satisfactions of loving relations and also that of sexual love have given us our most intense experiences of pleasure, and have 'thus furnished us with a pattern for our search for happiness' (Freud, 1930, p. 82). The 'weak' side of this technique of living is that 'we are never so defenceless against suffering as when we love, never so helplessly unhappy as when we have lost our loved object or its love' (1930, p. 82).

One would add here that the pattern of object relationships and how they are repeated in the transference gives us a clue as to the pattern by which we may seek happiness or constantly fail to achieve any. As an extreme example of this, one can see how those with a deprived history, whose early objects have been deeply unsatisfying and directly rejecting, may well repeat this pattern in their adult relationships, constantly avoiding the possibility of a lasting and satisfying close relationship, either with their partners or with their children. Another example can be seen with the narcissistic patient who cannot achieve lasting and fulfilling relationships, as they are impervious to the needs and wishes of the other.

Finally, one may turn to seek happiness in the enjoyment of beauty, through 'the beauty of human forms or gestures, of natural objects and landscapes and of artistic and even scientific creations' (Freud, 1930, p. 82). This aesthetic attitude 'offers little against the threat of suffering, but it can compensate for a great deal. The enjoyment of beauty has a peculiar, mildly intoxicating quality of feeling. Beauty has no obvious use; nor is there any clear cultural necessity for it. Yet civilization could not do without it' (1930, p. 82).

Freud concludes this section by suggesting that though we cannot fulfil the programme of becoming happy, imposed on us by the pleasure principle, we cannot give up our efforts to bring it nearer to fulfilment by some means or other (Freud, 1930, p. 83). There are many different paths by which we try to do this, some involving the negative path of avoiding unpleasure, others involving the positive path of gaining pleasure. But by none of these paths can we attain all that we desire, so that we can only find a reduced kind of happiness.

All kinds of different factors will go into directing an individual's choice of path towards seeking happiness. These include 'how much satisfaction he can expect from the external world, how far he is led to make himself independent of it, and, finally, how much strength he feels he has for altering the world to suit his wishes' (Freud, 1930, p. 83). The individual's own psychical constitution, or character, will place a decisive role in how he goes about looking for happiness. Freud makes the interesting point that any choice of path that is pushed to an extreme will 'penalize the individual to the dangers which arise if a technique of living that has been chosen as an exclusive one should prove inadequate' (1930, p. 84). Thus one might say that a flexible or elastic technique for living is the least susceptible to constant disappointment.

Much of the rest of *Civilization and Its Discontents* examines the sources of suffering, in particular those caused by the demands of civilization on the individual, who must give up a certain amount of individual freedom for the sake of the wider community. Civilized man (*Kulturmensch*) has exchanged a portion of his possibilities of happiness for a portion of security (Freud, 1930, p. 105). The need for such a 'social contract' comes from the fact that man is inherently aggressive, and that this aggression needs to be inhibited if people are to live with one another in a reasonable fashion. Neurosis is the price we pay for having to curb our drives in the service of cultural ideals. While sexuality has to be curbed and hence its importance as a source of happiness reduced by the demands of civilization, as indeed Freud argued in his earlier work on civilized sexual morality, what he adds here is that sexuality itself, with its innate bisexuality and also the coexistence of aggression, adds to the sources of frustration and suffering. Our innate bisexuality means that we cannot generally satisfy both male and female wishes, and our innate aggression affects the quality of our love relationships, introducing, for example, sadistic elements.

But is also the quality of our object relationships that in itself creates dilemmas: in the process of civilization we internalize aggression. 'Civilization, therefore, obtains mastery over the individual's dangerous desire for aggression by weakening and disarming it and by setting up an agency within him [the super-ego] to watch over it, like a garrison in a conquered city' (Freud, 1930, pp. 123–4). The sense of guilt produced once the superego has formed is what Freud calls 'the most important problem in the development of civilization' (1930, p. 134). It is the price we pay for our advance in culture and is responsible for a loss of happiness.

One could add that much psychoanalytic treatment is focused on dealing with the effects of an overly harsh superego, both by tackling its effects within the transference and also its effects on external relationships, as I will illustrate later with my first clinical example. In this sense, psychoanalysis aims to reduce suffering by tackling one of its most consistent sources.

Freud ends his account by pointing out the dilemmas produced by the inevitable tensions between the needs of the individual and those of the community. There is a struggle between two urges within each of us – the one towards the individual's personal happiness, and the other towards union with other human beings (1930, p. 141). The aim of happiness remains but is pushed into the background. One may observe that this view is in contrast to that of Charles Darwin (see McMahon, 2006, pp. 410–24), who put greater emphasis on the survival value of group cohesion. For him, natural selection favoured altruism. The social instinct of animals was a precursor of the moral instinct in man; altruism, sympathy and affection are favoured by evolution for group survival. While each generation has to struggle for life and against the forces of destruction, there was a kind of 'survival of the happiest'. Thus, as he writes in *On the Origin of Species*,

> When we reflect on this struggle, we may console ourselves with the full belief, that the war of nature is not incessant, that no fear is felt, that generally death is prompt, and that the vigorous, the healthy and the happy survive and multiply.
>
> (1859, p. 129)

Freud, in contrast, tended to see the situation with humans as involving an elemental tension between the forces of destruction, deriving from the death drive, and the life-enhancing forces of Eros, the life drive. He left it open at the end of his book which drive would be predominant in the future.

These eleven ways described by Freud through which individuals strive to attain happiness and keep suffering at bay give us a rich and complex basis for examining the nature of human happiness, both in the clinical setting and in the wider social context.

One overall theme which arises from reading Freud when he tackles the theme of happiness is its elusiveness and precariousness; just when one may attain a happy state, something may come up to snatch it away. This is illustrated in Freud's open letter to Romain Rolland on the occasion of the latter's seventieth birthday (Freud, 1936, pp. 238–48). Freud describes a disturbance of memory while visiting the Acropolis with his younger brother, when a symptom replaces or displaces a potentially happy experience. Freud describes how the two of them managed to arrive in Athens after various delays and doubts, as well as a strange period of depression when faced by the real possibility of achieving their aim. When they finally arrive, Freud describes how when

I stood on the Acropolis and cast my eyes around upon the landscape, a surprising thought suddenly entered my mind: 'So all this really *does* exist, just as we learnt at school!' To describe the situation more accurately, the person who gave expression to this remark was divided, far more sharply than was usually noticeable, from another person who took cognizance of the remark.

(1936, p. 241)

Freud connects the earlier depression with the idea of incredulity on the Acropolis, when he was unable to feel the kind of happiness and delight he would have expected to experience on achieving a long-cherished ambition. He asks why such incredulity should arise in something which promises such a high degree of personal pleasure. The answer is complex and involves an internal conflict going back to the past, to earlier times when he had already doubted that he would ever see the Acropolis, and had even doubted the reality of the place itself. Furthermore, he became aware of a sense of guilt attached to the fact that he had achieved something never felt to be possible, that he had been able to see something which his father would never had achieved. Thus the potential experience of happiness was prevented in part by some sort of Oedipal conflict.

By implication, one might expect that tackling such conflicts may help to address issues concerned with the experiencing of happiness. The following clinical material from the case of a young man in analysis several years ago illustrates how addressing the experience of happiness may encapsulate complex issues from the past and present in an analysis around Oedipal and other issues.

This involves a dream from the patient, who was caught up in a difficult sadomasochistic relationship with his girl friend, and saw at first no way out of the dilemma. The dream seemed to represent a turning point in this man's life, in that it seemed to reveal some kind of solution to his dilemma. It was also a turning point in the analysis, which ultimately helped him leave the relationship. I had the chance to follow him up at a point seven years later, and he referred to this dream and the session as a pivotal moment.

The man, in his late twenties, had experienced two weeks of extreme fatigue coupled with anger and irritability, which left him on waking from the dream.

The latter took place on a wide and uncrowded beach. A man, who resembled his father, but with wild red eyes, was beating up a little girl. He then threw her into the sea. The dreamer swam with difficulty because there were large waves, but managed to rescue the child. He brought her back to the beach, where he cared for her and attended her injuries. Then the dreamer was making love beautifully to a nurse in a hospital.

The patient woke up feeling happy, with a sense of relief and as if a burden had been lifted. He noted that the dream began with extreme violence but ended on a hopeful note. This was a welcome contrast to the general feeling of persecution and perplexity which had dogged him for some time. He felt as if a veil of oppression had been lifted. The girl who was being beaten reminded him that a baby sister had died soon after birth and her death had preceded his own birth by a year or two – for the dream girl was beaten to a pulp and could not possibly have survived. Although his father had not been excessively violent toward him as a child, the patient was aware of considerable anger with his father, which he also experienced towards me on occasions. As a young child he was probably very confused about what had happened to his sister. His mother mentioned her death to him on the anniversary of the child's death, but did not reveal the details as this was too upsetting for her. As a child, the patient had had the fantasy that the father had in reality killed the baby.

The beach seemed to be a large and secure place in the dream, as it had been in his childhood. The family's brief holidays were the only time that it was united. In the dream, the father wore swimming trunks. The patient recalled that his father was proud of the fact that he had a muscular body, which he kept fit, and was obsessed by his physique. His father's explanation for this attitude was that as a child he had been bullied by his elder brother (who beat him to a pulp) who, unlike him, later became a great success. When the patient's father came of age, he spent hours building up his strength until the day when he had his revenge by beating up his brother. The patient thought that his father could not stand the competition with his brother for he certainly experienced similar feelings coming his way – the father displayed quite openly a childish rivalry with his son, his eldest child.

The dream seems to represent the patient's struggle with aggressiveness and with a sadistic or harsh superego, represented by the father figure. But despite the father's violence, there was a rescue. The patient had swum against the tide, in spite of a powerful undercurrent pulling him out to sea. The patient (a well-read person) was reminded in the session of Ibsen's play *Little Eyolf*, in which the child Eyolf was drowned, pulled under the sea by the strong undertow. Eyolf had been abandoned by his parents who had a loveless marriage, and when the patient thought of his parents' marriage, he could not recall them displaying genuine affection. He said that they had thrown away affection for one another, as the battered child had been thrown away and discarded like so much dross. The patient himself had replaced the dead sister. From the analysis, it seemed that his mother had attached much hope to him to save the marriage and make up for the death. These hopes and expectations made him furious, as if he had to carry an unnecessary burden. He felt that, overall, the dream represented his new wish not to have a dead or beaten child, so that he did not have to go round with a burden of death and hate on his shoulders. He began to see that he did not have to take his dead sister's place, nor did he have to pretend she did not exist and so fight for his mother's attention.

Finally, there seemed to be something perverse in the dream, in that the beating of the child represented a sadomasochistic element, linked to his then difficult relationship. But the dream ended with a symbolically good intercourse which was, like the rescue, evidence of reparation.

The dream seemed to be a 'nodal' point in this man's analysis, in that he was not the same after it. It brought him a sense of relief, as if a burden had been lifted, and was felt to be important. On the one hand it was, like many dreams, quite unexpected on the other hand, it was produced as a result of previous work. The patient had begun to throw off his neurotic ties to the past and his compliance with a false notion of himself as a damaged man capable only of turbulent relationships with women; that is, there was some basic shift in his object relationships.

Of course, the feeling of happiness went, and soon other more negative emotions returned to plague him and had to be confronted, particularly when he actually began to separate from his troubled girl friend, but the memory of the session and the accompanying feelings of happiness, with all their associations and links to his past, helped him emerge from his conflictual situation. There was some kind of significant change. Happiness here was something about recognizing the emergence of positive material at a *moment bienheureux*, where past and present conflicts came together, but not in some idealized version of possibilities. One can begin to see from this material the basis of a psychoanalytic notion of happiness.

Other thinkers

One may continue to explore this question by first of all by starting with the roots of the word happiness itself. *Happ* in Old Norse and in Middle English means 'chance' or 'fortune', and *gehaep* in Old English means 'fitting', 'convenient' or 'orderly'. These roots give us what happens, a fortunate encounter, giving us also words such as 'happenstance', 'haphazard' and 'perhaps'. The roots of the word thus lead us to link happiness with fortune. Indeed, 'happiness has deep roots in the soil of chance' (McMahon, 2006, p. 11). Other languages also reflect this conjunction. Thus in French *bonheur* comes from *bon*, 'good', and old French *heur*, 'fortune' or 'luck'; Italian, Spanish and Portuguese take their versions (*felicita*, *felicidad* and *felicidade*) from the Latin *Felix*, 'luck' or 'fate'. The German *Glück* is the word both for happiness and fortune. The Greek word *eudaimonia* comprises *eu*, 'well' or 'good', and *daimon*, 'god', 'spirit' or 'demon'. So happiness involves having a good *daimon* or a favourable occult power watching over us. Yet of course such happiness may well be reversed by fate or chance or a bad encounter, by trauma one might add. For the Greeks, what happens to a person by luck – *Tuche* – is what does not happen through their own agency. The realm of *tuche* is what just happens; it is the element of human existence not controlled by humans (Nussbaum, 1986, p. 89 ftn.), and what makes human life fragile and vulnerable. It is what Lacan called the potentially traumatic encounter with the real (1973b, p. 55).

Incidentally, Schopenhauer (1851, p. 333) points out that as the external sources of happiness are by their nature exceedingly uncertain, precarious, fleeting and subject to chance, and can thus easily come to an end, happiness belongs to those who are naturally cheerful. Thus, as Freud also emphasized (1930, pp. 76–7), our possibilities of happiness are restricted by our constitution. There are undoubtedly some people who are just more capable of being consistently and lastingly happy, who feel happy in their core being, maybe even despite difficult early experiences. These are resilient personalities. There are those who are happy in circumstances where others are unhappy, and vice versa, so that one may say that two people in the same external situation need not be equally happy or unhappy. Happiness and misery, then, would depend more upon some internal disposition.

For Aristotle, *eudaimonia* is not found through a life of short-term pleasure, but has to be seen in the context of a whole life. 'For one swallow does not make a summer, nor does one day; and so too one day, or a short time, does not make a man blessed and happy' (Aristotle, 1925, p. 14). Indeed, rather than happiness, *eudaimonia* may be better translated as human flourishing, living well, and would seem to refer to taking an active part in life, being an active 'subject', even if human life is subject 'to' various hazards. Happiness for Aristotle does remain a somewhat precarious state – luck or fate may intervene at any moment to spoil things.

While one may talk of being happy one day and not the next, *eudaimonia* has more to do with the 'shape of one's whole life' (B. Williams, 1985, p. 34). It is for this reason that Aristotle based his ethical inquiry on looking at the nature of well-being and a life worth living in order to see what living a good life means.

For Aristotle, to be a happy human being was about goodness; happiness is an activity of the *soul* expressing *virtue*. Virtue, or excellence, refers to a kind of good or harmonious ordering of the soul. I shall return to Aristotle and some more general points about happiness, but is worth nothing that one can see here links to certain psychoanalytic views about happiness, such as those of Helene Deutsch (1989), for whom feelings of happiness were to be connected with the whole personality, assuming the harmonious cooperation of all the components of the ego. This is to be contrasted with transient feelings of pleasure and unpleasure, or moods. There is thus here again some notion of a happy disposition, which involves the capacity to achieve harmonious functioning.

Jean Parat distinguishes between 'moments of happiness' which are limited in time from more lasting 'periods of happiness' (1974, p. 564). The former refer to certain transitory, fragile yet intense experiences which may have rich associations with memory and fantasy, such as that described by Freud on the Acropolis, or when one is before a certain work of art or a landscape. The latter refers more to those experiences of happiness linked to a specifically invested object relationship. The object has both an 'object value' and a 'narcissistic value' (1974, p. 572), that is one is dealing with a couple relationship between two subjects who can value one another to various degrees.

Parat also cites the early maternal bond as providing such periods of happiness, and here one should add Winnicott's primary maternal preoccupation as an example of a special state of being in which a woman is happily devoted to her infant through a process of identification (Winnicott, 1956). Such a state would be described as an illness were it not for the fact of the pregnancy, as it appears in some ways such an abnormal period of sustained and overwhelming happiness.

Edith Jacobson (1957) gives a very detailed account of the nature of moods. For her they seem to represent a cross-section through the entire structure of the ego, lending a particular, uniform colouring to its manifestations for a longer or shorter time. They do not relate to a specific object, and in this sense are similar to Parat's moments of happiness, though moods for her can also be relatively long lasting. Moods can be distinguished from affective states, which are attached to specific drives, with libidinous or aggressive investments, and particular objects. However, affective states can be transformed into moods. Thus anger with someone specific can turn into an unhappy mood.

Self Psychology places particular emphasis on the need of the self for sustaining experiences, or 'selfobject experiences', which are necessary for the emergence, maintenance and completion of the self (Wolf, 1988, p. 14). That is, a person needs something from the environment around him or her, a positive response of particular kind in order to experience well-being or, one might add, sustained happiness. One can add the importance of a positive self and body image to the capacity to feel happy.

Attachment studies (Schore, 2003) emphasize the role of caregivers in facilitating the well-being of the child. A securely attached child has a mental representation of the caregiver as responsive in times of trouble. Such children feel confident and happy, are capable of empathy and of forming good attachments. Insecure attachments develop when the infants do not have a mental representation of a responsive caregiver in times of need, such as when they feel fearful or helpless, and they have to develop various abnormal strategies in order to elicit care. Deprived of good enough caretaking, such children have an impaired sense of their own emotional states, and their emotional regulation becomes distorted. The loss of the ability to regulate the intensity of their emotions may be the most far-reaching effect of early trauma and neglect.

Erich Fromm considered that happiness and unhappiness were more than states of mind and also were not to be confused with short periods of pleasure; instead, they were expressions of the whole organism, the total personality. 'Happiness is conjunctive with an increase of vitality, intensity of feeling and thinking, and productiveness; unhappiness is conjunctive with the decrease of these capacities and functions. Happiness and unhappiness are so much a state of our total personality that bodily reactions are frequently more expressive of them than our conscious feeling' (1949, pp. 181–2).

Helene Silberman, rather like Deutsch, links periods of sustained happiness to harmonious ego functioning. These are limited moments when various specific conditions come together:

> When such feelings of happiness overwhelm us, we find ourselves close to the recapture of narcissistic bliss of early childhood, now combined with the

wisdom of maturity. The ego shows maximum plasticity and mobility, swinging freely between past and present and fearlessly looking into the future. There is a deep sense of mastery, of achievement with minimal tension and maximal contentment and heightened pleasure – pleasure of an unusual illuminating quality . . . These feelings of happiness, although very personal and subjective, are not self-centred or constricted in narrow ego boundaries, but expansive, beyond one's transitional spheres.

(1985, p. 466)

Central to any psychoanalytic consideration of the nature of happiness must surely be the *developmental* perspective, the notion that how one experiences happiness may be different at different stages of life. There is thus clearly a difference between a baby's experience of happiness, and how one thinks about what this may mean, and the happiness experienced by a mature adult. One might indeed ask what it means for a baby to be happy, rather than, say, contented, satiated or at peace. However, it would seem reasonable to assume that the basis for subsequent potential happiness is at least laid down in the early years. All kinds of patterns in the way that happiness is expressed may occur. For example, if there are unhappy or depressed parents, then the baby may grow into a child who may feel they have to cheer up their parents, or be sort of an antidepressant for them. This would be a kind of neurotic 'false' happiness, perhaps related to a more severe form of false happiness as seen in mania, with the denial of depression. Older children can be seen to be more clearly happy or unhappy, depending upon their family and life experiences. Developmental achievements in children can produce intense moments of happiness. Adolescents are, of course, famously plagued by mood swings, alternating between happy and despairing states. It is only with early adulthood that one can see a more stable integration of moods and emotional states. Attitudes towards happiness vary enormously in middle and old age. There are those who approach ageing more serenely, seizing each moment as precious, and others who curse the onset of age and the approach of death, thus increasing their misery.

Putting a number of these contributions together, one could see more lasting periods of happiness as concerned with *moments of integration*, when various elements of the soul come together in some kind of harmonious way, or where the soul feels more at home. This can be seen to some extent in the next clinical example, which concerns a man in his forties nearing the end of a long analysis.

He had come into analysis because of a sense of emptiness and futility in personal and work relationships, as well as periods of depression. He had a traumatic early history, in that his ill manic-depressive mother was subject to repeated hospital admissions for quite florid, manic behaviour, followed by deep and disabling depressions. His father, a more stable but somewhat emotionally distant figure, spent periods away from the family home on various kinds of business. My patient, in fact, found some stability in attending a male boarding school, together with his younger brother to whom he was not that close; he learned there to hide his emotions and also to turn to academic achievement as a way of finding some self-regard. Despite these early difficulties he had managed to marry and have a successful career, but was always haunted by the ill mother.

The period of ending the analysis was, not surprisingly, emotionally difficult, yet also productive, as can be seen in this excerpt from a session a few months before the end.

He was worried about how he got entangled in relationships, muddled up and confused. He described some situations at work when he felt he was being drawn into behaving like a rival for his mother's attention, and linked this to his feelings about his younger brother, whom he felt was favoured by his mother. His mother had, in fact, had her first major breakdown after my patient's birth, and the theme of feeling responsible for her madness had been a major element of the analysis.

My patient then said that what he had gotten from the analysis was a way of fighting through all these problems without losing the thread any more. But he was fearful about how he was going to do this without coming to see me. I linked this fear to one we had frequently talked about before, about how to separate from a mad mother. He replied by suddenly remembering a fragment of a dream. This was that he had pain in the soles of his feet.

He said that this was a bit weird, and wondered what it meant. Something about pain, he added. I replied that maybe it was something about another kind of 'soul', and about a painful soul, and how he was going to deal with that kind of pain.

This led to him thinking about how he dealt with emotional pain, tending in the past to distance himself, although now he was more able to face conflicts, as he had described at his work. He said he needed to find a space to feel pain 'without disintegration and madness'. He was thinking about the next phase of his life. He mentioned a book he was reading about William Wordsworth and his sister, Dorothy, who were 'fused' with one another. That led onto more thoughts about him and his mother, what he had had to deal with, with her bizarre behaviour, how he had to defend himself against her intrusion, and also his fear of being 'fused' with her. However, he did feel that he could lead a life of his own. He could now feel he could be happy with his family, but he was also afraid of how the ending of the therapy was going to be, what kind of life he was going to live. He ended the session by wondering what the next phase of his life was going to be like.

While of course there was considerably more work to be done around the ending of the analysis, the patient was much more able to deal with conflicting emotions. As he put it, he now had a way of fighting through his problems without losing the thread, or one might say without being taken over by his mother's madness. As so often the case with such patients, one of the main tasks of the analysis is to sort out how much a patient is muddled up with the parent's madness, which becomes an alien presence, as it were. This work concerns separating the patient's own disturbance from that of their parent's disturbance, or of trying to diminish the unhappiness that gets passed down the generations. The patient was able to have more lasting periods of happiness with his family because, as he put it, he had begun to find a space to experience emotional pain; his dream was indicating that his soul could bear the pain.

Thus one can see that a psychoanalytic concept of happiness includes moments when there is an ability to experience happiness but linked to an ability to tolerate psychic pain; these would be genuine moments of integration, where the soul feels more at home. Here also, one reaches a psychoanalytic notion of mental health, which does not necessarily equate with freedom from symptoms. As Heinz Hartmann pointed out, it is 'often a difficult matter to decide whether the pedantry or ambition of an individual or the nature of his object choice are symptoms in a neurotic sense or character traits possessing a positive value for health' (1964, p. 5).

Health as understood by psychoanalysis consists of more than merely loss of symptoms, especially as it may be difficult to decide whether a given mental manifestation is in the nature of a symptom, or whether it is an achievement. For Hartmann, a healthy person in a psychoanalytic sense must have the capacity to suffer and to be depressed (1964, p. 6). Indeed, it would be unhealthy to be unable to admit to oneself the possibility of illness and suffering.

Winnicott (1986, pp. 71–9) also had the view that depression has value, even though depressed people suffer and may kill themselves. Depression as a normal phenomenon relates to mourning, to the capacity to feel guilt, and so to the maturational processes. Indeed, a person may come out of a depression stronger, wiser and more humble than before – provided, of course, that the depression has not been overwhelmingly damaging. As Winnicott emphasized, depression has within it the germ of recovery; it can be progress for a patient to experience depression rather than deny it, or project it. Clearly, this view is also linked to Klein's notion of the pivotal role of the depressive position in achieving whole-object relationships (Klein, 1952).

Jonathan Lear discusses the nature of happiness from both a psychoanalytical and a philosophical perspective, basing his argument on a close reading of Aristotle's *Ethics*, which provides a source of many essential arguments about the nature of happiness. Lear points out that happiness in Aristotle is 'systematically inconstant. People use it to designate what they don't yet have, what they are longing for, that which they have just lost and would like again. People tend to fantasize that if they just had this missing thing, it would make them happy. Thus, as Aristotle points out, the sick man longs for health and thinks that if only he can be healthy again he would be happy. In his sickness, he is oblivious to the thought that it would be a sign of his regaining health that he turns his attention to something else that is missing and begins to fantasize that it would give him happiness' (2000, p. 23).

Lear suggests that happiness for Aristotle is a perfect transference concept, a blank which holds a place for that which would satisfy our deepest longings, whatever they happen to be (2000, p. 24).

Lear offers a psychoanalytic interpretation of Aristotle's ethical enterprise by revealing underlying disruptive and disturbing elements in Aristotle's *Ethics*. He shows that Aristotle points out that most people are not and never will be happy; that happiness, as in Freud's *Civilization and Its Discontents*, is by and large an elusive condition, and that though happiness is human flourishing, it largely eludes people. Aristotle offers an ideal of the happy, contemplative life of the philosopher as a model for the few who are able to achieve it, yet this remains something of a ploy to eliminate the fundamental impossibility of achieving happiness, the basic 'discontent' at the heart of the attempt to find happiness. Yet despite these paradoxes, Aristotle's virtues as a thinker are great; his was a serious attempt to ground ethical life in a realistic understanding of human psychology, and he affirmed that ethical life cannot be based on a rule book.

Despite the kind of paradoxes revealed in Lear's account, happiness would appear to be a candidate for giving our lives some structure and justification, but the problem is that people disagree about what counts as happiness. Just considering personal happiness, the well-being of the individual, immediately leads one to think of the happiness of the other. After all, it is generally agreed that being on one's own – except for those few who strive for the solitary life – is not a happy experience, as Freud pointed out in his list of the ways of avoiding suffering. The solitary contemplative life of the philosopher does not seem all that convincing as an ideal of a happy man. On the contrary, being happy has something to do with being with others in a particular way. It is through certain kinds of relationship that one can begin to be happy, or at least to register one is happy, and in particular through the transference relationship that one can try to work this issue out in analysis. In this sense, analysis remains an essentially ethical activity, concerned with the quality of relationships, their impact on the other.

If being happy involves a certain kind of *connectedness*, one is then immediately faced by the issue of having to take the other's happiness into account when considering one's own happiness. If otherness comes in here, then so does concern for the other, and hence one is already dealing with ethical and moral issues, for example, how cruelty can undermine well-being.

This is also a field where one cannot avoid tackling difficult moral dilemmas. For example, one could ask if a Nazi could be happy at home while being cruel at work. As Robert Jay Lifton (1986) described in his masterly account of Nazi doctors, these men showed that this was indeed possible. He illustrates how through a process of 'doubling' the doctors were able to divide their selves into two functioning wholes, which did not necessarily connect. The kind paterfamilias could become the unfeeling sadist. This is different from splitting, where a part of the self is unavailable. These men made a sort of Faustian bargain, receiving benefits in exchange for their being caught up in the killing machine. Lifton shows how doubling enables an ordinary or even generally decent person to become actively involved in a murderous project. Thus, one can see that it is possible to pursue personal happiness through evil means. But is this then a kind of *negative* happiness, one which we would not really recognize as essentially human or humane? The latter, more *positive* kind of happiness must surely extend into the content of the person's thoughts and include their decent behaviour. Thus, already one is involved with complex human dilemmas such as the relationship between happiness and human good.

In general, the issue of happiness is of great concern to psychoanalysts, for people come to us suffering from all kinds of human distress and misery, and rightly expect us to help them with this distress. But as Lacan (1973) has pointed out, the analytic situation with regard to the demand for happiness and the relief of suffering is complex. The analyst offers a place of refuge, in which the patient hopes to be freed not only from his ignorance but also from his suffering. In this sense, happiness appears to be offered as a goal of our striving. But it would be wrong to imagine that happiness as such is actually offered or guaranteed, or that psychoanalysis can easily contribute directly to human happiness. Indeed, as Lacan put it,

> To make oneself the guarantor of the possibility that a subject will in some way be able to find happiness even in analysis is a form of fraud.
>
> (Lacan, 1973, p. 303)

That is, the demand for happiness is something to be analysed rather than gratified. As Lacan pointed out, Oedipus was happy to be married to Jocasta, but 'he doesn't know that in achieving happiness, both conjugal happiness and that of his job as king, of being the guide to the happiness of the state, he is sleeping with his mother . . . In fact, he has been duped, tricked by reason of the fact that he achieved happiness . . . [H]e enters the zone in which he pursues his desire' (1973, p. 304).

Desires disrupt the possibility for achieving lasting happiness. Yet the term *happiness*, as can be seen here, can be used to signify what can satisfy our deepest longings, even if, as with Lear's account, it eludes us. In this sense, the word 'happiness' itself can represent the unattainable. Furthermore, the possibility of masochism points to the fact that we can be happy being unhappy; we can desire suffering. In psychoanalysis we can also see by means of the transference relationship how often the deprived patient bites the hand that feeds, or else how any possibility of happiness can be undermined by powerful and destructive forces within the soul, or how an unrealistic desire for happiness can cause misery – that is, one may see how a search for happiness can cause suffering as much as suffering can be a constraint on happiness. I have argued that a capacity for experiencing some kind of happiness, however briefly, depends upon a capacity to suffer, to experience painful feelings. But there must be a point where that pain becomes so overwhelming that one is pushed into the territory of sheer misery.

It is through articulating the complex place of desires in the human condition that Lacan places the role of ethics in psychoanalysis, giving psychoanalysis its basic ethical position. 'Know your desire' is the kind of ethical aim, if there is one, in psychoanalysis rather than 'make me happy'. Put another way, the demand for happiness may arise from the superego, and so be full of guilt or else primitive and remorseless demands for satisfaction. Lacan distinguishes this from the truly ethical dimension of psychoanalysis, which can be captured in Freud's phrase, 'Wo es war, soll Ich werden'. In Strachey's version, this is translated as, 'Where id was, there ego shall be' (Freud, 1933, p. 80). Lacan emphasizes instead a more subtle meaning in the phrase, one which means something like 'So there where "it" was, "I" shall become, or shall come into being' (Lacan, 1973b, p. 44). That is, if there is an authentic analytic imperative, it is to talk, to face one's truth, to become whatever one is. This is not to be confused with the morality of the superego, with its restless and ruthless demands for happiness or misery. Perhaps one could say that one of the main aims of psychoanalysis is to help the patient disentangle the ethical imperative, or the ethics of truth, from moral or moralistic demands.

I have argued that happiness is not merely a passing mood but involves some-thing more lasting, or what the ancient Greeks in particular would see as referring to something about the refined craftsmanship of living, and involving issues of character and its link with virtue or excellence, and the quality of the soul. There is a need to add the developmental perspective, the way that time influences the way one deals with the issue of happiness. If there is an enduring state of hap-piness, how is this to be sustained? Is there only what one could call 'negative' happiness, that is, freedom from misery, pain and suffering? Or is there some kind of 'positive' happiness, a definite vision of what it is to be happy? If there is some positive vision of happiness, how is it related to religious happiness and ecstasy, what William James (1902, p. 48) defined as the most absolute and everlasting form of happiness?

But let me give an example, just for argument's sake, of what might well be clearly a happy experience, at least if all goes well, and that is of course the point – the joyful experience of the birth of a baby. Surely here we have a good example of personal happiness, what one could truly call 'deep' happiness (see Foot, 2001). Depth is a difficult concept to define in this context. The dictionary definition includes intensity of a feeling, its moral quality or state, and something about layers, going from a surface to a depth.

There is a complex mixture of anxiety, pleasure, risk, expectation and, finally, bliss when the baby is successfully born, which is the ultimately integrative moment, where the couple's endeavours have a clear and favourable outcome, the arrival of a new soul. In this sense the experience has many layers, and includes very intense feelings. The experience has intense meaning for the parents, even if it may well include all sorts of anxious and negative feelings. The risk of disas-ter only adds to the quality of happiness if the birth is successful. The parents' primary preoccupation with the child focuses their attention on the needs of the baby, which may well have biological, or evolutionary, roots. There is probably an evolutionary advantage in having happy parents who can focus on the care of the baby and are happy with the positive outcome. Perhaps this is a major source of altruism, which would favour family, and indeed social, cohesion.

The depth of the happiness at a successful birth can, of course, be ruined by the depth of grief over the loss of a child. It is difficult to define what we mean by the depth of happy or miserable experiences, but maybe it has something to do with the quality and meaning of the relationships surrounding the experiences, experiences which often involve the most basic human situations, life, birth, death, family and work. Depth here would seem to involve what one could call caring and passionate attachments, attachments about people for whom we care, whom we would deeply miss if they were not there, whom we value as separate yet connected people, whom we see as 'subjects' with a life of their own. Sexual fulfilment would also seem to have a place here, in so far as it is involved in a passionate attachment. It is a commonplace that sexual fulfilment without such an attachment leads to emptiness. Thus sexual enjoyment as such is not a lasting cause of happiness, however pleasurable in the moment.

All these considerations make it clear, I think, that happiness is not merely an inner state, but requires *otherness* for its achievement or expression. Such otherness involves having caring responses, which necessarily involve the risks of loss and unhappiness, splendor and misery.

But one may ask if there is a place for *aesthetic* experience, such as enjoyment of works of art or music, in achieving human happiness, when these experiences often do not directly involve a personal relationship. It was the great pessimist Schopenhauer who considered that we could find at least some temporary respite from the remorseless world of pain and unhappiness through contemplating great works of art. Before a great painting, or while listening to great music or while being within a great building one could find release from the storms of passion and the pressures of desire, or of the will. Freud also emphasized that we cannot do without such experiences. Indeed, a life deprived of artistic and musical experiences would be unhappy and unfulfilled. We need such experiences to feel complete. They not only take us out of ourselves, they help us to connect up with what is authentic. But they do this in a complex way, involving the joining up of different or conflicting elements. One way to understand this is through the representation of both positive and negative themes. James discusses this in the context of his descriptions of the variety of religious experience. He shows how an identification of religion with every form of happiness leaves out the essential peculiarities of religious happiness. In its most characteristic embodiments, James maintains that religious happiness is no mere feeling of escape. Genuine religious experience confronts the negative, whether it is in death, the devil or annihilation. He tries to illustrate this with an example from art:

> In the Louvre there is a picture, by Guido Reni, of St. Michael with his foot on Satan's neck. The richness of the picture is in large part due to the fiend's figure being there. The richness of allegorical meaning also is due to his being

there – that is, the world is all the richer for having a devil in it, *as long as we keep our foot upon his neck.* In the religious consciousness, that is just the position in which the fiend, the negative or tragic principle, is found; and for that reason the religious consciousness is so rich from an emotional point of view.

(1902, pp. 49–50)

That is, one can see the importance of keeping our foot on the devil, not allowing the negative to dominate, but accepting it has a place, indeed that it gives depth to our responses, and that happiness without its negative would be superficial and indeed illusory.

This makes a deep happy experience not merely a recreation of some childhood fantasy, as Freud originally proposed, such as the fantasy of a return to a situation of early maternal care, which has in it the notion of a perfect kind of unity of mother and baby, a blissfulness oneness. In the adult such wished-for happiness is more often than not associated with perverse gratification, enjoyment which excludes otherness.

Finally, there is the issue of how *creativity* and happiness may be related. As Winnicott (1971, pp. 65–85) emphasized, living creatively seems to be about living a worthwhile life, feeling enriched and not doubting life's possibilities. Klein (1952) emphasized reparation and restitution following the recognition of destructive impulses. It would certainly seem to be the case that there is often a fine line between creativity and destructiveness in producing works of art or science. In this sense, it is probably accurate to say that such creative achievements involve mixtures of happiness and misery; there may be joy in having a finished product, but considerable pain along the way that has to be surmounted.

* * *

In conclusion, one can now say that it would seem clear that happiness is not merely a mood, though a cheerful mood may be a component of a happy disposition. It is easier to define happiness 'negatively' as freedom from excessive suffering than it is to get hold of a 'positive' view of happiness. Happiness is an elusive concept; it can become an ideal for which we strive, and that very striving may cause us untold disappointment and loss. Such striving may even be hardwired into our brains. But if one were pushed to put forward a *positive* view, it would include techniques of living, or ways of life, that include lasting and passionate attachments, interspersed with various kinds of relatively brief but satisfying aesthetic experiences. The intensity of such experiences can make up for their brevity. Deep happiness also includes the risk of suffering. Too much suffering can lead to prolonged misery, but a certain amount of suffering can give 'shape' to happiness. Psychoanalytic treatment cannot promise happiness, but may enable the patient to be relieved of excessive misery. The excessive demands of the superego will need to be tackled, but what the patient then does with a freer psychic life is up them.

Happiness, then, consists of something more than just pleasurable experiences; as can be seen at crucial life events such as at the birth of a baby, it includes authentic attachments, the shape of a whole life, and is a kind of mixed state, which includes a certain amount of suffering. The expression of happiness may vary at different stages of the life cycle.

One could also say that happiness involves some lasting capacity to experience happy states, even if they may come and go; these states can emerge when past and present converge, and involve moments of integration of the soul, when the soul feels more at home, when psychic pain is more able to be tolerated. In addition, being happy is not just feeling good but involves caring responses in relation to others.

While an inquiry such as this may not be exhausting, and may fail to completely capture the nature of happiness, there is some consolation in the fact that, though, as Freud put it (1930, p. 76), it may not have been the intention of creation to make us happy; we are generally not always unhappy, and are even, at certain key moments in our life, particularly happy.

Chapter 8

Summary

I have proposed that when we talk about a person's soul, we are touching on something elemental, their essence, something irreducible, what makes them human, their sense of being a subject of experience, their unique *voice*, what goes deep within the person, much, of course, unconsciously. I have argued that to do without the notion of a soul, even if at the very least it is kept as a metaphorical expression for being alive, would be to lose too much that is precious about being human. Without something like souls, what are we? According to Wittgenstein, we could be automata; but he wonders, how do we then feel pain? (Wittgenstein, 1992) For those of us who deal with the extremes of human mental suffering, it is difficult to understand how people split off areas of their experience, can maintain often very strange states of mind or can behave in what appears to be completely against their best interests, unless one looks for explanations beyond physical events in the brain.

I have also explored how having a home implies both having a physical entity, the physical structure of the dwelling, the house, but also something that goes beyond the building blocks into the area of the interior of the soul. Having an idea of a psychic home, or 'soul home', is just as vital for a person as having a physical shelter; it is one of the most basic human needs. We need to feel at home in the world: it makes us feel secure, it provides the base from which we can explore. The loss of a sense of home is deeply traumatic, as is, of course, the loss of a house. Yet we need to leave home in order to find ourselves, in order to mature and have a firm sense of identity.

This sense of home as the ground of our being, the place we need in order to feel secure, is fundamental. Yet we often feel to a greater or lesser extent incomplete, divided and lacking a sense of the whole. There is a yearning for wholeness, for a home where we can feel truly ourselves, but this can also cause us considerable unhappiness, as I explored in the last chapter. Some carry a firm sense of home within, others need something external, yet others need a being that transcends daily life such as a God in order to feel complete. Whatever the nature of the home we seek, the fear of homelessness is never far from that of the sense of being at home.

I discussed how the word 'home' is a world for the poet Burnside and is both suffused by the commonplace, the world of everyday, yet also determined by the 'spirit', which the participants bring together to make a home. It provides a place in which to dwell and yet is fraught with hazards. Burnside points out that unless one takes account of the hazards, one may lose oneself or be wrecked; home, then, can become a catalogue of wrecks. Hence the need to retain a certain flexibility; home may provide a settlement for the spirit, or the soul, but also be too comfortable, too settled or cause you to risk losing what you are searching for.

In Chapter Three, I discussed, with illustrations, one of the most persistent themes in William Wordsworth's poetry, particularly in his early work and during the years he wrote his greatest poetry (between about 1795 and 1805) – that of home. He writes of yearnings for home, loss of home, intense homecomings, homes that are ruined and may become a shelter for the homeless, characters who have lost homes or who are homeless. Coincidentally, his life began to change significantly when, in 1794, he and his sister, Dorothy, set up home together for a few weeks, sealing their coming together after years apart, with her having led a life of drudgery in other peoples' homes, and he having led an itinerant life in England and France. It was not long before they were living in a permanent home, eventually settling back into the Lake District, their childhood home, where Wordsworth wrote his most intense poetry, including *Tintern Abbey* and the early versions of *The Prelude*.

I used Wordsworth's finding of a secure home after his years of wandering to illustrate the concept of a psychic home.

I have proposed that the notion of a psychic home consists of a number of different and interacting elements, including the physical interior of a home but internalized as a psychic interior. The notion of 'personal identity' refers to the development and then maintenance of a person's character, how they put together in some way their various multiple identifications, as well as including wider issues concerning a person's cultural and social influences. I suggest that the basic elements of the psychic home can be seen to provide a way of organizing the person's identity, or can be seen as intrinsic to any notion of identity, a theme developed in more detail in Chapter Four on identity.

Identity is a term used in many different ways and by a variety of disciplines. It has become a central issue of concern in contemporary debates about politics, ethics and culture. Issues of identity also touch upon the soul territory, that of each person's unique sense of who they are. Appiah even goes as far as to call 'soul making' the 'project of intervening in the process of interpretation through which each citizen develops an identity' (2005, p. 164).

Identity is a vitally important but complex and at times elusive or indeterminate concept. There are various fixed or constant elements in the development of our identity, which can become the source of integration and of a sense of permanence, of achievement and coherence, whether that be as a person and/or as a psychoanalyst; and there are still issues about the nature of identity that challenge our thinking, such as its link with the processes of identification, the question of whether or not unity is an illusion or a real possibility. De M'Uzan has suggested that one can talk of a 'spectrum of identity' (2005, p. 18), that the sense of I-ness is neither in the ego nor the other, but distributed along both, which matches my own picture of the human subject as being organized between the individual and the network of others.

I have proposed that one of the constant elements is that of the psychic home and that this provides a basis for a sense of identity, for crucial questions such as 'Who am I?' 'Who do I look and act like?' 'Which religion and nationality am I?' They indicate a search for a place in life, an identity which provides a relatively stable sense of home, and that provides the core of the elusive and precarious notion of identity, whatever its complex vicissitudes, however much the human subject is distributed between other subjects.

I have discussed that there are different ways that identifications may come together, or fail to come together, and that will make for different character structures, and different issues for the human subject's own sense of identity, including their sexual identity. That is, there are all kinds of ways that identifications can sit around in the soul, lodge there, feel alien or feel more settled and at home; various ways that the identifications can be bound together in some kind of containing membrane; various ways that the identifications, within and between subjects, interact. For this reason, identity can be fluid, stable or unstable, open to change or resistant to change, depending upon the way that the identifications are organized.

I concluded that what has came out of considering the various psychoanalytic and other contributions to identity is how identity as an issue is complex and potentially precarious, involving steering a path between different polarities, different sources of identification, but that in addition, charting a course along this difficult path requires holding a creative tension between possible positions, not holding fast to just one single way. However, feeling at home with a flexible notion of identity does not appeal to everyone. People vary as to how much the psychic home remains for them the only true home, and how much they need to pull away from it.

What contemporary accounts of identity in other disciplines repeatedly focus on is the notion of identity as plural, multiple, merging one with another, rather than, as it were, facing each other from separate corners. In addition, though identity involves individuals, their identity is formed under multiple influences. Identities involve having a position within our society and in relation to a history, a lineage. Certain markers of identity may be visible or can appear through inquiry – whether that is from a country of origin, race, religion or ideological standpoint.

One can see an identity as involving the taking up of a particular position, depending upon different social roles or different histories. But taking up a position requires a starting point, or a frame of reference or at least some scaffolding. This is where I have suggested that the notion of a psychic home comes in, as the starting point for the complex and indeed lifelong task of forming an identity, whether as a psychoanalyst or outside one's professional life.

In reconsidering the soul concept in Chapter Five, I suggested that the word 'soul' seems to be both abstract and yet also powerfully emotive. It can be approached from a number of different angles, from philosophy, religion, sociology, literature and neuroscience. No one discipline has the monopoly on understanding the soul concept, hence the need for a multidisciplinary approach to the soul territory. This applies to psychoanalysis as much as other disciplines. In trying to describe and define such an elusive and complex issue as the human soul, too much focus on metapsychology can divert us from reaching the heart of the issue.

While not undertaking an encyclopaedic history of the soul concept, I did emphasize three crucial 'moments' in the history of the soul: (1) Plato's foundational picture of the soul in his metaphor of the cave, in addition to his tripartite division of the soul linking up the soul with both the pursuit of knowledge and an ethical pursuit of the good; (2) the place of the soul in Hellenistic and then Christian thought and its linking with spiritual transformation, or *transformation of the soul*; and (3) the gradual disconnection of the soul from spiritual transformation with the scientific revolution, the development of a mercantile culture and the thought of Descartes. The latter, what Foucault called for convenience the '*Cartesian moment*' (2001, p. 68) has had profound effects on how we picture the soul. Until that point, philosophy and spiritual transformation, knowledge and human value, tended to be linked. From then on, there develops a radical *split* between knowledge and spiritual transformation, between the world of the spirit and the material world, a split which I have suggested needs some sort of attention in our overly materialist society.

I discussed how, taking our cue from Plato, one can say that the soul is the image of convergence; it is what coheres, it is our name for *what makes for the sense of inner unity*, the 'form' of convergence, to borrow from Aristotle, even though we do not understand how this occurs, even though we still do not understand the link between the inner unity and the brain processes occurring simultaneously or in parallel. We are aware of this sense of unity from time to time, particularly when we feel at home in our body and our selves, when the sense of who we are 'takes residence' and gives us a firmer sense of identity; for this reason, one might talk of a human being providing a home for the soul. But the sense of unity is an elusive experience, difficult to tie down, capable of fleeing from us. It is in part linked to the unified stream of consciousness, but at least since Freud we know that consciousness is only a fraction of the soul's activity and indeed of the brain's activities. Traditionally, one could sense this inner unity when looking into a man's eyes, the eyes being the 'mirror' of the soul. I suggested in the opening chapter that, from the experience of death, what is essentially human, the link with others, as revealed by the nature of the fading gaze, dies with the body. I suggested there that from a psychological point of view, we call *that which links with others* the human soul. The live gaze, that which reflects back to the other, reveals the essence of a man, their character, their depth, their value, the 'weight' of their soul, to use a rather medieval image.

In considering the so-called hard problem about how one leaps from nerve impulses to human emotions, I argued that there are various ways of dealing with this dilemma. One may come down on one side of the divide, the mental or the physical, proposing either an idealist or a materialist solution; or accept a dualist position, where both the mental and physical are relevant in different ways; or propose a solution where some merger of the mental and physical is posited, some synthesis of both; or propose a solution that we are made of one kind of material, but that we perceive this in two different ways, appearing material from the outside but mental from the inside; or propose a solution common to religious thought where there exists another entity, such as the immortal soul, which is independent of physical properties; or advance yet another way of thinking which does not close off any solution, but which *holds the tension* between different proposals without making a final decision. I personally favour the latter approach in a field where there is so much that is still puzzling. If we still cannot even bridge the gap between the nerve impulse and the feeling, how on earth can we be too dogmatic about the nature of mental events? And, in the end, all these considerations only give us a partial view of the human world, which has more to do with the meaning and value of human stories. In the meantime, we need to turn to a variety of disciplines if we are to find some clarity in this complex field.

I discussed how one can see why understanding complexity, emergence and networks may well add to our understanding of brain processes, possibly even psychological self-organization. We do not know how the brain is organized to function as a whole, though we know it appears to do this quite well, in fact remarkably well, mostly at an unconscious level. The many individual elements just do work, both together and in parallel, making sensation, movement and so on run smoothly. One could see that consciousness might just be the emergent property of networks of neurones firing, until a tipping point is reached and a person has a conscious experience. It sounds like an interesting idea, though as yet there is no evidence that consciousness works like this. Indeed, it is still possible that the firing of neurones and having a conscious experience are different and incommensurable phenomena.

In Plato's metaphor of the cave, the prisoners remain shackled and cut off from the light, but they are at least huddled together so as to mitigate their loneliness. Once one of them is freed from their shackles and reaches the bright light of true being, they are transformed into a new state, no longer cut off from the light, and in touch with a higher region; their souls have reached a higher stage of development, reminiscent of the religious grades of the soul's upward ascent. I suggested that this latter state is less like loneliness and more like solitude; the move from one state to the other was a main theme of Chapter Six.

There is a difference between loneliness and solitude, though with some overlap. Loneliness is about being cut off from others, even in their presence. In solitude, one often requires being alone, yet I am by myself with myself in some kind of *internal dialogue*, very much part of the soul territory. Since loneliness and solitude are so much a part of the psychoanalyst's work, I used the psychoanalytic experience to explore the loneliness–solitude dimension. In addition, I used Freud's fort/da observation to explore different aspects of the way that the child deals with maternal absence.

I suggested that there is always a tension, or strain, between the mother as mere physical object and the mother as an elusive human presence, capable of appearing and disappearing when she wants to, or needs to, whether it is to go to the father or elsewhere, the mother who stirs up the child's yearnings and desires. In the fort/da one can see the working out of the difference between mother as material object and the mother as elusive human presence; out of this difference one can see human subjectivity, with all its dilemmas and possibilities, beginning to emerge. The task of the developing child, as well as that of the analytic patient, is, in a sense, to come to the realization that the mother is not a mere physical object, or at least not an object under the child's omnipotent control, but a subject with a mysterious life of her own, relating to other subjects, the father and others. The dawning of this realization is never easy; there is always a certain amount of strain involved in the process of coming to terms with the mother's elusiveness, more so when the mother's absence is prolonged, or her return highly problematic. Prolonged absences may result in a deep sense of loneliness. The symbolization of absence makes solitude bearable; merely feeling absence, without the capacity to symbolize it, plunges the subject into loneliness.

Storr (1988, p. 174), in his book on solitude, also discusses late Beethoven as an exemplar of the late or third period in an artist's development. The last quartets, for example, are less concerned with communication, are unconventional in form, display an absence of rhetoric and explore remote areas of experience. Such work is expressive of deep inward experience, very much the theme of last works.

One may suppose that as a result of the artist achieving a point in their life where their identity is firm enough to be able to face their own dissolution, these last works convey in their form and expression what is unattainable; that human happiness, while achievable in brief moments, cannot last, though the yearning for it may persist. Faced by approaching death, the artist, or indeed analyst, becomes ever aware that happiness and integration are transient, loneliness in some form inevitable.

This then led onto considering more specifically the complex issue of human happiness in Chapter Seven. Happiness is an elusive concept. It may be easier to define 'negative' happiness as an absence of suffering. It can become an ideal for which we strive, and that very striving may cause us untold disappointment and loss. Such striving may even hardwired into our brains. But if one were pushed to put forward a *positive* view, it would include techniques of living, or ways of life, that include lasting and passionate attachments, interspersed with various kinds of relatively brief but satisfying aesthetic experiences. The intensity of such experiences can make up for their brevity. Deep happiness also includes the risk of suffering. Too much suffering can lead to prolonged misery, but a certain amount of suffering can give 'shape' to happiness, and seems to reach into the depths of the human soul. Psychoanalytic treatment cannot promise happiness, but may enable the patient to be relieved of excessive misery. The excessive demands of the superego will need to be tackled, but what the patient then does with a freer psychic life is up to them.

I have described at various points in the text the experience of contemplating a Rembrandt self-portrait in order to grasp the essence of the human soul trying to communicate to another soul. I have described how Rembrandt's eyes seem to take you into the picture, into the depths. Unlike a mirror, which reflects your own image back to you, the Rembrandt urges you to reflect into yourself in the act of being drawn into his image. Repeated visits are like drawing from some primal source of light and intensity, leaving you changed in some way, both uplifted and more melancholy. Repeated visits do not exhaust the depths of the experience; in this sense, the portrait is always 'more' than it appears. Perhaps here one is touching what religious thought would see as the sacred element of the soul.

It was certainly easier to talk of the soul when religious belief was virtually taken for granted. The context for talking about the soul has, of course, significantly changed, though some of the language may still be shared with religious thought.

Perhaps music is a more appropriate medium to capture what I have been trying to convey, though of course I am limited here to words. It is generally accepted that music does touch the inner depths, though there is no agreement about how this occurs and what precisely is touched. Malcolm Budd takes to pieces a number of musical theories, which purport to show how music communicates emotions, though he does agree in the end that music 'reaches as far as the inner world of emotion itself' (1985, p. 176). He also quotes Elgar's dedication on the score of his violin concerto, 'Herein is enshrined the soul of ...' This secret dedication was likely to be to the 'soul-mate' of his later years, Alice Stuart-Wortley. If the soul can be given a voice, then surely this violin concerto would be a candidate. As would the plainsong chant of Hildegard of Bingen – 'Columba aspexit'. The chant creates a sense of sublime serenity and spirituality.

Roger Scruton points out himself that he uses the word 'soul' on several occasions to try to capture the essence of Mozart's music. Mozart's is not a simple soul; his music 'explores every mood, every character, every turn of the human spirit' (2009, p. 88).

It would be both simplistic and untrue to propose that music always evokes particular feelings. A sad-sounding piece of music may in fact produce a feeling of great satisfaction. Very occasionally a piece of music dominated by one sort of feeling may evoke a similar feeling in the listener. Perhaps the last movement of Tchaikovsky's *Pathetique* symphony is just one of those pieces.

But the response in the listener to music is a complex affair, involving cognitive and emotional aspects. The music will tend to evoke some feelings in the listener, usually of a general kind, often pleasurable, sometimes linked to memories, or even past memories of previous performances of the piece. There may be recognition of a pattern conveyed by the music, or surprise at a new pattern that emerges from the music, or there may be a sense of a journey, with the music taking the listener along. That journey may be a long one, as with Wagner, and may involve a trip through the darker recesses of the soul or otherworldliness, as with Mahler, but can be uplifting of the human spirit, food for the soul.

As Martha Nussbaum (2001, p. 266) has pointed out in her discussion of music and emotion, Proust connects the sense of otherworldliness with music. Perhaps he alone of writers is capable of grasping the essence of music in words. As he put it in his novel, during the break in a concert, when people were talking, in a passage which provides a suitable place to end my own explorations of the soul territory,

> But what was I to make of their words, which like all spoken human words seemed so meaningless in comparison with the heavenly musical phrase that has just been occupying me? I was really like an angel fallen from the delights of Paradise into the most insignificant reality. And just as certain creatures are the last examples of a form of life which nature has abandoned, I wondered whether music were not the sole example of the form which might have served – had language, the forms of words, the possibility of analysing ideas, never been invented – for the communication of souls.
>
> (Proust, 1923, p. 237)

References

Akhtar, S. (2007), 'The trauma of geographical dislocation: Leaving, arriving, mourning and becoming', in *The Geography of Meanings*, ed. by M. Hooke and S. Akhtar, pp. 165–90, London: International Psychoanalytical Association.

Appiah, K. A. (2005), *The Ethics of Identity*, Princeton, NJ: Princeton University Press.

Arendt, H. (1963), *Eichmann in Jerusalem*, New York: Viking Press; Penguin Books, 1977.

Aristotle (1925), *The Nicomachean Ethics*, trans. by D. Ross, Oxford: Oxford University Press, 1980.

Augustine (1467), *Concerning the City of God Against the Pagans*, trans. by H. Bettenson, Harmondsworth: Penguin Books, 1972.

Augustine (1949), *The Greatness of the Soul*, trans. by J. Colleran, Westminster, MD: Longmans.

Aurelius, M. (1916), Loeb Classical Library, Cambridge, MA: Harvard University Press.

Auster, P. (1982), *The Invention of Solitude*, Santa Fe NM: Sun.

Bachelard, G. (1958), *The Poetics of Space*, trans. by M. Jolas, Boston: Beacon Press, 1969.

Baker, M. and Goetz, S., eds. (2011), *The Soul Hypothesis*, New York: Continuum.

Balint, M. (1968), *The Basic Fault*, London: Tavistock.

Barrett, W. (1959), *Irrational Man*, New York: Anchor Books.

——— (1987), *Death of the Soul*, Oxford: Oxford University Press.

Bauman, Z. (2004), *Identity*, Cambridge: Polity Press.

Bellow, S. (1994), *It All Adds Up*, New York: Viking Penguin.

Benjamin, J. (1988), *The Bonds of Love*, New York: Pantheon.

——— (1998), *Shadow of the Other*, New York: Routledge.

Bennett, M. and Hacker, P. (2003), *Philosophical Foundations of Neuroscience*, Oxford: Blackwell.

Benvenuto, B. and Kennedy, R. (1986), *The Works of Jacques Lacan: An Introduction*, London: Free Association Books.

Berkeley, G. (1710), *The Principles of Human Knowledge*, ed. by G. Warnock, London: Fontana, 1962.

Berlin, I. (1999), *The Roots of Romanticism*, ed. by H. Hardy, London: Chatto and Windus.

Bettelheim, B. (1983), *Freud and Man's Soul*, London: Chatto and Windus.

Bion, W. (1970), *Attention and Interpretation*, London: Tavistock.

Blanchot, M. (1955), *The Space of Literature*, trans. by A. Smock, Lincoln: University of Nebraska Press, 1982.

Bonhoeffer, D. (1970), *Letters and Papers from Prison*, ed. by E. Bethege, New York: Touchstone.

Bowlby, J. (1988), *A Secure Base: Clinical Application of Attachment Theory*, London: Routledge.

Breen, D. (1993), 'General introduction', in *The Gender Conundrum*, ed. by D. Breen, pp. 1–39, London: Routledge and Institute of Psychoanalysis.

Brentano, F. (1982), *Descriptive Psychology*, trans. by B. Muller, London: Routledge, 1995.

Britton. R. (2009), 'Mind and matter: A psychoanalytic perspective', in *The Organic and Inner World*, ed. by R. Doctor and R. Lucas, pp. 1–14, London: Karnac.

Budd, M. (1985), *Music and the Emotions*, London: Routledge, 1992.

Buechler, S. (1998), 'The analyst's experience of loneliness', *Contemporary Psychoanalysis* 34:91–113.

Burnside, J. (2011a), *Black Cat Bone*, London: Cape Poetry.

—— (2011b), 'Interview', *Agenda* 45:42–38.

Butler, J. (1990), *Gender Trouble*, London: Routledge.

Celenza, A. and Gabbard, G. (2003), 'Analysts who commit sexual boundary violations: A lost cause?' *Journal of the American Psychoanalytic Association* 51:617–36.

Cassirer, E. (1955), *The Philosophy of Symbolic Forms, Vol. 1*, trans. by R. Mannheim, New Haven: Yale University Press.

Corbin, A. (1990), 'Backstage', in *A History of Private Life, Vol. IV*, ed. by M. Perrot, trans. by A. Goldhammer, pp. 451–668, Cambridge, MA: Harvard University Press.

Crick, F. (1994), *The Astonishing Hypothesis: The Scientific Search for the Soul*, New York: Touchstone.

Damasio, A. (1994), *Descartes' Error*, New York: G. P. Putnam.

—— (2010), *Self Comes to Mind: Constructing the Conscious Brain*, London: William Heinemann.

Darwin, C. (1859), *On the Origin of Species*, Harmondsworth: Penguin Books, 1968.

Davidson, D. (1980) Essays on Action and Events by Donald Davidson, Oxford: Clarendon Press.

Defoe, D. (1722), *Moll Flanders*, ed. by J. Mitchell, Harmondsworth: Penguin Books.

de Mare, H. (1999), 'Domesticity in dispute: A reconsideration of sources', in *At Home: An Anthropology of Domestic Space*, ed. by I. Cieraad, pp. 13–30, Syracuse: Syracuse University Press.

de M'Uzan, M. (2005), *Aux Confins de l'Identite*, Paris: Gallimard.

—— (2009), 'The uncanny, or "I am not who you think I am" ', in *Reading French Psychoanalysis*, (2010), ed. by D. Birksteed-Breen, S. Flanders, and A. Gibeault, pp. 201–9, London: Routledge.

Dennett, D. (1991), *Consciousness Explained*, London: Allen Lane.

Deutsch, H. (1989), 'On satisfaction, happiness and ecstasy', *International Journal of Psycho-analysis* 70:715–23.

Dolto, F. (1994), *Solitude*, Paris: Gallimard.

Durkheim, E. (1912), *The Elementary Forms of Religious Life*, trans. by K. Fields, New York: Free Press.

Ellis, D. (1985), *Wordsworth, Freud and the Spots of Time*, Cambridge: Cambridge University Press.

Engelman, E. (1976) *Berggasse 19: Sigmund Freud's Home and Offices, Vienna, 1938: The Photographs of Edmund Engelman*, New York: Basic Books.

Erikson, E. (1956), 'The problem of ego identity', *Journal of the American Psychoanalytic Association* 4:56–121.

—————— (1959), *Identity and the Life Cycle*, New York: Norton.

Fonagy, P. and Target, M. (1996), 'Playing with reality: 1. Theory of the mind and the normal development of psychic reality', *International Journal of Psycho-analysis* 77: 217–33.

Foot, P. (2001), *Natural Goodness*, Oxford: Clarendon Press.

Foucault, M. (1994), *Essential Works, Ethics*, ed. by P. Rabinow, Harmondsworth: Penguin, 2000.

—————— (2001), *The Hermeneutics of the Subject*, trans. by G. Burchell, New York: Picador, 2005.

Freud, S. (1900), *The Interpretation of Dreams*, in J. Strachey (ed.) (1953–73), *The Standard Edition of the Complete Psychological Works of Sigmund Freud*, Vol. 4 (S. E. 4), London: Hogarth Press and Institute of Psychoanalysis.

—————— (1908), 'Civilized sexual morality and modern nervous illness', S. E. 9, pp. 179–204.

—————— (1914), 'The unconscious', S. E. 14, pp. 161–215.

—————— (1916–17), *Introductory Lectures on Psychoanalysis*, S. E. 16, pp. 243–463.

—————— (1918), 'From the history of an infantile neurosis', S. E. 17, pp. 3–122.

—————— (1919), 'The uncanny', S. E. 17, pp. 217–56.

—————— (1920), *Beyond the Pleasure Principle*, S. E. 18, pp. 3–64.

—————— (1921), *Group Psychology and the Analysis of the Ego*, S. E. 18, pp. 67–143.

—————— (1923), *The Ego and the Id*, S. E. 19, pp. 3–63.

—————— (1930), *Civilization and Its Discontents*, S. E. 21, pp. 57–145.

—————— (1933), *New Introductory Lectures on Psycho-analysis*, S. E. 22, pp. 3–182.

—————— (1936), 'A disturbance of memory on the Acropolis', S. E. 22, pp. 238–48.

—————— (1941 [1926]), 'Address to the Society of B'nai Brith', S. E. 20, pp. 271–4.

—————— (1950), *Project for a Scientific Psychology*, S. E. 1, pp. 282–397.

—————— (1985), *The Complete Letters of Sigmund Freud to Wilhelm Fliess 1887–1904*, trans. and ed. by J. Masson, Cambridge, MA: Harvard University Press.

—————— and J. Breuer (1895), *Studies in Hysteria*, S. E. 2, pp. 3–309.

Fromm, E. (1949), *Man for Himself*, London: Routledge, 1986.

Fromm-Reichmann, F. (1990), 'Loneliness', *Contemporary Psychoanalysis* 26:305–29.

Fuss, D. (2004), *The Sense of an Interior*, London: Routledge.

Gale, J. (2000), 'The dwelling place of meaning', in *A Therapeutic Approach to Care in the Community*, ed. by S. Tucker, London: Jessica Kingsley.

Gill, S. (1989), *William Wordsworth: A Life*, Oxford: Oxford University Press.

—————— (2004), 'Introduction', *William Wordsworth: Selected Poems*, pp. xiv–xxviii, Harmondsworth: Penguin.

Goetz, S. and Taliaferro, C. (2011), *A Brief History of the Soul*, Oxford: Wiley-Blackwell.

Graham, J. (1991), *Region of Unlike*, NJ: Echo Press.

Green, A. (1983), 'The dead mother', in *On Private Madness*, pp. 142–73, London: Hogarth, 1986.

—————— (1993), *The Work of the Negative*, trans. by A. Weller, London: Free Association Books, 1999.

——— (1997), 'The intuition of the negative in playing and reality', *International Journal of Psycho-analysis* 78:1071–84.

Greenacre, P. (1958), 'Early psychical determinants in the development of the sense of identity', *Journal of the American Psychoanalytical Association* 6:612–27.

Hall, C. (1990), 'The sweet delights of home', in *A History of Private Life, Vol. IV*, ed. by M. Perrot (1987), trans. by A. Goldhammer, pp. 47–94. Cambridge, MA: Harvard University Press.

Hall, S. (1990), 'Cultural identity and diaspora', in *Identity and Difference*, ed. by K. Woodward, pp. 51–9, London: Sage.

Hall, S. and du Gay, P. (eds.) (1996), *Questions of Cultural Identity*, London: Sage.

Hampshire, S. (1989), *Innocence and Experience*, Harmondsworth: Allen Lane.

Hartmann, H. (1964), *Essays on Ego Psychology*, London: Hogarth Press and Institute of Psychoanalysis.

Heidegger, M. (1926), *Being and Time*, trans by J. Maquarrie and E. Robinson, Oxford: Basil Blackwell, 1962.

——— (1971), *Poetry, Language, Thought*, trans. by A. Hofstadter, New York: Harper and Row.

Hinshelwood, R. (1997), *Therapy or Coercion*, London: Karnac Books.

Hollander, M. (2002), *An Entrance for the Eyes: Space and Meaning in Seventeenth-Century Dutch Art*, Berkeley: University of California Press.

Hume, D. (1740), *A Treatise of Human Nature*, ed. by L. Selby-Bigge, Oxford: Clarendon Press, 1888.

Humphrey, N. (2011), *Soul Dust: The Magic of Consciousness*, London: Quercus.

Hunt, L. (1990), 'The unstable boundaries of the French Revolution', in *A History of Private Life, Vol. IV*, ed. by M. Perrot, trans. by A. Goldhammer, pp. 1–45. Cambridge, MA: Harvard University Press.

Husserl, E. (1954), *The Crisis of European Sciences*, trans. by D. Carr, Evanston: Northwestern University Press, 1970.

Jackson, H. (1958), *Selected Writings, Vol. 2*, New York: Basic Books.

Jacobson, E. (1957), 'Normal and pathological moods: Their nature and functions', *Psychoanalytic Study of the Child* 12:73–113.

——— (1964), *The Self and the Object World*, Madison, CT: International Universities Press.

James, W. (1890), *The Principles of Psychology*, New York: Dover, 1950.

——— (1902), *The Varieties of Religious Experience*, Harmondsworth: Penguin Books, 1985.

Jones, E. (1954), *Sigmund Freud, Life and Work, Vol. 1*, London: Hogarth Press.

——— (1961), *The Life and Work of Sigmund Freud (Abridged)*, Harmondsworth: Penguin.

Judt, T. (2005), *Post War: A History of Europe Since 1945*, London: Heinemann.

Kant, I. (1781), *The Critique of Pure Reason*, trans. by M. Weigelt, Harmondsworth: Penguin, 2007.

Kennedy, R. (1984), 'A dual aspect of the transference', *International Journal of Psycho-analysis* 65:471–83.

——— (1997), *Child Abuse, Psychotherapy and the Law*, London: Free Association Books.

——— (1998), *The Elusive Human Subject*, London: Free Association Books.

——— (2007), *The Many Voices of Psychoanalysis*, London: Routledge and Institute of Psychoanalysis.

Kierkegaard, S. (1846), *Concluding Unscientific Postscript*, trans. by D. Swenson and W. Lowrie, Princeton, NJ: Princeton University Press, 1941.

Klauber, J. (1976), 'Elements of the psychoanalytical relationship', in *Difficulties in the Analytic Encounter* (1981), pp. 45–62. New York: Jason Aronson.

―――― (1981), *Difficulties in the Analytic Encounter*, New York: Jason Aronson.

Klein, M. (1952), 'Some theoretical conclusions regarding the emotional life of the infant', in *Envy and Gratitude and Other Works*, pp. 71–4ff, London: Hogarth Press and Institute of Psychoanalysis.

―――― (1963), 'On the sense of loneliness', in *Envy and Gratitude and Other Works*, pp. 300–13. London: Hogarth Press and Institute of Psychoanalysis.

Lacan, J. (1966), *Ecrits*, Paris: Le Seuil.

―――― (1973a), *The Ethics of Psychoanalysis*, trans. by D. Potter, London: Tavistock/Routledge, 1992.

―――― (1973b), *The Four Fundamental Concepts of Psychoanalysis*, trans. by A. Sheridan, Harmondsworth: Penguin, 1979.

―――― (1975), *The Seminar of Jacques Lacan, Book 1: Freud's Papers on Technique*, ed. by J.-A. Miller, trans. by J. Forrester, Cambridge: Cambridge University Press, 1988.

Laufer, E. and Laufer, M., eds. (1989), *Developmental Breakdown and Psychoanalytic Treatment in Adolescence*, New Haven: Yale University Press.

Lear, J. (2000), *Happiness, Death and the Remainder of Life*, Cambridge, MA: Harvard University Press.

Lichtenstein, H. (1977), *The Dilemma of Human Identity*, New York: Jason Aronson.

Lifton, B. (1994), *Journey of the Adopted Self*, New York: Basic Books.

Lifton, R.J. (1986), *The Nazi Doctors*, New York: Basic Books.

Locke, J. (1690), *An Essay Concerning Human Understanding*, ed. by P. Nidditch, Oxford: Clarendon Press, 1975.

Loewald, H. (1971), 'On motivation and instinct theory', *Psychoanalytic Study of the Child* 26:91–128.

Luria, A. (1973), *The Working Brain*, Harmondsworth: Penguin Books.

Maalouf, A. (1996), *On Identity*, trans. by B. Bray, London: Harvill Press, 2000.

Malafouris, L. (2008), 'Between brains, bodies and things: *Tectonoetic* awareness and the extended self', *Philosophical Transactions of the Royal Society B* 363.1499:1993–2002.

Malcolm, N. (1984), 'The causal theory of mind', in *Consciousness and Causality*, by D. Armstrong and N. Malcolm, pp. 66–102, Oxford: Basil Blackwell.

Mallett, S. (2004), 'Understanding home: A critical review of the literature', *Sociological Review* 52:62–89.

May, S. (2011), *Love, A History*, New Haven: Yale University Press.

McGilchrist, I. (2009), *The Master and His Emissary*, New Haven: Yale University Press.

McMahon, D. (2006), *The Pursuit of Happiness*, London: Allen Lane.

Mitchell, J. (1982), *Feminine Sexuality*, ed. by J. Mitchell and J. Rose, London: Macmillan.

Montaigne, M. de (1580), 'On solitude', in *The Complete Works*, trans. by D.M. Frame, London: Everyman Library, 2003.

Nagel, T. (1979), *Mortal Questions*, Cambridge: Cambridge University Press.

―――― (1986), *The View from Nowhere*, New York: Oxford University Press.

Neiman, S. (2002), *Evil in Modern Thought*, Princeton, NJ: Princeton University Press.

Niebuhr, R. (1941), *The Nature and Destiny of Man*, London: Nisbet.

Nussbaum, M. (1986), *The Fragility of Goodness*, Cambridge: Cambridge University Press.

————— (1994), *The Therapy of Desire*, Princeton, NJ: Princeton University Press.

————— (2001), *Upheavals of Thought*, Cambridge: Cambridge University Press.

Padel, R. (1992), *In and Out of the Mind*, Princeton, NJ: Princeton University Press.

Page, J. (2003), 'Gender and Domesticity', in *The Cambridge Companion to Wordsworth*, ed. by S. Gill, pp. 125–41, Cambridge: Cambridge University Press.

Papadopoulos, R. (2002), 'Refugees, home and trauma', in *Therapeutic Care for Refugees*, ed. by R. Papadopoulos, London: Karnac.

Parat, J. C.-J. (1974), 'Essay on happiness', *Revue Française de Psychanalyse* 38:561–608.

Parsons, M. (2000), *The Dove That Returns, the Dove That Vanishes*, London: Routledge.

————— (2006), 'Ways of transformation', in *Psychoanalysis and Religion in the 21st Century*, ed. by D. M. Black, pp. 117–31, London: Routledge, New Library of Psychoanalysis.

Pass, P. (2011), 'The Plight of Dwelling: "Settlements" and the Making of Home', *Agenda* 45.4:45–9.

Perelberg, R. (1999), 'The interplay between identifications, and identity in the analysis of a violent young man', *International Journal of Psycho-analysis* 80:31–45.

Perrot, M., ed. (1987), *A History of Private Life, Vol. IV*, trans. by A. Goldhammer, Cambridge, MA: Harvard University Press, 1990.

Pigeaud, J. (2006), *La Maladie de l'Ame*, Paris: Les Belles Lettres.

Plato (1914), *The Apology, Phaedo, Phaedrus*, in *Plato, Vol. 1*, Loeb Classical Library, Cambridge, MA: Harvard University Press.

————— (1927), *Charmides, Alcibiades, Hipparchus, The Lovers, Theages, Minos, Epinomis Vol. 12*, Loeb Classical Library, Cambridge, MA: Harvard University Press.

————— (1990), *The Theatatus*, trans. by M. Levett, Indianapolis: Hackett.

————— (1992), *The Republic*, trans. by G. Grube, Indianapolis: Hackett.

Proust, M. (1923), *The Prisoner*, trans. by C. Clark, London: Allen Lane.

————— (1927), *Time Regained*, trans. by A. Mayor (1970), London: Chatto and Windus.

Quinodoz, J.-M. (1993), *The Taming of Solitude*, trans. by P. Slotkin, London: Routledge, New Library of Psychoanalysis.

————— (1996), 'The sense of solitude in the psychoanalytic encounter', *International Journal of Psycho-analysis* 77:481–96.

Ramachandran, V. (2011), *The Tell-Tale Brain*, London: William Heinemann.

Rice, C. (2007), *The Emergence of the Interior*, London: Routledge.

Ricoeur, P. (1990), *Oneself as Another*, trans. by K. Blaney, Chicago: University of Chicago Press.

Robertson, J. (1958), *Young Children in Hospital*, London: Tavistock.

Rorty, R. (1980), *Philosophy and the Mirror of Nature*, Oxford: Basil Blackwell.

Rosen, C. (2002), *Beethoven's Piano Sonatas*, New Haven: Yale University Press.

Rybczynski, W. (1986), *Home: A Short History of an Idea*, New York: Viking Penguin.

Ryle, G. (1949), *The Concept of Mind*, London: Hutchinson.

Said, E. (1993), *Culture and Imperialism*, London: Chatto and Windus.

————— (2006), *On Late Style*, London: Bloomsbury.

St Augustine (1467), *Concerning the City of God Against the Pagans*, trans. by H. Bettenson, Harmondsworth: Penguin Books, 1972.

Schopenhauer, A. (1851), *Parerga and Paralipomena, Vol. 1*, trans. by E. Payne, Oxford: Oxford University Press, 1974.

Schore, A. N. (2003), *Affect Regulation and the Repair of the Self*, New York: Norton.

————— (2012), *The Science of the Art of Psychotherapy*, New York: Norton.

Scruton, R. (2009), *Understanding Music*, London: Continuum.

Searle, J. (1997), *The Mystery of Consciousness*, London: Granta.

Sen, A. (2006), *Identity and Violence: The Illusion of Destiny*, Harmondsworth: Penguin Books.

Sherrington, C. (1940), *Man on His Nature*, Cambridge: Cambridge University Press.

Silberman, H. (1985), 'On Happiness', *Psychoanalytic Study of the Child* 40:457–72.

Steedman, C. (1995), *Strange Dislocations: Childhood and the Idea of Human Interiority, 1780–1930*, Cambridge, MA: Harvard University Press.

Steiner, G. (1978), *Heidegger*, London: Fontana.

——— (1989), *Real Presences*, Chicago: University of Chicago Press.

Steiner, J. (1993), *Psychic Retreats: Pathological Organizations in Psychotic, Neurotic and Borderline Patients*, London: Routledge and Institute of Psychoanalysis.

Storr, A. (1988), *Solitude*, London: Andre Deutsch.

Strawson, P. (1985), *Skepticism and Naturalism*, London: Methuen.

Sylvester, D. (2000), *Looking Back at Francis Bacon*, London: Thames and Hudson.

Taylor, C. (1989), *Sources of the Self*, Cambridge, MA: Harvard University Press.

Tillich, P. (1963), *The Eternal Now*, London: SCM Press.

Vendler, H. (1995), *Soul Says*, Cambridge, MA: Harvard University Press.

——— (2010), *Dickinson, Selected Poems and Commentaries*, Cambridge, MA: Harvard University Press.

Vidler, A. (1992), *The Architectural Uncanny*, Cambridge, MA: MIT Press.

Wainrib. S. (2012), 'Is psychoanalysis a matter of subjectivication?' *International Journal of Psycho-analysis* 93:1115–35.

Ward, K. (1998), *In Defence of the Soul*, Oxford: Oneworld.

Weil, S. (1986), *Simone Weil: An Anthology*, Harmondsworth: Penguin.

Williams, B. (1972), *Morality*, Cambridge: Cambridge University Press.

——— (1985), *Ethics and the Limits of Philosophy*, London: Fontana Book.

Williams, R. (2005), *Grace and Necessity*, London: Morehouse.

Wilson. A. (1986), 'An outline of work with families', in *The Family as In-Patient*, ed. by R. Kennedy, A. Heymans, and L. Tischler, London: Free Association Books.

Winnicott, D. (1941), 'The observation of infants in a set situation', in *Through Paediatrics to Psychoanalysis: Collected Papers*, pp. 52–69, London: Hogarth Press and Institute of Psychoanalysis, 1975.

——— (1949), 'Mind and its relation to the psyche-soma', in *Through Paediatrics to Psychoanalysis: Collected Papers*, pp. 243–54. London: Hogarth Press and Institute of Psychoanalysis, 1975.

——— (1956), 'Primary maternal preoccupation', in *Collected Papers*, pp. 300–5, London: Hogarth Press and Institute of Psychoanalysis.

——— (1958), 'The capacity to be alone', *International Journal of Psycho-analysis*, 39:416–20.

——— (1960), 'The parent-infant relationship', in *The Maturational Processes and the Facilitating Environment*, pp. 37–55, London: Hogarth Press, 1965.

——— (1963), 'Communicating and not communicating', in *The Maturational Processes and the Facilitating Environment*, pp. 179–92, London: Hogarth Press, 1965.

——— (1965), *The Maturational Processes and the Facilitating Environment*, London: Hogarth Press and Institute of Psychoanalysis.

——— (1969), 'The use of an object', *International Journal of Psycho-analysis* 50: 711–16.

——— (1971), *Playing and Reality*, London: Tavistock.

——— (1986), *Home Is Were We Start From*, Harmondsworth: Penguin Books.

Wittgenstein, L. (1953), *Philosophical Investigations*, trans. by G. Anscombe et al., Oxford: Oxford University Press, 2009 rev. ed.

——— (1992), *Last Writings on the Philosophy of Psychology, Vol. 2*, ed. by G. Von Wright and H. Nyman, trans. by C. Luckhart and M. Aue, Oxford: Blackwell.

Wolf, E. (1988), *Treating the Self*, New York: Guilford Press.

Wolfe, T. (1941), *The Hills Beyond*, New York: Signet Classics, 1968.

Wollheim, R. (1984), *The Thread of Life*, New Haven: Yale University Press.

Woodward, K., ed. (1997), *Identity and Difference*, London: Sage.

Woolf, V. (1925), *Mrs Dalloway*, London: Folio Edition, 2011.

Wordsworth, J. (1995), *The Prelude: The Four Texts*, Harmondsworth: Penguin.

Wordsworth, W. (1977), *The Poems, Volume One*, ed. by J. Hayden. Harmondsworth: Penguin Books.

Wordsworth, W. and Coleridge, S. (1805), *Lyrical Ballads*, ed. by D. Roper, London: Collins.

Wu, D. (2002), *Wordsworth: An Inner Life*, Oxford: Basil Blackwell.

Young, J. Z. (1987), *Philosophy and the Brain*, Oxford: Oxford University Press.

Zeki, S. (2004), 'The asynchrony of visual perception', in *Human Brain Function*, ed. by R. Frack et al., London: Elsevier.

——— (2009), *The Splendors and Miseries of the Human Brain*, Oxford: Wiley-Blackwell.

Index

music 4, 52, 57, 135, 144–5; music and
  soul 144–5
M'Uzan, M. de 19, 46, 140

Nagel, T. 49, 74, 75
narrative 10, 26, 27, 55, 57, 62, 67, 82
National Gallery 2, 75, 87
Neimann, S. 17–18
neuronal networks 80, 142
neuroscience 2, 8, 9, 66, 74, 75, 79, 81,
  141; and soul 74–81
neurosis 22, 104, 120, 122
Niebuhr, R. 18
Nietzsche, F. 18, 117
Nussbaum, N. 68, 116, 126, 145

object relationships 121, 122, 126
Odyssey 13, 47
Oedipus complex 57, 58, 59

Padel, R. 66
Page, J. 34, 35
Papadopoulos, R. 12
Parat, J. 127–8
Parsons, M. vii, 60–1, 96, 109
Perelberg, R. 56, 57
Perrot, M. 21, 22
personalization 54
Pigeaud, J. 6
Plato 11, 67, 68, 69, 70, 71, 72, 89, 141;
  and soul 11, 67, 68–70, 89
Plotinus 71
Plutarch 68
private life 21–5
Proust, M. 77, 141
psyche 5, 18, 24, 28, 54, 56, 59, 66, 68,
  69, 78, 109
psychic home 2, 11, 13, 15, 24, 25–33,
  34–44, 45, 46–8, 49, 50, 55, 57, 61, 64,
  89, 138, 139, 140; and identity 46–8,
  51, 139, 140
psychic retreat 27–8
psychoanalysis and soul 83–8
psychoanalytic setting 28, 29, 84, 90, 95,
  97, 102, 114
psychoanalytic treatment 28–32, 84, 123,
  136, 144

Ramachandran, V. 74
Rembrandt, H. 2, 3, 7, 9, 21, 75, 81, 84,
  87, 144
Rice, C. 23, 24
Ricoeur, P. 49

Rolland, R. 123
Rorty, R. 73
Rosen, C. 113
Rybczynski, W. 20–1
Ryle, G. 8, 10

Said, E. 45, 61, 62, 113
Saki 114
Schopenhauer, A. 117, 126–7
Schore, A. 79
science 3, 5, 9, 72, 74, 136
Scruton, R. 144
Searle, J. 75
self 10, 14, 16, 17, 18, 19, 24, 27, 51, 52,
  53, 54, 55, 66, 67, 71, 72, 73, 74, 79,
  80, 81, 84, 98, 106, 128
Sen, A. 45, 48, 63
Seneca 68
sexuality 22, 23, 45, 47, 59, 118, 121, 122
Shakespeare, W. 15, 16, 49, 77
Shelley, P. 117
Sherrington, C. 10
Silberman, H. 128–9
Sinatra, F. 50
Socrates 11, 68, 69
solitude 11, 23, 44, 89–135
soma 28, 54, 78
soul 1–12, 14, 16–19, 23, 24, 26, 40, 42,
  43, 44, 45, 56, 63–74, 81, 83–8, 89, 97,
  98, 113, 114, 115, 117, 127, 129, 130,
  131, 133, 134, 137–45; and home 65,
  70, 131, 137, 138; and religion 71, 72,
  73, 77, 81, 86, 141, 142, 144
spectrum of identity 46, 57, 108, 140
Spinoza, B. 74
split brain 48
spirit 2, 5, 16, 17, 18, 44, 66, 67, 68, 70,
  81, 86, 126, 139, 141, 144, 145
spirituality 68, 86, 144
Steedman, C. 24
Steiner, G. 15, 87
Steiner, J. 27
Storr, A. 113, 114
Strachey, J. 134
Strawson, P. 77
subject (human) 3, 4, 5, 8, 9, 10, 13, 14,
  18, 21, 24, 25, 26, 46, 49, 50, 52, 53,
  55, 56, 57, 59, 63, 77, 79, 81, 82, 83,
  84, 85, 86, 88, 89, 90, 91, 92, 97,
  102, 103, 104, 105, 108, 112, 116, 118,
  126, 127, 129, 133, 135, 138, 140, 143
subjective organization 56–7
subjective position 85